The Distribution of Wealth – Growing Inequality?

The Distribution of Wealth – Growing Inequality?

Michael Schneider

Honorary Research Fellow, Federation University Australia

Mike Pottenger

The University of Melbourne, Australia

J.E. King

Emeritus Professor, La Trobe University, Australia and Honorary Professor, Federation University Australia

Edward Elgar
PUBLISHING

Cheltenham, UK • Northampton, MA, USA

Published by
Edward Elgar Publishing Limited
The Lypiatts
15 Lansdown Road
Cheltenham
Glos GL50 2JA
UK

Edward Elgar Publishing, Inc.
William Pratt House
9 Dewey Court
Northampton
Massachusetts 01060
USA

A catalogue record for this book
is available from the British Library

Library of Congress Control Number: 2016949906

This book is available electronically in the **Elgar**online
Economics subject collection
DOI 10.4337/9781783476442

ISBN 978 1 78347 643 5 (cased)
ISBN 978 1 78347 644 2 (eBook)

Typeset by Servis Filmsetting Ltd, Stockport, Cheshire

Contents

Preface to the First Edition

Michael Schneider

This book is the first to provide a comprehensive treatment of the personal distribution of wealth in its modern sense, namely the distribution between people of (to put it briefly) a country's stock of marketable assets. If the subject matter is important, why has a book on it not been published before? I attempt here to provide an answer.

To adopt William Stanley Jevons's aphorism, originally related to 'the laws of consumption', if the laws of the distribution of wealth 'are developed by no other science, they must be developed by economists' (Jevons [1871] 1957, p. 39). But as Harold Demsetz put it, '[e]conomists usually take the bundle of property rights as a datum and ask for an explanation of the forces determining the price and the number of units of a good to which these rights attach' (Demsetz, 1967, p. 47). The vast majority of economists, especially those of the present day, have preoccupied themselves with either the allocation of resources or, to a lesser extent, the utilisation (employment) of resources. Only a small proportion have devoted their time to the study of distribution. Of these, most have been concerned with analysing the distribution of income, between either classes or persons. Only a few have examined the personal distribution of wealth.

One of the reasons for the unequal allocation of labour among economists has been the relative paucity of data relating to the distribution of wealth, at least until very recent times. But one suspects this is not the only reason. The claims of economics to be a science have been supported by the belief that allocation and utilisation of resources are value-free, a belief which can be sustained if one is prepared to ignore, for example, the fact that in a market economy, resource allocation is determined not according to 'one person, one vote', but 'one (distributed) dollar, one vote'. Distribution theories, involving as they must the making of interpersonal comparisons, are more difficult to divorce from explicit reference to values. This gives them a faintly disreputable air in the eyes of some economists, as does their potential for challenging the *status quo*. Working in the area of distribution is thus for an economist a challenging task. It does not follow, however, that it is a task which need not be undertaken. On the contrary, the well-being of persons depends greatly on the share they obtain of both national income and national wealth.

Given the universal relevance of the subject matter of this book, I have tried as far as possible to make it accessible to the general reader; diagrams and equations are very few and far between. I have nonetheless eschewed the 'dumbing down' which has increasingly afflicted the modern world.

The closest approximation to an antecedent to this book is to be found in the chapter in Atkinson and Bourguignon (2000) entitled 'The Distribution of Wealth', by James B. Davies and Anthony F. Shorrocks. My acknowledgements begin with an appreciation of the generosity of Tony Shorrocks in unhesitatingly sending me a draft of that chapter two years prior to its publication. The forthcoming publication of that chapter, in turn, was originally drawn to my attention by Ed Wolff, to whom also I consequently owe a debt of gratitude. And I am particularly indebted to Tony (now Sir Anthony) Atkinson, who generously read the drafts of two chapters of this book when it was in its infancy, and magnanimously encouraged what must have then seemed to him an unpromising project. Atkinson (in the United Kingdom) and Wolff (in the United States) have been leaders among those dedicated individuals who have beavered away transforming unfriendly statistics into meaningful pictures of the distribution of wealth, to whom I take this opportunity of paying tribute.

As may be apparent, this book has been substantially influenced by the *Weltanschauungen* both of James Meade, Professor of Political Economy at Cambridge and Fellow of Christ's College at the time when I was a postgraduate student at Christ's, and of Amartya Sen, a contemporary of mine at Cambridge; I should like to acknowledge my debt also to the Shell Company, one of whose scholarships enabled me to study at Cambridge in the first place. The book has in addition benefitted from discussions, sometimes at the Boxing Day Test cricket in Melbourne, with Jack (J.J.C.) Smart, who taught me philosophy when I was an undergraduate at the University of Adelaide.

This book was conceived during a discussion with Edward Elgar, to whose unwavering support over the subsequent years I should like to attest. At Edward Elgar Publishing my main dealings have been successively with Jane Croft (before she moved elsewhere), Julie Leppard, Alexandra Minton and Suzanne Mursell, all of whom willingly provided assistance when it was needed – my thanks go to each, as well as to two anonymous helpful referees and an anonymous eagle-eyed proofreader.

I should like to acknowledge also the assistance provided by librarians at three splendid libraries, namely the Borchardt Library at La Trobe University, the Cambridge University Library, and the Marshall Library in Cambridge. The fruitful time that I spent at the latter two libraries was facilitated by a grant of six months' study leave by La Trobe University.

Assistance with some part or parts of the book has been provided by colleagues at La Trobe University, namely economists Harry Burley, Buly Cardak, Lionel Frost, John Kennedy, Rod Maddock, Imad Moosa, Roman Peretiatko, Neil Perry, David Prentice, Suzanne Sommer and Bill Stent, and philosophers Tim Oakley and Janna Thompson, by Wylie Bradford (Macquarie), Harold Demsetz (University of California at Los Angeles), Jamie Galbraith (Texas), Geoff Harcourt (Cambridge), David Johnston (Wilfred Laurier), Laurence Kotlikoff (Boston, and National Bureau of Economic Research), Race Mathews (Monash), Michael McClure (Western Australia), Kevin McElwaine, Gay Meeks (Cambridge), Ann Morrow (Melbourne), John Nevile (New South Wales), John Power (Melbourne), Jack Reilly, Peter Saunders (New South Wales), Tony Sheehan (Parliament House, Melbourne), by Monica Hodgkinson and Colleen Stoate (secretaries at La Trobe), and by Rosemary Moore (*quondam* secretary at La Trobe).

I am indebted above all, however, to two people. One is my long-standing colleague and friend John King, who, encouraging the project from the beginning, has provided innumerable ideas during lengthy conversations, many taking place during our bushwalking excursions while we were on 'recreation leave', and has read and incisively commented on more drafts than he probably cares to remember. The other is my supportive wife Margaret, who has shared with me the daunting task of preparing the indexes and tricking a computer into presenting them as we wish, whose non-economist comments during discussions of the book incited me to think laterally, and whose moral support has been invaluable.

Michael Schneider
June 2003

Preface to the Second Edition

Michael Schneider

Nine years after the Edward Elgar publication of *The Distribution of Wealth* in 2004, John King suggested that the time had come for a new edition incorporating an update of the personal distribution of wealth figures featuring in that book's Chapter 3. When I expressed doubts about my ability to carry out this task, John suggested I approach Andrew Leigh for suggestions of a co-author. An opportunity for this approach occurred at the Melbourne launch of Andrew's *Battlers and Billionaires* (Leigh, 2013). It produced immediate results, in the form of an introduction there and then to Mike Pottenger, with whom I formed a rapport that quickly led to an agreement that we would co-author the new book. When Edward Elgar Publishing suggested that the second edition should concentrate on growth in inequality in the personal distribution of wealth, we happily agreed, with my wife Margaret coming up with the new title *The Distribution of Wealth – Growing Inequality?* Eighteen months later, having been diagnosed with liver cancer (emanating from an eye melanoma), with Mike's agreement I invited my long-standing friend and colleague John King to join us as a co-author; happily he accepted.

Our principal purpose in writing this book is to determine whether, in the countries for which data are available, the personal distribution of wealth has changed over time, and if so, whether the change has been in the direction of greater inequality or greater equality. The first edition threw some light on the answer to this question, at least up to 2002, though this was not the main focus of that book, as will be apparent from the Preface to it (reproduced here above). While much of the argument of the earlier book has been retained in this one, it has throughout been recast so as to focus on change over time in the personal distribution of wealth. In some cases the revisions have been so substantial as to almost consider this a separate book, rather than a second edition.

One of the problems I encountered in writing the earlier book was a paucity of data relating to the distribution of wealth. In the mere ten or so years since then there has been a huge increase in available data relating to the personal distribution of wealth, though it has to be said that much of it is not very reliable; as Thomas Piketty (2015a, p.2) put it with respect to 'the evolution of income and wealth distributions', although 'we have too little historical data at our disposal to draw definitive judgements . . . at least we have substantially more evidence than we used to'. One wonders if this increase in evidence is related to a widespread perception that in recent years there has been a rapidly growing inequality in the personal distribution of wealth. More specifically, a massive increase in available data occurred in 2013 when Thomas Piketty published *Le capital au XXI siècle* (an English translation appeared in 2014, under the title *Capital in the Twenty-First Century*). In this book Piketty also set out to explain changes in the distribution of wealth by economic class from time immemorial to the present; an assessment of his explanation, and of its implications for changes over time in the personal distribution of wealth, is to be found in Chapter 5 of this book. Elsewhere, however, this book does not attempt to deal with the distribution of wealth by economic class, important though that topic is. Likewise, this book does not attempt to cover distribution of wealth by cohorts identified by income, age, education, sex or race, important though these topics are.

As in the case of the first edition, given the universal relevance of the subject matter of this book, we have tried as far as possible to make it accessible to the general reader; diagrams and equations are very few and far between, and technical matters relating to the measurement of the personal distribution of wealth have been relegated to an Appendix. We have nonetheless eschewed the 'dumbing-down' which has continued to afflict the modern world.

We would like to acknowledge that assistance with some part or parts of this book has been provided not only by those who are listed in the Preface to the first edition, but also by Dan Ariely, Danny Dorling, John Wilkinson and (from Edward Elgar Publishing Limited) Edward Elgar, Matthew Pitman and Harry Fabian.

Michael Schneider
January 2016

Preface to the Second Edition

Mike Pottenger and John King

As Michael Schneider noted in his Preface to the first edition of this book, it was 'the first to provide a comprehensive treatment of the personal distribution of wealth in its modern sense, namely the distribution between people of . . . a country's stock of marketable assets' (see above). The first, but by no means the last! Our contributions notwithstanding, the new edition (and the shift in the focus of this edition that warranted a new title) is very much Michael's work. He read and approved the final draft that we completed for him in January 2016, and eight of the nine chapters are substantially revised and updated versions of the 2004 text. Even the new Chapter 5, on 'Determinants of Changes in the Distribution of Wealth', consists very largely of the paper that he presented at the December 2014 conference of the Society of Heterodox Economists in Sydney (Schneider and Pottenger, 2014), and of revisions he made to that work following the conference.

His voracious appetite for any and all new work done in this field made the task of preparing a second edition a constantly evolving one, punctuated by long discussion and debate. Had Michael been in better health, he would no doubt have preferred to delve deeper into the ongoing discussion about the role of policy in shaping the distribution of wealth.

We are very grateful to have had the opportunity to work with and learn so much from such a persistent and perceptive scholar.

Mike Pottenger
John King
February 2016

1. Introduction

let a palace arise beside the little house, and it [the latter] *shrinks from a little house to a hut* (Karl Marx, [1849] 1977, p. 216)

This book is about the distribution of wealth among persons, described by statisticians as the size distribution of wealth, and the way this distribution has changed over time. Why is the distribution of wealth important? How can the distribution of wealth be measured? How unequal is this distribution in practice, and has the degree of inequality changed over time? What factors determine the degree of inequality? What criteria can be used to rank alternative distributions of wealth? What instruments are available to a government that wishes to change the distribution of wealth? How is the distribution of wealth related to the aggregate amount of wealth? These are the questions to which this book provides answers. The answers have many dimensions, notably economic, statistical, ethical, political, sociological and legal.

'Distribution' and 'wealth' may each be interpreted in more than one way. We accordingly begin by stating explicitly how these terms are used in this book. First, we basically follow John Stuart Mill in defining 'wealth' as 'all useful or agreeable things which possess exchangeable value' (Mill, [1848] 1965, p. 10), the definition that in the context of economics is said to have 'been most widely accepted' (*Oxford English Dictionary*, 2015). Second, we define a distribution (in general) as '[t]he way in which a particular measurement or characteristic is spread over the members of a class', and the 'the distribution of wealth' in particular as being '[t]he division of the aggregate [wealth] . . . of any society among its individual members' (*Oxford English Dictionary*, 2015).[1] We next discuss each of these concepts in more detail.

1.1 WHAT IS MEANT BY WEALTH?

Wealth is not the same thing as income. While income is a flow concept, wealth is a stock concept. That wealth is a stock, not a flow, is implicit in Mill's definition. Mill, however, did not spell this out, the distinction between stocks and flows being first clearly established, as its fervent advocate Irving Fisher acknowledged (Fisher, 1896, pp. 532–3), by Edwin Cannan. While Cannan did not publish anything on this distinction until 1893 (Cannan, 1893, p. 14), in an unpublished article entitled 'The Two Wealths', inspired by a study of the accounts of a British railway company and 'read in a somewhat amplified but less symmetrical form to the Oxford Economic Society on March 1 1887' (Cannan, 1897, p. 280), Cannan made the distinction as clearly as anyone has done since:

> It is, in fact, universally recognised, that an individual's capital exists at a point in time, and not in a length of time, and that his income exists in a length of time and not at a point of time. The same distinction, surely, is to be found between the capital and the income of a community; a community has a certain amount of income in the year 1886 and a certain amount of capital at 10 a.m. on the 1st of June 1886, but it has not a certain amount of income at 10 a.m. on the 1st of June, nor a certain amount of capital in the course of the year 1886. (Cannan, 1897, p. 281)

Given that wealth is a stock, what does it comprise? The word 'wealth' is derived from 'weal', a state of well-being,[2] but over time it came to be identified with possession of the durable objects on which well-being depends, and to be measured by the exchangeable value of these objects. The wealth of a country, as Jack Revell (1965, p. 368) pointed out, 'consists of two elements – the value of tangible assets located in the country and the net total of claims on overseas residents', the second element comprising tangible assets owned by domestic residents but located outside the country minus tangible assets located in the country but not owned by its citizens. The wealth of an economic unit within a country, such as an individual, can also be seen as consisting of two elements – in this case, the value of tangible assets owned by the individual and the net total of the individual's claims on tangible assets, the second element comprising financial assets net of liabilities.[3]

Some of the objects which make up a country's wealth are owned communally (public sector wealth), while the remainder are owned privately (private sector wealth). Private sector wealth assumes a private property system, the key features of which were neatly summarised by Harold Demsetz (1965, p. 62) as follows:

> Crucially involved is the notion that individuals have control over the use to which scarce resources (including ideas) can be put, and that this right of control is saleable or transferable. A private property right system requires the prior consent of 'owners' before their property can be affected by others. The role of the body politic in this system is twofold. Firstly, the government or courts must help decide which individuals possess what property rights and, therefore, who has the power to claim that his rights are affected by others.

Secondly, property rights so assigned must be protected by the police power of the state or the owners must be allowed to protect property rights themselves.

Stewart (1991, p. 99) provided a concise summary of the view taken by the 1975 Royal Commission on the Distribution of Income and Wealth in the United Kingdom on the calculation of private sector wealth, namely that it should in principle include not only:

> marketable wealth which includes all assets for which a value can immediately be realised, net of liabilities . . . plus value of occupational and state pension rights, . . . [but also] the net worth of the company sector, collective wealth of the public sector (eg schools, hospitals and local authority housing), the value of human wealth (eg the value to an individual of the investment in his education and training), contingent rights to forms of income other than [occupational and state] pension rights . . . (eg child benefit and income-related benefits) and the value of restricted access to certain assets like subsidised tenancies.

However, measuring the value of all but the first of these types of assets, and dividing the result between individuals, both involve such conceptual and practical problems that actual calculations of the personal distribution of wealth are most commonly based on marketable wealth alone. Nonetheless, some of the empirical studies outlined in Chapter 3 include one or more of the additional types of assets referred to by the 1975 Royal Commission; their authors' reasons for such inclusions are discussed in that chapter.

Marketable wealth may take any one of a number of forms, some of which are more liquid than others, in the sense that they can be exchanged for money quickly with little if any loss of potential value. Housing is a relatively illiquid form of marketable wealth, while more liquid forms include cash, and other financial assets ranging in liquidity from money at call to shares. In this book the composition of wealth is discussed only in so far as it has a bearing on the distribution of wealth, to which we now turn.

1.2 WHAT IS MEANT BY THE DISTRIBUTION OF WEALTH?

The principal concern of this book is neither the distribution of wealth between the owners of land, labour and capital, commonly known as either the 'factor' or the 'functional' distribution of wealth, nor the distribution of wealth between generations, namely the intertemporal distribution of wealth.[4] Rather, the book is principally concerned with what may be referred to either as the 'personal distribution of wealth' or as the 'size distribution of wealth'. The term 'size distribution of wealth' is useful in that it is an application of a precise statistical term describing the frequency distribution of some characteristic of a population according to size. To this bloodless statistical term, however, we prefer the 'personal distribution of wealth', though 'personal' needs to be interpreted broadly, because in some contexts it is more appropriate to talk about the distribution of wealth not between individuals but between households, a distinction treated in more detail in Chapter 2.

A useful benchmark for measuring the personal distribution of wealth is a society in which every individual possesses the same amount of wealth. In such a society wealth can be said to be equally distributed. In every other case the distribution of wealth can be said to be unequal – though measuring the degree of inequality is no easy matter, as will become apparent in Chapter 2.

The distribution of wealth shares with public goods the characteristic that whatever is enjoyed by one member of a society is enjoyed by all. Just as it is impossible for one member of a society to experience a high level of defence provision and another member of the same society to experience a low level, so it is impossible for one member of a society to experience an equal distribution of wealth and another member of the same society simultaneously to experience an unequal distribution of wealth.[5] On the other hand, while increasing the level of defence provision inescapably involves an opportunity cost, this may or may not be true of (say) reducing the degree of inequality in the distribution of wealth, depending on whether or not the consequence is a lower amount of wealth in the aggregate and/or a lower level of national income.[6] This question is examined extensively in Chapter 8.

It is also commonly the case that a very unequal distribution of wealth is 'a public bad, as it creates a kind of society that decreases the welfare of all – most obviously, through the crime it engenders and, less proximately, through the lack of community that it engenders' (Roemer, 1994a, p. 461); though a very unequal distribution of wealth may not be accompanied by crime if there is a sufficiently authoritarian regime.

1.3   WHY IS THE DISTRIBUTION OF WEALTH IMPORTANT?

There is by now a substantial literature on the distribution of income; the interested reader is referred in particular to *Handbook of Income Distribution*, volume 1 (2000) and volume 2A (2015), edited by Anthony B. (Tony) Atkinson and François Bourguignon. A separate study of the distribution of wealth might appear superfluous if it were true that the distribution of wealth is the same as the distribution of income. In fact, however, the distribution of wealth is always more unequal than the distribution of income.

The distribution of wealth also need not necessarily mirror that of income. This fact is illustrated by calculations reported in an article by Donald L. Lerman and James D. Mickesell, based on the 1983 United States Survey of Consumer Finances data, showing that 'in 1983 the correlation coefficient between income and wealth for all U.S. households was [only] .49' (Lerman and Mickesell, 1988, p. 789), and that '[i]f income is measured net of the yield from net worth (i.e., if capital gains, IRA income,[7] dividends, interest, and rent are removed from total income), the income-wealth correlation between income and wealth of all families falls to .26' (Lerman and Mickesell, 1988, p. 789). This relatively low correlation between the distribution of wealth and the distribution of income reflects the fact that some people, notably the elderly, are typically 'asset rich but income poor', while others, notably young adults, are typically 'income rich but asset poor'. The lifecycle hypothesis proposed by Modigliani and Brumberg (1954) attributes inequality in the distribution of wealth to this relationship, on the basis that an individual's holdings of assets increase throughout their life, such that the distribution of wealth at any single point in time is likely to capture those who are younger and relatively poor but will become wealthier, and those who are older and relatively wealthy but were once poorer.

As Peter Whiteford puts it, following similar comments made by the Australian Bureau of Statistics, compared with net worth a 'more comprehensive measure of total household resources' (Whiteford, 2014, page not numbered) is to be found in the combination of net worth and income. Given the relatively low correlation between the distribution of wealth and the distribution of income, the distribution of total resources among households may be less unequal than the distribution of either wealth or income. Whiteford provides an example of this using figures from the Australian Bureau of Statistics for 2009–10, when the ratio of the top 20% to the bottom 20% for net worth was 62.0, for disposable income was 5.10, and for net worth when households are ranked by disposable income (that is, for the ratio of net worth of the top 20% of disposable incomes to the net worth of the bottom 20% of disposable incomes) was only 3.2; this apparently puzzling result is explained in part by the fact that a large component of net worth, namely house ownership, was distributed more equally than disposable income. But it is illegitimate of Whiteford to conclude that 'these figures suggest that wealth is actually more equally distributed than income when the joint distribution of income and wealth is used'

(Whiteford, 2014, page not numbered); they show only that resources are more equally distributed than wealth (and income). Unfortunately, neither the Australian Bureau of Statistics nor Whiteford notes that the distribution of total household resources among households can alternatively be measured by disposable income when households are ranked by net worth. Figures from the Australian Bureau of Statistics for 2009–10 show that by comparison with a ratio of the top 20% to the bottom 20% for net worth of 62.0, the ratio of disposable incomes for the top 20% by net worth to disposable incomes for the bottom 20% by net worth was 10.9, a reduction from 62.0, as is to be expected, but not a ratio that suggests such a degree of equality as does the ratio resulting when the Australian Bureau of Statistics and Whiteford measure of the distribution of total household resources is used.

The distribution of wealth is important in its own right because the well-being of individuals is affected by their wealth independently of their income. To take a simple example, consider a society in which the distribution of income is equal, but half the population has wealth and half does not. The well-being of those possessing wealth will exceed that of those without wealth for a number of reasons. Those possessing wealth will be better able to purchase a home in a secure environment, and will find it easier to cope with an adverse economic event such as loss of an uninsured asset. They will be able to sustain a higher consumption level after retirement. They will be able to leave more to their children. Given these economic advantages, they have the option of making do with less income than those without wealth, so as to be able to enjoy more leisure. They are likely to enjoy a higher social status, particularly if their wealth takes a conspicuous form, such as an expensive house in a prestigious locality. And the more wealthy the individual, the greater the political power they are likely to enjoy, not only if the wealth takes the form of media ownership, but also through the ability to influence political parties through contribution of funds.

Of course possessing wealth carries with it some disadvantages. As Lisa A. Keister (2000, pp. 7–8) put it:

> Excess wealth can attract unwanted media attention and solicitations of various kinds. In some cases, wealth can invite security threats and may produce social isolation. Moreover, wealth ownership may dampen achievement motivation and performance in both those who have created wealth and those who stand to inherit it.

But from the point of view of well-being these disadvantages of wealth are far outweighed by the advantages; as the entertainer Sophie Tucker expressed it, 'I've been rich, and I've been poor. Believe me, rich is better' (quoted in Keister, 2000, p. 8). The distribution of well-being thus depends not only on the distribution of income, but also on the distribution of wealth.

1.4 HAS THE DISTRIBUTION OF WEALTH BECOME MORE OR LESS UNEQUAL OVER TIME?

Over time the advantages initially enjoyed by the wealthy may be enhanced, for three reasons in particular. First, the more wealthy one is, the greater the capacity one has to save out of income and add to wealth; indeed, as demonstrated by Tony Aspromourgos (2015, pp. 291–3), a sufficient condition for increasing inequality in the pre-tax distribution of wealth over time is that the saving rate of the wealthy exceeds the saving rate of the poor. Second, wealth has the capacity to generate more wealth. Many forms of wealth are accompanied by interest or dividend payments which allow wealth to increase. In addition, those possessing wealth will find it easier to borrow from a bank for investment purposes – 'to him that hath shall be given'. Third, as shown in Piketty (2014), historically, compared with the growth rate of income from other income sources, the growth rate of the return on wealth has been substantially greater. Though in a private property society a necessary condition for an individual's wealth to generate wealth is a set of institutional arrangements which provide effective protection of both property rights and property transactions, as Hernando De Soto (2000) stressed, this is a condition lacking in many Third World countries. However, lawmakers in developed countries have enabled the wealthy to prosper '[b]y making assets fungible, by attaching owners to assets, assets to addresses, and ownership to enforcement, and by making information on the history of assets and owners easily accessible' (De Soto, 2000, p. 58).

1.5 INEQUALITY IN THE DISTRIBUTION OF WEALTH AND POVERTY

It may seem obvious that there is a connection between inequality in the distribution of wealth on the one hand and poverty on the other, but the closeness of the connection depends on how 'poverty' is defined. The definition to be found in the *Oxford English Dictionary* (2015) reads '[t]he condition of having little or no wealth or few material possessions'. It follows from this definition that if two societies have the same distribution of wealth among those who are not in poverty, the distribution of wealth will be more unequal in that society with the greater proportion of its population in poverty. However, the most that can be said of the obverse proposition, namely that of two societies, the one with the greater proportion of its population in poverty will have a more unequal distribution of wealth, is that it is likely to be true, because alternatively inequality could be concentrated among those who are not in poverty.

It should be noted that the term 'poverty line', though obviously related to 'poverty', is commonly used to refer to a level not of wealth but of income; the *Oxford English Dictionary* (2015) defines it as 'the estimated minimum income needed to purchase the necessities of life'. Since the publication of Adam Smith's *Wealth of Nations*, at least, it has been widely recognised that the concept of 'means of subsistence' contains a conventional element that has resulted in its content increasing over time as societies become more affluent. Eventually this resulted in the term 'poverty line' being changed from an absolute to a relative measure. In Australia, for example, while in 1966 Ronald Henderson and his co-workers at the Melbourne University Institute of Applied Economic and Social Research specified a poverty line in absolute terms, in 1975 the Report of the Commission of Inquiry into Poverty headed by Henderson defined it as a fraction of the average wage, adjusted for family size. Estimating the proportion of the population that falls below the 'poverty line' has thus become a partial measure of inequality in the distribution of income (Henderson et al., 1975). Similarly, estimating the proportion of the population that is in poverty, defined, say, as possession of zero or negative net wealth, could be used as a partial measure of inequality in the distribution of wealth.

1.6   ASPECTS OF THE DISTRIBUTION OF WEALTH NOT CONSIDERED IN THIS BOOK

In the first edition of this book (Schneider, 2004a, p. 53), it was noted that unfortunately it was not

> possible to say much about the world distribution of wealth, though it is possible to say something about it as a result of the recent Branko Milanovic and Shlomo Yitzhaki (2002) study of the world distribution of income. This study both estimated the Gini coefficient for the world distribution of income to be 0.659, and found that the Gini coefficient for the distribution of income did not exceed 0.6 for any individual country other than Namibia. Even if the Gini coefficient for the distribution of wealth of 0.93 resulting from a sample survey in Sweden is disregarded as an outlier, a number of estimates of Gini coefficients for the distribution of wealth in individual countries in recent times

have exceeded 0.8, and taking into account also the fact that these coefficients are typically double those for the distribution of income, it seems reasonable to conclude that the Gini coefficient for the world distribution of wealth is at least as high as 0.9.

Subsequent research reported in Davies et al. (2011) has shown that the suggested Gini coefficient figure of 0.9 for the world distribution of wealth is probably too high. While Davies et al. (2011) include, as already noted, a comparison of the distribution of wealth in 20 countries, the declared goal of the article is 'to try to estimate the global distribution of household wealth' (ibid., p. 223) for the year 2000, which as the authors point out 'requires imputation of both wealth levels and distribution to the countries with missing data' (ibid., p. 223). The authors met this requirement by making use of the best available data for each country, and by making the figures for each country comparable with those for other countries by using purchasing power parity exchange rates. They concluded that the global distribution of wealth in 2000 did not differ greatly from the distribution of wealth in the group of 20 countries for which reasonably good distribution of wealth figures existed, the Gini coefficient for the global distribution of wealth being 0.802, and for the group of 20 (which they estimate accounts for 75% of global wealth) being 0.796. They further found that the wealth shares of the 10%, 5% and 1% wealthiest adults were 70.7%, 56.7% and 31.6% respectively, and that the wealth share of the 50% poorest was as little as 3.7%. Alternatively, using official exchange rates as the basis of their calculations, 'which is appropriate if attention is focused on the rich and super rich' (ibid., 2011, p. 250), the authors arrived at a Gini coefficient for the global distribution of wealth of 0.892, and a wealth share of the wealthiest 10% of adults of 85%.

Beyond these observations, we do not intend to delve any deeper into the question of how wealth is distributed *between* countries, or how that distribution of wealth between countries has changed over time. Similarly, this book does not explore the distribution of wealth between populations based on other characteristics such as gender or race. Though it is likely that analysis of the distribution of wealth in these dimensions could yield important insights into the nature of the distribution of wealth, this edition, like the first, focuses primarily on aggregate measures of the distribution of wealth between cohorts of individuals or households, and inequality in that distribution within countries.

1.7 PLAN OF THIS BOOK

Chapter 2 explains why measuring the distribution of wealth is by no means straightforward, and describes and compares measures which are commonly used, such as the Lorenz curve, the Gini coefficient, and the wealthiest x per cent share in total wealth. Chapter 3 summarizes the known facts about the distribution of wealth, drawing on studies both of changes in the distribution of wealth in particular countries over time and of country-by-country differences in the distribution of wealth at particular points in time. Chapter 4 discusses the relative importance of the factors that determine the distribution of wealth, addressing in particular the question of the extent to which unequal distributions merely reflect the age structure of the population, each individual's wealth increasing up to the age of retirement and decreasing thereafter. Chapter 5 examines theories leading to the conclusion that the distribution of wealth changes over time, notably that advanced recently by Thomas Piketty in *Capital in the Twenty-First Century* (2014). Chapter 6 grapples with the thorny problem of how to rank alternative distributions of wealth, and Chapter 7 deals with the means by which the distribution of wealth can, if desired, be changed. Chapter 8 examines the evidence for and against the proposition that making the distribution of wealth less unequal would lead to a smaller amount of wealth in the aggregate. Chapter 9 outlines the principal conclusions to be drawn from the preceding chapters.

NOTES

1. Note that the *Oxford English Dictionary* defines distribution in the context of political economy as the distribution not of wealth in particular but of 'the produce of the industry' in general. That this definition can apply to the wealth of all society is demonstrated by the quotations included in the *Oxford English Dictionary*.
2. '[T]he suffix th indicates a state or condition, so that "wealth" indicated a state or condition of being well, . . . just as "health" indicated a state of being healed' (Cannan, 1914, p. 3). There was a time, however, when 'weal' did not require a suffix.
3. Since the focus of this book is on the personal distribution of wealth, the fact that government bonds and 'outside' money involve a liability of the private sector as a whole is here ignored.
4. For a discussion of the intergenerational distribution of wealth see Meade, 1976, chapter IX.
5. This point is made by Meade (1976, p. 17).
6. This is a simplification of reality in that it ignores the administrative costs of changing the distribution of wealth, in the direction of either less or more inequality.
7. 'IRA income' stands for the 'individual retirement arrangement income' received by United States citizens who set up their own superannuation scheme.

2. Measuring inequality in the distribution of wealth

an inequality measure calls for a numerical scale (F.A. Cowell, 1977, p. 13)

If one is to determine whether over time there has been growing inequality in the distribution of wealth, one must first have a measure of change in inequality. To measure change in inequality over time, in turn, one must have a measure of the level of inequality at any one point in time.

Measuring the inequality of observations in any unequal distribution necessarily involves making a value judgement about what kind of inequality matters. Taking the distribution of wealth as our example, we now demonstrate how the choice of method for measuring inequality can lead to different conclusions about whether inequality is increasing or decreasing.

The measures most commonly used to assess inequality in the distribution of wealth are relative ones. But a measure of inequality may alternatively be an absolute one. We illustrate the difference between these two categories of measures by taking a simple case, namely a society consisting of two individuals, A and B. If the wealth of Individual A equals the wealth of Individual B, one can say without fear of contradiction that the level of inequality is zero. Suppose now, however, that at time t the wealth of Individual A is 90 and that of Individual B is 10, and that at time $(t + 1)$ the wealth of Individual A is 99 and that of Individual B is 11. A relative measure of distribution would show the degree of inequality in these two situations to be the same (in both cases Individual A is nine times as wealthy as Individual B). By contrast, an absolute measure would focus on the gap between the wealth of Individual A and that of Individual B; since this gap increases from 80 at time t to 88 at time $(t + 1)$, the conclusion that follows is that there is a greater degree of inequality at time $(t + 1)$ than at time t.

Suppose, alternatively, that starting from the same situation at time t the situation at time $(t + 1)$ is one in which the wealth of Individual A is 98 and that of Individual B is 12. In this case a relative measure of distribution would show the degree of inequality to have decreased (because Individual A at time $(t + 1)$ is not nine times but only 8.2 times as wealthy as Individual B), whereas an absolute measure would show the degree of inequality to have increased (given a gap at time (t + 1) of 86 compared with the initial gap of 80). Such contradictory cases led Kolm to entitle his seminal 1976 article on measures of distribution 'Unequal Inequalities'. This case is an illustration of the fact that a set of figures may represent a decrease in inequality in relative terms but an increase in inequality in absolute terms. Given the focus of this book on changes in inequality over time, however, it is worth noting that if an ascending set of figures represents an increase in inequality in relative terms, mathematically it must represent an increase in inequality in absolute terms also.

While an absolute measure of inequality in the distribution of wealth can be applied equally to one country at two different points in time or to two countries at one point in time, its use is less likely to have political ramifications in the latter case than in the former. The poor in the wealthier of two countries may not complain that the absolute gap between them and the rich is greater than that between the poor and the rich in the poorer country, knowing that they are in the richer country anyway, and perhaps also not knowing about the (disadvantageous to them) relative size of the two gaps, due to imperfect communications between countries. However, if the level of wealth of everyone in a country increases between the two points in time by the same percentage, the poor may notice that the gap between them and the rich has increased, and protest. This actually happened for example in the case of income distribution in May 1968 in France, when under the Grenelle agreements that followed a workers' general strike all payrolls were increased by 13 per cent, so that 'laborers earning 80 pounds (sic) a month received 10 pounds more, whereas executives who already earned 800 pounds a month received 100 pounds more' (Kolm, 1976, p. 419), leading labourers to feel cheated even though they were ten pounds a month better off and relatively speaking no worse off than before.

It has been contended that at least in some contexts one of these two measures may be preferable to the other. Atkinson and Brandolini (2010) argued that in analysing world distribution of income there are three reasons for re-examining the use of a relative as opposed to an absolute measure, and in their measures of inequality included an 'absolute Gini coefficient', based on absolute as opposed to relative mean differences (for a description of the 'Gini coefficient' see the next section of this chapter). They went on to note regretfully of global income distribution studies that '[a]t the empirical level, however, relative measures predominate' (2010, p. 3). Unfortunately, too, no study has as yet applied an absolute measure to the distribution of wealth. In preparing this book we have not found sufficient data to do so ourselves, either, and present primarily relative measures, though we acknowledge the importance of considering the ramifications of changes in absolute wealth inequality.[1]

Measuring inequality in either income or wealth distribution involves a second problem, namely that of choosing the unit whose wealth is to be the basis of calculation. Wealth may be seen as distributed between individuals, as has been assumed up to this point, but it may also be seen as distributed between households, and the assessment of inequality will depend on which unit is used. Suppose, for example, that a community consists of only two households, A and B. Suppose further that while each household possesses equal wealth, they possess an unequal number of members, say with one member in Household A and ten members in Household B. While a household measure of wealth distribution would show perfect equality, the individual measure would show substantial inequality (though this would also depend upon the distribution of Household B's wealth between its members). Alternatively, suppose that Household B has ten times as much wealth as Household A. In this case the individual measure of wealth distribution would show complete equality, whereas the household measure would show great inequality. Since both measures are open to the objection that they inadequately reflect the welfare implications of any particular wealth distribution, some investigators have used as the basis of their studies an 'equivalised' household, in which a weight is attached to each household member determined by age; for example, a ten-member household containing several young children might be regarded as equivalent to not ten but (say) five individuals. Since the attached weights are apt to vary substantially from one investigator to another, and given variation in household characteristics within and between different societies, this makes comparisons between such studies unreliable. This shortcoming does not, however, apply to comparisons over time in studies where the weights are fixed. For now, we continue our discussion in the context of individual wealth.

A limitation of empirical studies of the distribution of wealth that needs to be noted is that the available data are often insufficient to enable a comprehensive measure of inequality to be derived. A desirable characteristic of a comprehensive measure of inequality is that it is sensitive to any change in the distribution of a quantity, such as wealth. Thus if the distribution of wealth between any two individuals changes (if some wealth is transferred from an Individual A to an Individual B, for example), there will be a consequent change in the measure of inequality.

There are cases where existing distributional measures of inequality may not capture important aspects of changes in the nature of that inequality. For example, if the richest person and the poorest person in a distribution swap places, the distribution will appear not to have changed, even though the experience of the individuals will have changed dramatically. Existing distributional measures of inequality are insensitive to the scale of such 'churning': whether the wealthiest individual in a distribution swaps places with the poorest, or the individual immediately above the median swaps places with the individual immediately below it, the result will be the same, in that the measure of inequality will not change. Distributional measures are also insensitive to the frequency of such churning: in two different distributions, richer and poorer people may be swapping places more or less frequently without any substantial difference between the distribution measures of inequality. Thus, in scenarios like these, while the distributional measure accurately reflects the fact that inequality between abstract individuals in a population remains unchanged, this can conceal substantial volatility and differences between the nature of inequality in different distributions.[2] A measure of inequality that reflected the situation of not abstract but actual individuals would show an increase in churning as a decrease in inequality; more individuals would enjoy a period of prosperity. The additional churning required to offset a given increase in inequality would of course be a matter of judgement.

Since sensitivity to any change, including a mere swap of positions, is not a characteristic of a partial measure of inequality, any partial measure must be regarded as second-best; as Branko Milanovic puts it in a comparable context, if a comprehensive measure of inequality is available, a partial measure 'will be (as the saying goes) history' (Milanovic, 2005, p. 10).

2.1   COMPREHENSIVE MEASURES OF INEQUALITY

Extending our analysis beyond two individuals, we now suppose that a quantity of wealth x is distributed between a number of individuals n. Distribution is equal if every individual possesses the quantity x/n. All other distributions of x are unequal. If n is 2, the degree of inequality is measured by the extent to which the fraction assigned to either person, and therefore to the other, departs from one half. If n is greater than 2, however, measuring inequality is not so straightforward. Compare, for example, the following three abstract distributions of wealth, each with three individuals:

Distribution A: (4, 4, 4)
Distribution B: (2, 5, 5)
Distribution C: (3, 3, 6)

While Distribution A is clearly an example of equality, it is not immediately obvious which of Distributions B and C is the more unequal, or indeed what it would mean to say that one is more unequal than the other.

We begin our response to this problem by noting that the distribution of wealth can be illustrated by thinking in terms of probability. The distribution of wealth is described for any society by the combination of each level of wealth with the probability that a randomly chosen individual will hold that amount of wealth, a probability given by the ratio of the number of wealth-holders who actually hold that amount of wealth to the total number of wealth-holders. In an equal distribution, the likelihood of an individual possessing an equal share of wealth (the total wealth of society divided by the number of individuals in that society) would be 100 per cent, or a probability of 1. This is true of Distribution A. In the case of Distribution B, the probability of an individual possessing 2 units of wealth is one-third, and the probability of an individual holding 5 units is two-thirds, and in the case of distribution C, the probability of an individual possessing 3 units of wealth is two-thirds, and the probability of an individual holding 6 units is one-third. To take a real-world (and common) scenario, consider the distribution of wealth in Great Britain in 1968 as depicted in Figure 2.1, in which most individuals hold relatively low or

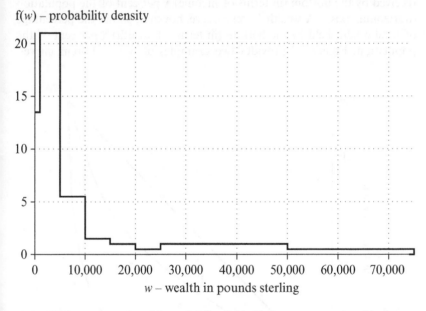

$f(w)$ – probability density

w – wealth in pounds sterling

Note: While most segments of the probability density line cover a range of wealth of £5,000, the first segment covers a range of only £1,000, and the last two segments a range of £25,000. Probabilities do not add up to 100 per cent because approximately 56 per cent of the population were not recorded as having any wealth.

Sources: This figure is based on Table 1 in Atkinson and Harrison (1974, p.134), which provides data on the distribution of wealth in Great Britain in 1968.

Figure 2.1   Distribution of wealth in Great Britain in 1968 measured by probability density (%)

zero amounts of wealth. In this figure, on the horizontal axis *w* represents wealth (in thousands of pounds sterling), and on the vertical axis $f(w)$ (an example of what is known as a probability density function) shows the probability that a randomly chosen wealth-holder will hold that amount of wealth. The figure shows, for example, the probabilities of a randomly chosen wealth-holder having wealth in the range of zero to £1,000, £1,000 to £5,000, and £5,000 to £10,000 are 13.5 per cent, 21.5 per cent and 5.5 percent respectively.

The comprehensive relative measure of inequality in the distribution of wealth most commonly used is the Gini coefficient. A diagrammatic illustration of the application of the Gini coefficient to measurement of the distribution of wealth is to be found in what we shall call a 'wealth Lorenz curve'. Lorenz curves were originally designed, by Max Otto Lorenz (1905), to show the percentage of total income (vertical axis) received by the bottom (in terms of income) *x* per cent of the population (horizontal axis).[3] A wealth Lorenz curve, however, shows the percentage of total wealth held by the bottom (in terms of wealth) *x* per cent of the population. Figure 2.2 provides two examples of wealth Lorenz curves.

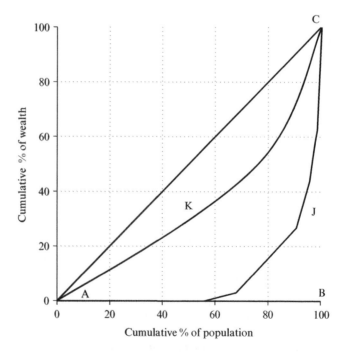

Figure 2.2   Distribution of wealth depicted by a Lorenz curve

The 'J' curve is as close a representation of the probability density function illustrated in Figure 2.1 as the data allow.

One boundary of wealth Lorenz curves is the line of complete equality, depicting the situation in which all units hold the same amount of wealth; since in this case x per cent of the population holds x per cent of total wealth, the line of complete equality runs from the origin (A) to point C, the latter representing 100 per cent of both total population and total wealth.[4] The other boundary is the remaining two sides (AB) and (BC) of the triangle ABC. The Lorenz curve ABC illustrates maximum inequality, BC representing 100 per cent of the wealth of a country being held by one person and AB representing none being held by anyone else.

The relationship between a Lorenz curve and the Gini coefficient is as follows. By definition the Gini coefficient is the arithmetic mean of all the differences between the (say) n members of a series divided by twice the mean of the members of the series;[5] it has the convenient property of lying between zero, representing complete equality, and one, representing maximum inequality. As Corrado Gini demonstrated in an article published in 1914, when the area between a Lorenz curve and the line of complete equality is divided by the area of the triangle of which the line of complete equality forms the hypotenuse, the result is the Gini coefficient.[6] Thus if one wealth Lorenz curve lies everywhere closer to the line of complete equality than another, its Gini coefficient is the lower of the two, and it represents a more equal distribution of wealth. In Figure 2.2, for example, where a second Lorenz curve labelled K has been drawn so as to lie everywhere closer to the line of complete equality than the 'J' curve, the area AKC is clearly a lower fraction of area ABC than is area AJC.

However, the situation may not be as simple as that illustrated by Figure 2.2. Two wealth Lorenz curves representing a single country at different points in time, or two countries at a single point in time, may intersect. An example of this is to be found in Figure 2.3, where the two series (2, 5, 5) and (3, 3, 6) are illustrated by the wealth Lorenz curves ADC and AEC respectively. Suppose now that ADC and AEC are the wealth Lorenz curves for a country at two points in time, t and $(t + 1)$ respectively. Compared with ADC, AEC lies closer to the line of complete equality for the bottom half of the population, but it lies further away for the top half of the population. As the eminent economist Richard T. Ely put it as long ago as 1903, possibly influenced by his member of staff Lorenz, 'there may be movements of both concentration and diffusion going on simultaneously and one has to be balanced against the other' (Ely, 1903, p. 257). How is this 'balance' to be achieved? One way of comparing the distribution of wealth at the two points in time in our example is to compare the areas between ADC and AEC on the one hand and the line of complete

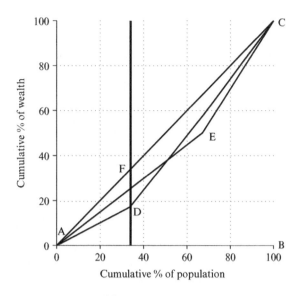

Figure 2.3   Intersecting wealth Lorenz curves

equality on the other; since inspection of Figure 2.3 suggests these areas are equal, we can surmise that the degree of inequality in the distribution of wealth is the same in the two countries. A surer way is to calculate the Gini coefficient, which turns out to be 0.25 in both cases. When it is not possible to tell by inspection which, if either, of two intersecting Lorenz curves is further away from the line of complete equality, in order to discover which Lorenz curve represents the greater degree of inequality we have to calculate the Gini coefficient of each.

We turn now to a complication which can be ignored if Lorenz curves are to be used to measure inequality in the distribution of income but cannot be ignored if they are to be used to measure inequality in the distribution of wealth. The number of individuals who have negative net income (resulting from realised capital losses outweighing income from other sources) is typically negligible (crises such as that in the United States during the 1929 Wall Street Crash being the exceptions that prove the rule). By contrast, a group as large as the bottom 10 per cent of the population may have negative net wealth, owing more than they own.[7] Thus negative values, though ignored when Lorenz curves are used to measure inequality in the distribution of income, have to be taken into account if Lorenz curves are to be used to measure inequality in the distribution of wealth.

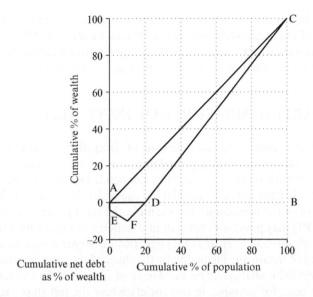

Figure 2.4   Wealth Lorenz curves where some individuals/households have zero or negative wealth

Let us start with a society in which individuals/households possessing positive net wealth all have the same amount, but some individuals have zero net wealth. Tracing down to the left from point C in Figure 2.4, the wealth Lorenz curve for such a society would meet the horizontal axis at a positive point, such as point D representing 20 per cent of the population (the last quintile), indicating that 20 per cent of the population have zero net wealth, and thereafter follow the horizontal axis to the origin. The Gini coefficient would thus be the area ADC divided by the area ABC, namely 0.2. Note that a transfer of some members of the poorer group to the richer group would reduce the Gini coefficient.

Now consider a society in which some individuals have negative net wealth. After meeting the AB line at (say) point D, the wealth Lorenz curve for this society would dip below it, each point on it between the vertical axis and D representing a ratio of cumulative net debt to national wealth in percentage terms. If the net debt of the poorest individual, for example, equals 4 per cent of national wealth, starting from point A the Lorenz curve first moves to point E, the latter lying approximately on the vertical axis in the case of a large population. Thereafter it slopes downward until the first individual with positive net wealth is reached, after which it turns upward. In this case the Gini coefficient would be measured by the ratio of the sum of the areas ADC and ADFE divided by the area ABC.[8]

The Gini coefficient is not the only comprehensive measure of inequality. Alternatives are discussed in the Appendix to this chapter.

2.2   PARTIAL MEASURES OF INEQUALITY

Given that a comprehensive measure of inequality cannot always be obtained, due to lack of data, partial measures have their place. The distribution of wealth is often measured by the percentage of total wealth held by the top 1 (percentile), 10 (decile), 20 (quintile), 25 (quartile), 30, 40 or 50 per cent of the population. For example, the top 1 per cent (often designated as P1) may possess 40 per cent of a nation's wealth, or the top 10 per cent (which we shall refer to as D1) may possess 60 per cent, and so on. A deficiency of measuring inequality by the share of the top x per cent is that it sheds no light whatsoever on the degree of inequality for the remaining (1-x) per cent; for example, in one society where the top 10 per cent possesses 60 per cent of total wealth, the distribution of wealth between the remaining 90 per cent of the population may be perfectly equal, whereas in another society where the top 10 per cent possesses 60 per cent of the total wealth, the next 10 per cent may possess the whole of the remainder. But this is often the only measure available, and despite its deficiency we nonetheless make use of it.

The distribution of wealth is also often measured, alternatively, by the percentage of total wealth held by more than one of the top percentiles, deciles, quintiles, or quartiles of the population. While this measure is subject to the same deficiency as the previous one, in that it says nothing about the distribution of wealth in the remaining percentiles, deciles, quintiles, or quartiles, it is subject to a further deficiency in that it provides more than one measure of inequality; for example, data for the top percentile may show inequality increasing over time, while data for the next percentile shows inequality decreasing over time. This measure only produces unambiguous results if the share data for all measured elements of the top 50 per cent of the population move over time in one direction, and the share data for all measured elements of the bottom 50 per cent of the population move over time in the other direction.

In some cases data are available for all percentiles, deciles, quintiles or quartiles. In this case distribution can be measured by the wealth ratio of the top x per cent to the bottom x per cent. This has the advantage that it provides a single figure for inequality, measuring the average (mean) wealth possessed by the top group divided by that possessed by the bottom group.

For such ratios, in the limiting case of equality between the two groups, the measure of inequality would take a value of one, and the greater the inequality between the two groups, the greater the amount by which the measure would exceed one.

Take, for example, the ratio of the top 50 per cent to the bottom 50 per cent (let us call it the 50/50 ratio), which in the case of the distribution of wealth commonly comes out to be something like 15. Since the number of persons in each of these groups is by definition the same, this implies that the average (mean) person in the top group possesses 15 times as much wealth as the average (mean) person in the bottom group, thereby providing a single measure of inequality that is easy to understand. On the other hand, while providing a measure of inequality for the whole population, the 50/50 ratio is insensitive to all changes in distribution confined to members of either the top or the bottom group.

While wealth data in some cases do not permit calculation of the 50/50 ratio, they may permit calculation of the ratio of the top 40 per cent to the bottom 40 per cent (the 40/40 ratio), which commonly comes out to be something like 20. Since the number of persons in each of these groups is again by definition the same, this implies that the average (mean) person in the top 40 per cent possesses 20 times as much wealth as the average (mean) person in the bottom 40 per cent. While providing a measure of inequality for 80 per cent of the population, the 40/40 ratio is, however, insensitive to all changes in distribution confined to members of either the top 40 per cent, the middle 20 per cent or the bottom 40 per cent. And the lower the percentage of the population represented in the wealth ratio, the less reliable this ratio is likely to be as a proxy for inequality in the distribution of wealth for the population as a whole. Further, when measuring the 40/40 ratio for available wealth data, we find it to be particularly volatile in cases where wealth inequality is high, which makes this measure of wealth inequality ironically less useful the greater the level of inequality. Nonetheless, the 40/40 ratio may be preferred to the 50/50 ratio in cases where excluding those close to the median (whom we might deem 'ordinarily wealthy') may be desirable in order to compare the wealth of the 'rather' wealthy and the 'rather' poor. Despite its deficiencies, we regard the 'wealth ratio' measure of inequality as the partial measure that most closely approximates a comprehensive measure, and use it wherever it is available.

Partial measures of inequality, too, can be depicted by means of a Lorenz curve diagram. Take, for example, the Lorenz curve going through the point D in Figure 2.3. The vertical line representing the bottom one-third and top two-thirds of the population, going through point D, splits the Lorenz curve into two parts. The relative wealth of the top two-thirds of the population is measured by the actual area to the right of this line between the Lorenz curve and the line of perfect equality, CDF, divided by its maximum value, the result in this case being 5/6, and the difference between the actual and maximum ratios being 1/6. Alternatively, the relative poverty of the bottom one-third of the population is measured by the actual area to the left of this line between the Lorenz curve and the line of perfect equality, ADF, divided by its maximum value, the result in this case being 1/6, and the difference between the actual and maximum ratios again being 1/6. Such 'difference' figures could be called 'partial Gini coefficients' – partial because they do not provide information about distribution within either the top or the bottom section of the population.

Now that we have explored the difficulties involved in measuring inequality in the distribution of wealth, we turn in the next chapter to the attempts that have actually been made to measure it, focusing on single countries over time, though also sometimes looking at different countries at given points in time.

APPENDIX TO CHAPTER 2: ALTERNATIVE COMPREHENSIVE MEASURES OF INEQUALITY

Given that the Gini coefficient is more sensitive to changes in the middle than in the upper and lower ranges of distribution, it is not surprising that it is not the only comprehensive relative measure of inequality to have been applied to the distribution of wealth.[9] One alternative measure is the coefficient of variation. In the example used in the body of the chapter, Distributions B (2, 5, 5) and C (3, 3, 6) both have an arithmetic mean (total wealth divided by number of individuals) of 4, and their dispersion as measured by their standard deviation (the square root of the average squared deviations of each observation from the mean) is in both cases equal to the square root of 2. The coefficient of variation measures the standard deviation relative to the mean multiplied by 100. In the case of our example, as Distributions B and C both have the same mean and standard deviation, they also share the same coefficient of variation (the square root of 1/8 multiplied by 100). By contrast, in the case of the equal distribution (4, 4, 4), while the mean is again 4, the standard deviation is obviously zero, yielding a coefficient of variation that is also zero, reflecting the fact that there is no variation in wealth between individuals in this distribution. Partly because the coefficient of variation is more sensitive to changes in the upper than in the middle and lower ranges of distribution and partly because it is unbounded, the coefficient of variation is less commonly used as a comprehensive relative measure of inequality in the distribution of wealth than the Gini coefficient is. Another comprehensive relative measure is the relative mean deviation, which measures the sum of the absolute deviations from the mean divided by the total. For both Distributions B (2, 5, 5) and C (3, 3, 6) this measure produces a figure of 4/12, that is to say 1/3.

Where the two distributions are more complex than in our example, however, the Gini coefficient, coefficient of variation, and relative mean deviation measures may produce different rankings. It was for this reason that Atkinson and Harrison commented with respect to these measures that they

> give different weight to different parts of the distribution, and mean in effect that one has to examine the underlying Lorenz curves in order to understand what is going on. To this extent the value of using summary measures is diminished. (Atkinson and Harrison, 1978, p. 124)

Also subject to this limitation are alternative summary relative measures such as the relative interquartile range. The relative interquartile range measure makes use of the concept of the median value, namely that value of which it is true that as many observations lie above it as lie below it; this measure is the difference between the median wealth of the richer half of the population and the median wealth of the poorer half, divided by the median wealth of the whole population. For example, for the distribution (2, 3, 4, 5, 6, 7, 8) this measure produces a figure of $(7 - 3)/5$, that is to say 4/5.

Further, since Vilfredo Pareto put forward what was to become known as Pareto's Law, attempts have been made to find a statistical distribution to which the distribution of income or wealth approximates; in addition to Pareto's Law, these parametric approaches include an exponential index and Theil's entropy index.[10] We look at these in turn. Pareto's Law arose out of Pareto's finding that for the societies he examined the number of persons (N) above each income level (x) was approximately described by the equation $N = A/x\alpha$, with inequality varying inversely with the value of α, which is sometimes referred to as the Pareto index.[11] In a pioneering paper Dwight B. Yntema (1933) calculated the value of α, as well as seven other measures of inequality, for ten sets of wealth distribution data collected between 1859 and 1923, relating to Australia, the United States, France, the United Kingdom, Massachusetts and Wisconsin, concluding that they all lay within the rather narrow range of 1.03 to 1.54.[12]

The exponential measure (E) comes from James B. (Jim) Davies (1979), drawing on M.C. Wolfson (1977), where it is defined as the log of (the sum of the exponentials of one minus the wealth of each individual divided by the mean, all divided by the number of individuals), which is to say

$$E \equiv \ln\left(\frac{1}{n}\sum_{i=1}^{n}\exp\left(1 - \frac{w_i}{\mu}\right)\right) \qquad (2.1)$$

The exponential measure represented by equation (2.1) was proposed by Davies as a supplement to the coefficient of variation and the Gini coefficient on the grounds that while the coefficient of variation is in practice most sensitive to changes in the upper range and the Gini coefficient is most sensitive to changes in the middle range (as we have already noted), the exponential measure is most sensitive to changes in the lower range.

In turn, Theil's entropy index, applied to the distribution of wealth, can be expressed as the sum of the wealth of each individual divided by the mean multiplied by the log of that ratio, all divided by the number of individuals. Although Theil's entropy index has been widely used, notably in measurement of concentration in industry, as well as by W. Norton Grubb and Robert H. Wilson (1992), and James K. Galbraith (1998) to measure the distribution of income, it has not as yet been applied to measurement of the distribution of wealth.[13]

NOTES

1. It is possible to derive a measure of inequality including both absolute and relative elements. Thus Kolm, having categorised relative measures of inequality as 'rightist' and absolute measures as 'leftist', went on to derive the conditions for a measure involving elements of both, which he categorised as 'centrist'.
2. See, for example, Ravallion (2006) for an example of churning in developing economies.
3. The title of the article by Max Otto Lorenz in which Lorenz curves were first drawn is 'Methods for Measuring Concentration of Wealth', but Lorenz's use of the term 'wealth' rather than 'income' only reflects the fact that he regarded these terms as alternative ways of describing the same flow.
4. We follow the convention of economists in applying the term 'curve' even when the relationship is linear.
5. This is the way the Gini coefficient is defined in Camilo Dagum (1987).
6. For an account of the origins of the Lorenz curve and the Gini coefficient, and of how Gini was possibly inspired by the Lorenz curve to replace other measures of inequality he had already derived by what is now known as the Gini coefficient, see Schneider (2004b).
7. See Chapter 3 for examples of the bottom 10 per cent of the population having negative net wealth. We are indebted to Tony Atkinson for drawing our attention to the importance of this distinctive feature of the distribution of wealth, and to the likelihood that it would lead to complications with respect to measurement. Figure 2.4, together with the accompanying text, is a response.
8. Where negative net wealth exists, a Gini coefficient greater than one is a theoretical possibility. Suppose, for example, that a society's total wealth is all held by the one individual, and that in addition this individual has a financial asset representing the net debt of another individual. In this admittedly unrealistic case, the Gini coefficient would be greater than one.
9. Note, however, that Dagum (1987, p. 531) argued that, when properly interpreted, the Gini coefficient is not subject to this bias.
10. For a summary of parametric approaches, see Giorgi (1999, pp. 252–4).
11. While Pareto (1897, p. 312) stated that the slope α of the line depicting his equation logarithmically is a negative index of inequality, the surrounding text makes it clear that he defined inequality as a low per capita income.

12. Yntema's article was one of the sources of inspiration for H.O.A. Wold and P. Whittle (1957), who constructed a model justifying the application of Pareto's Law to the distribution of wealth.

13. With the exception of the exponential index, these measures of inequality and several others are discussed in a technical – but not too technical – way in Cowell (1977), their properties being usefully summarised in Table 3–1 (Cowell, 1977, pp. 72–3). See also Cowell (2003) for a discussion of the relationship between this measure of inequality and others. An alternative source which assumes a higher level of mathematical knowledge on the part of the reader is the 1999 book edited by Jacques Silber.

3. Empirical studies of the distribution of wealth

There are basically two ways of collecting . . . information: 1 You can ask for it. 2 You can make them give it to you. Neither method is wholly satisfactory since, in the first case, some people may choose not to give the information, or may give it incorrectly, and in the second case, the legal requirement for information may not correspond exactly to the data requirements of the social analyst. (Cowell, 1977, pp. 106–7)

Data on the distribution of wealth, like other data, come from sources which belong to one of the two main categories listed by Cowell. First, there are data collected on a voluntary basis by sample survey. Second, there are the figures collected by governments on a compulsory basis, notably census and estate data, though census data rarely include figures on wealth. Each of these basic data collection sources has its own deficiencies, making a comparison where figures based on one source are compared with figures based on the other source of limited validity. This caution also applies, though to a lesser extent, to a comparison where figures are based on the same basic source, as there may be variability in definitions used in the collection of the data.

Variability of data sources is one of three principal reasons why comparisons between distributions of wealth may have limited validity. A second reason is that distribution of wealth data differ not only according to nature of source, but also according to the unit whose wealth is measured. The unit whose wealth is measured may be either an individual or a household, and as noted in Chapter 2 a measure of inequality among individuals may be equivalent to quite a different measure of inequality among households. In addition, there may be differences in the way individuals and households are defined.

Third, distribution-of-wealth data differ according to the method by which they are estimated. In the few cases where a country has a wealth tax, estimates of the distribution of wealth can be made on the basis of the wealth data provided to the taxation department. Otherwise, some estimates of the distribution of wealth are made according to the estate multiplier method, some on the basis of sample surveys, and some according to the investment income method. We next briefly outline the nature of each of these methods.

In the case of the estate multiplier method, the raw data come from a sample of estates classified by size and the age and sex of the deceased. Estimates of wealth distribution are made by

> [a]ssuming that those of a particular age and sex dying in a given year are representative of the living population, . . . [and] 'blowing up' the estate data by a mortality multiplier equal to the reciprocal of the mortality rate. In other words, if the mortality rate for a particular male age group is 1 in 1,000, we assume that for every man who died at this age in a given year, there are 999 alive in similar circumstances and multiply the numbers and values of estates in this age group by 1,000. (Atkinson and Harrison, 1978, p. 8)

Commonly an adjustment is made for differential mortality rates according to social class. However, estate data, being collected for taxation purposes, are liable to underestimate wealth, to varying degrees, and generally cover only that part of the population which possesses wealth in excess of a certain amount.

In the case of the sample survey method, as the term suggests the raw data come from the wealth holdings of a sample of the population that is intended to be representative of the population as a whole. Even if the raw data are accurate with respect to those included in the sample, which they may not be, due in particular to non-response of a non-random nature, it is unlikely that any sample will be completely representative of the population as a whole. In the case of the investment income method (alternatively known as the income capitalisation method), recourse is 'made to statistics on investment incomes, from which estimates of the wealth which generated these incomes can be calculated' (Harrison, 1979, p. 1). The essence of this method

> is to apply a 'yield multiplier' to work back from the distribution of investment income to the distribution of wealth: if, for example, the yield is thought to be 5 per cent, the multiplier is 20, so that an investment income of £5,000 would be assumed to correspond to wealth of £100,000. The yield multiplier varies with the form in which wealth is held and the normal procedure has been to calculate a weighted average yield based on the composition of wealth indicated by the estate duty statistics. (Atkinson and Harrison, 1978, pp. 11–12)

The principal deficiencies of this method are outlined in detail by Harrison (1979, pp.19–20). They include in particular the guesswork involved in estimating the 'yield multiplier' (reciprocal of the yield) to be applied to each investment income.

We now turn to studies of wealth distribution based on one or more of these estimation methods. We postpone until later in this chapter discussion of country studies based on distribution of wealth figures available for only one point in time, beginning instead with country studies that cover not only the distribution of wealth at one point in time but also changes therein over time. Arguably reliable measurements of the distribution of wealth date back to the eighteenth century in the cases of four countries, namely Denmark, Norway, the United Kingdom[1] and the United States, to the nineteenth century in the cases of France and Sweden, and to the twentieth century in the cases of Australia, Belgium, Canada, Finland, Ireland, Italy, Japan, New Zealand, the Republic of Korea, West Germany, and Switzerland. A summary of findings on changes in the distribution of wealth in seven of these countries is to be found in the first section of this chapter. The following seven sections look at further information relating to the distribution of wealth in these countries, one by one. Subsequent sections discuss the distribution of wealth in other countries for which data are available. The last section draws some conclusions. As noted in the introduction, since the focus of the book is on the personal distribution of wealth, this chapter does not include reference to studies of the distribution of wealth according to cohorts identified by (say) class, income, age, education, sex or race.

Data relating to changes in a country's distribution of wealth over time need to be treated with caution because sources and/or methods of interpreting them may change from one year to the next. Particular caution should be exercised when any comparisons are made between countries. While for most countries data relate to the distribution of wealth between households, for a substantial minority they relate to the distribution of wealth between individuals, and as noted in Chapter 1, while empirical studies of the distribution of wealth most commonly include in their measurement of wealth marketable assets only, some studies include additional types of assets. Data sources also differ widely between studies, as do the assumptions made as to how the data should be interpreted. For these reasons, in this chapter the distribution of wealth in different countries is only explicitly compared where those producing the figures have themselves judged that the data warrant making a comparison.

3.1   LONG-RUN TRENDS IN THE DISTRIBUTION OF WEALTH

In attempting to identify long-run trends in the distribution of wealth for different countries, we begin by presenting a measure of the share of total wealth held by the wealthiest 5% of the population in Denmark, France, Norway, Sweden, Switzerland, the United Kingdom and the United States, from 1740 to 2003 (Table 3.1), derived from data published by Ohlsson et al. (2006).[2] Data on the wealthiest 10%, derived from Piketty (2014), are

Empirical studies of the distribution of wealth 29

Table 3.1   Wealth share (%) of the wealthiest 5% in Denmark, France, Norway, Sweden, Switzerland, the United Kingdom and the United States, 1740–2003

Year	Den	Fra	Nor	Swed	Switz	UK	USA
1740						86.9	
1774							41.0
1789	80.0		70.0				
1800				90.6			
1807		70.2					
1810						85.3	
1817		71.9					
1827		73.1					
1837		71.2					
1847		72.4					
1857		74.5					
1860							49.0
1867		72.7					
1875						84.0	
1877		76.0					
1887		76.5					
1902		78.5					
1904		78.2					
1906		81.1					
1907		78.5					
1908	78.0			75.2			
1910		79.2				87.0	
1911		80.2				87.0	
1912		79.2	69.2				
1913		78.2					
1915	74.2				68.7		
1917	74.0						
1919	72.5				62.3		
1920	66.2			79.2			
1921	67.5				64.0		
1923	68.2					82.0	
1925	68.1	69.2			64.6		82.1
1927		70.4					81.3
1929		71.9			66.6		78.9
1930		71.6	70.6	77.3			79.2
1933		68.5					
1934					67.9		
1935		68.7		70.8			
1936		68.2			68.1		77.4

Table 3.1   (continued)

Year	Den	Fra	Nor	Swed	Switz	UK	USA
1938		65.2			73.3	77.2	
1939	70.5	66.4					
1940		64.7			67.6		
1941		62.1			69.4		
1943		63.2					
1944	68.4	64.8					
1945		62.1		65.4	64.3		
1947		55.8		63.4	65.4		
1948		56.9	62.4	63.1			
1949	58.2	59.4		61.9	65.0		
1950	56.0	60.1		60.6		74.4	
1951	56.0	58.7		59.0	66.3	73.7	
1953	55.7	60.9			66.6	71.3	
1955	55.2	58.9			67.3	72.4	
1957	51.8	57.7			67.4	69.1	
1960	50.3	54.2	51.0			59.5	
1962	50.7	55.2				54.9	53.1
1964	50.9	57.8				59.0	
1966	47.1			46.9		55.7	
1967	47.0					56.3	
1969					66.8		
1970	47.7			42.1		53.9	
1972	48.0					56.9	
1973			44.0			51.5	
1975	50.5			44.3		46.5	
1976			42.3			49.0	
1978				39.8		37.0	
1979			42.1	38.6		37.0	
1981				35.9	56.6	36.0	
1982			45.5	37.0		36.0	
1983			44.4	37.0		37.0	56.1
1984		46.7	42.6	36.0		35.0	
1986			43.0	35.3		36.0	
1988			43.2	39.1		36.0	
1989			42.9	40.3		35.0	59.0
1991			42.7	38.2	56.6	35.0	
1992			40.3	39.3		38.0	60.0
1993				40.7		38.0	
1994		44.6	42.2			39.0	
1995	53.9		41.9			38.0	60.3
1996	53.0		42.5			40.0	
1997			43.4		58.0	43.0	

Table 3.1   (continued)

Year	Den	Fra	Nor	Swed	Switz	UK	USA
1998			47.0			40.0	59.4
2000			47.5	42.2		44.0	
2001			46.1	39.8		42.0	
2002			46.9	40.1		45.0	
2003						40.0	

Source: Ohlsson et al. (2006), Table 1, pp. 18–20, and Table 2, pp. 21–2.

next presented, covering France, Sweden, the United Kingdom and the United States, for the period 1810 to 2010 (Table 3.2).[3] In interpreting and analysing these trends, in chapter sections 3.2 to 3.8 we draw on additional data for each of the countries covered by Ohlsson et al. (2006). Then, in subsequent chapter sections we add a discussion of available data for countries other than those included in Ohlsson et al. (2006), including some comparative studies; again, we emphasise that because of the different sources and/or methods used to gather these data, the validity of comparisons across countries is likely to be questionable.

Table 3.1 shows that over the period 1740–1913 for France the percentage share in total wealth of the wealthiest 5% rose from the low seventies in 1807–67 to the high seventies to low eighties in 1877–1913. On the other hand, the four observations for the United Kingdom show virtually the same percentage for 1911 as for 1740, with in between a fall followed by a rise. The paucity of observations makes it difficult to infer anything for the other four countries (there are no data for Switzerland), though for Denmark and Norway there is very little change between 1789 and the early twentieth century, and for Sweden there is not a rise but a marked fall between 1800 and 1908.

By comparison with the 1920s, by the end of the 1950s inequality in the distribution of wealth as measured by the wealthiest 5% share was markedly less for Denmark, France, Norway, Sweden and the United Kingdom. Thus in these countries the personal distribution of wealth so measured became less unequal between the 1920s and the 1950s. The exception is Switzerland, where the distribution of wealth remained relatively constant until 1969, but became less unequal between that year and 1981 (in the case of the United States there are no figures for this period, making comparisons over time impossible).

Between 1960 and 2003 there was an upward drift in inequality in the distribution of wealth from 1966 in the case of Denmark, 1979 in the case of Norway, 1991 in the case of the United Kingdom, and 1983 in the case

*Table 3.2   Wealth share (%) of the wealthiest 10% in France, the
United Kingdom, the United States and Sweden, 1810–2010*

Year	Fra	Swed	UK	US
1810	79.9	83.9	82.9	58.0
1820	81.8			
1830	83.2			
1840	80.4			
1850	82.4			
1860	83.7			
1870	81.8	87.2	87.1	71.0
1880	84.6			
1890	84.7			
1900	87.3			
1910	88.5	88.2	92.0	81.1
1930	80.0	83.6	85.0	73.4
1940	75.8	83.2		66.4
1950	72.8	77.3	76.0	65.7
1960	69.9	63.2	71.5	67.0
1970	62.0	54.7	64.1	64.2
1980	61.8	53.4	62.6	67.2
1990	61.0	57.7	64.0	68.7
2000	62.1	57.8	68.5	69.7
2010	62.4	58.8	70.5	71.5

Source: Piketty (2014), Technical Appendix, Table S10.1.

of the United States; no clear trend is discernible in the cases of France
and (again) Switzerland.

In the case of some of the countries reported by Ohlsson et al., there is
more recent information available on the wealth holdings of the wealthiest
5%. Data published in Wolff (2012) provide more recent figures for the
wealth share of the wealthiest 5% in the United States, and suggest that
while the wealthiest 5% held 59% of the wealth in the United States in 2001
and 2004 (suggesting relatively little change in this proportion from 1989
until 2004, as evidenced by Ohlsson et al.'s data in Table 3.1), that share of
wealth increased to 62% in 2007, and 63% in 2010.

Table 3.2 reproduces the wealth share (%) of the wealthiest 10% figures
as shown in Table S10.1 in the Technical Appendix to Piketty (2014). Only
in the case of France are these figures strictly comparable in the sense that
they are based on a single source. These data are not directly comparable
with those in the previous tables, in that they show the percentage share in
total wealth of not the wealthiest 5% but the wealthiest 10%.

All in all, despite their different basis in terms of the wealthiest percentage used, the data in Table 3.2 show a remarkable consistency with those in Table 3.1. In the case of all four countries the wealth share of the wealthiest 10% increased between 1810 and 1910. The wealth share of the wealthiest 10% also declined between 1910 and the 1970s in the case of the United States, between 1910 and the 1980s in the cases of the United Kingdom and Sweden, and between 1910 and the 1990s in the case of France. In each case, after reaching a minimum, the wealth share of the wealthiest 10% in total wealth started to increase in the final decades of the twentieth century.

In the following seven sections of this chapter we record and comment on the additional information on the distribution of wealth currently available for the seven countries discussed in this section, in each case starting with the wealthiest 1% and next wealthiest 4% data to be found in Ohlsson et al. (2006) that provided the basis for the wealthiest 5% data reported in this section, and following this up with data from other studies, where these exist.

3.2 DENMARK

Table 3.3 shows the share of total wealth of the wealthiest 1% and the next wealthiest 4% of the population of Denmark, over the period 1789–1996.

What this table indicates is that the fall in the wealth share of the wealthiest 5% in Denmark between 1915 and 1996 (see Table 3.1) was largely due to the fall in the wealth share of the wealthiest 1%, from 47.0% in 1915 to a minimum of 24.6% in 1967, though it rose somewhat thereafter, to 27.2%. The wealth share of the next wealthiest 4% remained relatively constant over this period, falling from 27.2% in 1915 only to a minimum of 22.3% in 1966, before rising to 25.8% in 1996.[4]

3.3 FRANCE

Table 3.4 shows the share of total wealth (%) of the wealthiest 0.1%, wealthiest 1% and next wealthiest 4% of the population in France over the period 1807–2010.

Table 3.4 indicates that the rise in the wealth share of the wealthiest 5% of the population in France between 1807 and 1913 (see Table 3.1) was largely due to the rise in the wealth share of the wealthiest 1%, because the wealth share of the next wealthiest 4% remained relatively constant over the period 1807–87, and thereafter actually fell to lower levels. A further

Table 3.3   *Wealth share (%) of the wealthiest 1% and the next wealthiest 4% in Denmark, 1789–1996*

Year	Top 1%	Next 4%
1789	56.0	24.0
1908	46.3	31.7
1915	47.0	27.2
1917	44.1	27.9
1919	42.6	26.9
1920	37.2	29.0
1921	39.7	27.8
1923	39.9	28.3
1925	38.7	29.4
1939	41.7	28.8
1944	39.2	29.2
1949	31.3	26.9
1950	29.6	26.4
1951	29.7	26.3
1953	29.5	26.2
1955	29.5	25.7
1957	27.2	24.6
1960	26.4	25.6
1962	26.9	23.8
1964	27.6	23.3
1966	24.8	22.3
1967	24.6	22.4
1970	24.8	22.9
1972	25.3	22.7
1975	25.9	24.6
1995	26.9	27.0
1996	27.2	25.8

Source: Ohlsson et al. (2006), Tables 1 and 2, pp. 18–23.

implication is that the rise over this period in the wealth share of the wealthiest 1% of the population in France was in part due to a rise in the wealth share of the wealthiest 0.1% of the population.

Table 3.4 also indicates that the fall in the wealth share of the wealthiest 5% of the population in France between 1919 and 1994 (see Table 3.1) was largely due to a fall in the wealth share of the wealthiest 1% of the population, because the wealth share of the next wealthiest 4% of the population actually rose over this period. Further implications are first, that the fall in the wealth share of the wealthiest 1% of the population over this period was in part due to a fall in the wealth share of the wealthiest 0.1% of the

Table 3.4   *Wealth share (%) of the wealthiest 0.1%, the wealthiest 1% and the next wealthiest 4% in France, 1807–1913*

Year	Top 0.1%	Top 1%	Next 4%
1807		43.4	26.8
1810	17.1		
1817		44.5	27.4
1820	19.0		
1827		45.2	27.9
1830	17.1		
1837		43.8	27.4
1840	15.5		
1847		47.9	24.5
1850	19.4		
1857		49.5	25.0
1860	18.3		
1867		48.0	24.7
1870	18.3		
1877		47.1	28.9
1880	21.1		
1887		48.7	28.5
1890	20.2		
1900	28.1		
1902		51.6	23.9
1904		54.4	23.8
1906		59.8	21.3
1907		54.5	24.0
1909		56.8	22.4
1910	29.0		
1911		57.7	22.5
1913		54.9	23.3
1920	23.1		
1925		44.6	24.6
1927		47.6	22.8
1929		50.2	21.7
1930	22.4	50.3	21.3
1933		44.9	23.6
1935		46.1	22.6
1936		45.8	22.4
1938		42.0	23.2
1939		42.9	23.5
1940	13.7	38.7	26.0
1941		34.9	27.2
1943		36.8	26.4
1944		38.3	26.5

Table 3.4   (continued)

Year	Top 0.1%	Top 1%	Next 4%
1945		35.3	26.8
1947		29.9	25.5
1948		30.4	26.5
1949		34.0	25.4
1950	12.1	33.6	26.5
1951		33.0	25.7
1953		32.6	28.3
1955		31.5	27.4
1957		32.3	25.4
1960	11.5	29.5	24.7
1962		30.3	24.9
1964		31.3	26.5
1970	7.0		
1980	6.7		
1984		21.6	25.1
1990	6.4		
1994		21.3	23.3
2000	7.0		
2010	7.2		

Source: Ohlsson et al. (2006), Tables 1 and 2, pp. 18–23, and Piketty (2014), Technical Appendix, Table S10.1.

population, and second, that by contrast the wealth share of the wealthiest 0.1% of the population actually rose between 2000 and 2010.

3.4   NORWAY

Table 3.5 shows the share of total wealth of the wealthiest 1% and the next wealthiest 4% of the population of Norway, over the period 1789–2002.

Table 3.5 implies that the fall in the wealth share of the wealthiest 5% of the population in Norway between 1930 and 1992 was due to falls in the wealth shares of both the wealthiest 1% and the next wealthiest 4%, but that the rise in the wealth share of the wealthiest 5% of the population between 1992 and 2002 was largely due to a rise in the wealth share of the wealthiest 1% of the population, because over this period the wealth share of the next wealthiest 4% actually fell.

Table 3.5   Wealth share (%) of the wealthiest 1% and the next wealthiest 4% in Norway, 1789–2002

Year	Top 1%	Next 4%
1789	47.0	23.0
1911/12	37.2	32.0
1930	37.6	33.0
1948	34.6	27.8
1960	25.5	25.5
1973	21.5	22.5
1976	19.5	22.8
1979	18.5	23.6
1982	18.0	27.5
1983	17.5	26.9
1984	18.0	24.6
1986	18.7	24.3
1988	18.9	24.3
1989	18.9	24.0
1991	18.8	23.9
1992	17.5	22.8
1994	19.9	22.3
1995	20.0	21.9
1996	20.6	21.9
1997	21.6	21.8
1998	25.9	21.1
2000	26.6	20.9
2001	25.2	20.9
2002	25.4	21.5

Note: Ohlsson et al. list a top 1% figure for 1912 and a next 4% figure for 1911.

Source: Ohlsson et al. (2006), Tables 1 and 2, pp. 18–23.

3.5   SWEDEN

Table 3.6 shows the share of total wealth of the wealthiest 1% and the next wealthiest 4% of the population of Sweden, over the period 1800–2002.

Table 3.6 indicates that both the fall in the wealth share of the wealthiest 5% of the population in Sweden between 1800 and 1981 and its rise thereafter were due in part to a fall and subsequent rise in the wealth share of the wealthiest 1% and in part to a fall and subsequent rise in the wealth share of the next wealthiest 4%.

Changes in the distribution of wealth in Sweden have also been estimated

Table 3.6   Wealth share (%) of the wealthiest 1% and the next wealthiest 4% in Sweden, 1800–2002

Year	Top 1%	Next 4%
1800	51.9	38.7
1908	53.5	21.7
1920	51.5	27.7
1930	50.0	27.3
1935	42.8	28.0
1945	37.7	28.3
1947	34.7	28.7
1948	34.1	29.0
1949	33.2	28.7
1950	32.8	27.8
1951	32.2	26.8
1966	23.4	23.5
1970	20.1	22.0
1975	20.7	23.6
1978	19.4	20.4
1979	17.1	21.5
1981	16.2	19.7
1982	17.3	19.7
1983	18.1	18.9
1984	16.5	19.5
1986	16.2	19.1
1988	18.6	20.5
1989	19.7	20.6
1991	16.0	22.2
1992	16.5	22.8
1993	17.8	22.9
2000	19.5	22.7
2001	17.8	22.4
2002	18.4	22.3

Source: Ohlsson et al. (2006), Tables 1 and 2, pp. 18–23.

by Roland Spånt, for two periods, namely 1920–75 and 1975–83 (see Spånt, 1978, and Spånt, 1987), and by Lars Bager-Sjögren and N. Anders Klevmarken (1998) for the period 1983/84–1992/93.

Spånt's estimates for each of eight years during the period 1920–75 are based on samples of household tax returns in which, Spånt noted, the most wealthy are over-represented; since taxable assets include only those assets that are marketable, pension rights are ignored. The results are set out in Table 3.7.

Table 3.7   Households' percentage shares of total wealth, Sweden,
              1920–75

Year	Top 1%	Top 2%	Top 5%	Top 10%	Top 20%	Last 80%*
1920	50	60	77	91	100	0
1930	47	58	74	88	98	2
1935	42	53	70	84	97	3
1945	38	48	66	82	96	4
1951	33	43	60	76	92	8
1966	24	32	48	64	82	18
1970	23	31	46	62	84	16
1975	17	24	38	54	75	25

Note: * The last column has been added, calculated on the basis of the previous column,
with all figures rounded to nearest integer.

Source: Spånt (1987), Table 3.8, p. 60.

Spånt's figures for the wealth share of the wealthiest 1% and wealthiest 5% on the whole support those derived by Ohlsson et al., in that they show a fall for the period 1920–75. Spånt himself commented that his table shows that the distribution of net wealth in Sweden became very much more equal over the period 1920–75, the greatest losers in terms of percentage share being the wealthiest 2%, and the greatest gainers being the poorest 95%. He added:

> These figures refer to wealth at tax values. It seems that the same tendencies apply to wealth at market prices or if allowance could be made for under-declaration. The trend towards greater equality would probably have been still stronger if the measure of wealth had been extended to include claims on private and public pension funds and so on. (Spånt, 1987, p. 59)

Spånt (1987, p. 60) also noted that the proportion of households declaring some form of wealth 'rose from one-fifth in 1920 to three-fourths in 1975'.

Spånt's conclusions relating to changes in the distribution of wealth between 1975 and 1983, by contrast, are confined to the share held by those within the wealthiest 2%, and are based on estimates of the effect of the rapid inflation experienced by Sweden during this period on the market value of different types of assets. Table 3.8 sets out his results. Spånt commented on this table:

> Considering the inertia normally characterizing the distribution of wealth, the changes estimated here are remarkably large. It is the wealthiest 0.2 per cent of households that have gained by the changes of value occurring since 1975.

40   The distribution of wealth – growing inequality?

Table 3.8   Households' percentage shares of total wealth, Sweden, 1975 and 1983

Year	Top 0.1%	Top 0.2%	Top 0.5%	Top 1%	Top 2%
1975	6	8	12.5	17	24
1983	8	10	14.5	19.5	26

Source: Spånt (1987), Table 3.11, p. 68.

(Spånt, 1987, p. 68; '0.1 per cent' would be more accurate than '0.2 per cent' if the reference is to greatest percentage gain)

Spånt's estimates are at variance with the data derived by Ohlsson et al., which show a continuing fall in the wealth share of the wealthiest in Sweden over the period 1975–83.

Bager-Sjögren and Klevmarken (1998) based their findings on data derived from two sets of random household surveys. The 'Household Market and Nonmarket Activities' (HUS) survey collected figures during the following six months for household wealth on 31 December 1983, 1985 and 1992. They compared these figures with those obtained from the HINK survey, administered by Statistics Sweden and largely derived from tax returns, conducted annually from the mid-1970s. The HINK figures exclude owner-occupied houses and consumer durables from the definition of wealth. Bager-Sjögren and Klevmarken first excluded these items from the HUS figures, for purposes of comparison for each of the years 1983–84, 1985–86 and 1992–93. Arguing that measures of inequality depend substantially on whether or not these items are included, Bager-Sjögren and Klevmarken then produced 'extended wealth' HUS figures based on their inclusion. Their results, using the coefficient of variation, the Gini coefficient and the relative interquartile range as measures of inequality, are summarised in Table 3.9.

Commenting on the non-extended wealth cases, Bager-Sjögren and Klevmarken wrote:

The three measures do not give the same picture of changes in inequality during the period of observation. The measures more sensitive to the tails of the distribution, the coefficient of variation and the Gini coefficient[,] indicate an increase in the inequality of net wealth, while the relative interquartile range shows no increase or even a decrease. Any increase in inequality should thus come from the extreme tails of the distribution. (Bager-Sjögren and Klevmarken, 1998, p. 484)

They cautioned, however, that except in the case of the Gini coefficient for the HINK data, the standard errors of estimation are so large as to

Table 3.9   Measures of household wealth inequality using HINK and HUS data, Sweden, 1983/84 to 1992/93

Measure of inequality	1983/84	1985/86	1992/93
Coefficient of variation (HINK)	2.18	2.47	2.90
Gini coefficient (HINK)	0.85	0.88	0.92
Relative interquartile range (HINK)	5.90	5.32	6.09
Coefficient of variation (HUS)	1.79	3.87	3.36
Gini coefficient (HUS)	0.74	0.93	0.76
Relative interquartile range (HUS)	2.71	2.90	2.58
Coefficient of variation (extended wealth)	1.14	2.06	2.25
Gini coefficient (extended wealth)	0.52	0.59	0.58
Relative interquartile range (extended wealth)	1.38	1.44	1.54

Source: Bager-Sjögren and Klevmarken (1998), Tables 3 and 4, pp. 483 and 485.

make the estimated changes in the distribution of wealth not statistically significant. In the extended wealth case, the 'inequality of net wealth shows a modest increase from the beginning of the 1980s to the beginning of the 1990s' (ibid., p. 484), though in the case of the coefficient of variation measure the standard errors are 'very large'.

The Bager-Sjögren and Klevmarken results are broadly consistent with the Ohlsson et al. data in that the latter indicate an increase in inequality in the distribution of wealth in Sweden from about 1981.

3.6   SWITZERLAND

Table 3.10 shows the share of total wealth of the wealthiest 1% and the next wealthiest 4% of the population of Switzerland, over the period 1915–97.

Table 3.10 implies that the fall in the wealth share of the wealthiest 5% of the population in Switzerland between 1969 and 1981 (see Table 3.1) was due to falls in the wealth shares of both the wealthiest 1% and the next wealthiest 4%.

3.7   UNITED KINGDOM

Table 3.11 shows the share of total wealth of the wealthiest 1% and the next wealthiest 4% of the population of the United Kingdom over the period 1740–2003.[5]

Table 3.11 implies that both the fall in the wealth share of the wealthiest

Table 3.10   Wealth share (%) of the wealthiest 1% and the next wealthiest 4% in Switzerland, 1915–97

Year	Top 1%	Next 4%
1915	42.3	26.4
1919	36.4	25.9
1921	38.1	25.9
1925	40.7	23.9
1929	42.0	24.6
1934	40.4	27.5
1936	40.1	28.0
1938	44.4	28.9
1940	40.4	27.2
1941	41.5	27.9
1945	37.1	27.2
1947	38.3	27.1
1949	37.8	27.2
1951	39.0	27.3
1953	40.0	26.6
1955	41.5	25.8
1957	41.9	25.5
1969	41.6	25.2
1981	33.0	23.6
1991	33.6	23.0
1997	34.8	23.2

Source: Ohlsson et al. (2006), Tables 1 and 2, pp. 18–23.

5% of the population in the United Kingdom between the 1920s and 1991, and its subsequent rise, were largely mirrored by the behaviour of the wealth share of the wealthiest 1% of the population, and by the behaviour of the wealth share of the next wealthiest 4% of the population from 1950, though by contrast the latter remained relatively constant from the 1920s until 1938, and had actually risen substantially by 1950.

We next derive further information about the distribution of wealth in the United Kingdom from not only the sources drawn on by Ohlsson et al. (2006) but also some additional sources. Most of these sources used the estate multiplier method.

The estate multiplier method was applied by Peter H. Lindert to large samples of probate inventories taken for selected years over the period 1670 to 1875 from four regions in England and Wales; the probate inventories measured 'wealth for persons from all classes above paupers' (Lindert, 1986, p. 1131). Lindert's distribution of wealth estimates, which are

Table 3.11   Wealth share (%) of the wealthiest 1% and the next wealthiest 4% in the United Kingdom, 1740–2003

Year	Top 1%	Next 4%
1740	43.6	43.3
1810	54.9	30.4
1875	61.1	22.9
1911	69.0	18.0
1923	60.9	21.1
1925	61.0	21.1
1927	59.8	21.5
1929	55.5	23.4
1930	57.9	21.3
1936	54.2	23.2
1938	55.0	22.2
1950	47.2	27.2
1951	45.8	27.9
1953	43.6	27.7
1955	44.5	27.0
1957	43.4	25.7
1960	33.9	25.6
1962	31.4	23.5
1964	34.5	24.5
1966	30.6	25.1
1967	31.4	24.9
1969	31.1	25.3
1970	29.7	24.2
1972	31.7	25.2
1973	27.3	24.2
1975	22.7	23.8
1976	24.4	24.6
1978	20.0	17.0
1979	20.0	17.0
1981	18.0	18.0
1982	18.0	18.0
1983	20.0	17.0
1984	18.0	17.0
1986	18.0	18.0
1988	17.0	19.0
1989	17.0	18.0
1991	17.0	18.0
1992	18.0	20.0
1993	18.0	20.0
1994	19.0	20.0
1995	19.0	19.0

Table 3.11   (continued)

Year	Top 1%	Next 4%
1996	20.0	20.0
1997	22.0	21.0
1998	22.0	18.0
2000	23.0	21.0
2001	22.0	20.0
2002	24.0	21.0
2003	21.0	19.0

Source: Ohlsson et al. (2006), Tables 1 and 2, pp. 18–23.

Table 3.12   *Percentage shares of aggregate marketable net worth, England and Wales, 1670–1875*

Year	Households Top 1%	Individuals* Top 5%
1670	48.9	84.6
1700	39.3	81.9
1740	43.6	86.9
1810	54.9	85.3
1875	61.1	84.0

Note: * 'Individuals' refers to the adult population only.

Source: Lindert (2000), Table 2, p. 181, based on Lindert (1986), Table 4, p. 1145.

summarised in Table 3.12, imply a degree of inequality during the period 1670 to 1875 which is high compared with that in the twentieth century. However, they do not display any clear rising or falling trend in inequality in the distribution of wealth over the period 1670 to 1875. Lindert concluded that the absence of any such clear rise or fall 'resulted from the near balancing of two strong trends: a broad-based tendency toward greater concentration of both income and wealth versus the egalitarian consequences of the diminishing importance of land and of the title-landed class' (ibid., p. 1147).

The absence of data relating to paupers does not detract materially from Lindert's study, as paupers may be assumed to have accounted for a relatively small proportion of the population during the relevant period. By contrast, Board of Inland Revenue records, on which most estimates of the distribution of wealth in Great Britain from 1911 onwards rely, have generally if not always covered the wealth at death of less than half of the total population, the remainder being officially labelled the 'excluded population'. Where the 'excluded population' is substantial, unadjusted application of the 'estate multiplier' method to a whole population suffers from the deficiency that those whose wealth at death is not recorded are implicitly assumed to have no wealth. The resulting measurement of the distribution of wealth among the whole population thereby exaggerates the actual degree of inequality.

Using such information as he could obtain, Henry Clay (1925) attempted to rectify this deficiency by making an estimate of the wealth held by the 'excluded population'. A subsequent valuable addition to knowledge about the distribution of wealth came with the calculation of national balance sheet accounts estimating the value of individual components of wealth held by the private sector, first produced by Revell (1967) for the years 1957–61. However, while national balance sheet accounts provide an independent estimate of total wealth, they do not provide much information on the proportion of this wealth which is held by the 'excluded population'. Those who have estimated the distribution of wealth in Great Britain have still had to make an educated guess as to this proportion.

The earliest estimates of the distribution of wealth in Great Britain during the twentieth century are for the years 1911–13, though these apply only to England and Wales, and only to the population aged 25 and over. Revell (1965), drawing for pre-Second World War figures on Kathleen Langley (1950), who drew on George Daniels and Henry Campion (1936), who in turn drew on Clay (1925), and using the estate multiplier method unadjusted for social class, obtained for the period 1911–13 to 1960 the figures for the distribution of wealth (excluding pension rights) set out in Table 3.13. When compared with Lindert's figures for 1875, Revell's figures for 1911–13 suggest an increase in inequality in the distribution of wealth, though given the different bases of calculation it would be rash to conclude that this is what actually happened.

Estimates covering a more extended period, namely 1923 to 1973, were subsequently made by Atkinson and Harrison, their prime consideration being consistency. These estimates, based on the estate multiplier method adjusted for social class and applied to the adult population (defined as at least 23 years of age in 1923 and reduced linearly to at least 18 in 1973), include occupational pension rights, but not 'social property' such as state pension rights. As Atkinson and Harrison briefly explained, the latter 'type of wealth has been excluded, not because we believe it to be unimportant, but because it raises serious conceptual problems which we do not feel have been adequately resolved, and partly because it is typically

Table 3.13   Individuals' percentage shares of total wealth, England and
              Wales, 1911–13 to 1960

Year	Top 1%	Top 5%	Top 10%	Last 90%
1911–13	69	87	92	8
1924–30	62	84	91	9
1936–38	56	79	88	12
1954	43	71	79	21
1960	42	75	83	17

Source: Revell (1965), Table 6, p. 379.

Table 3.14   Individuals' percentage shares of total wealth, England and
              Wales, 1923–38

Year	Top 1%	Top 5%	Top 10%	Top 20%	Last 80%*
1923	60.9	82.0	89.1	94.2	5.8
1924	59.9	81.5	88.1	93.8	6.2
1925	61.0	82.1	88.4	93.8	6.2
1926	57.3	79.9	87.4	93.2	6.8
1927	59.8	81.3	88.3	93.8	6.2
1928	57.0	79.6	87.2	93.1	6.9
1929	55.5	78.9	86.3	92.6	7.4
1930	57.9	79.2	86.6	92.6	7.4
1936	54.2	77.4	85.7	92.0	8.0
1938	55.0	76.9	85.0	91.2	8.8

Note: * The last column has been added, on the basis of the previous column.

Source: Atkinson and Harrison (1978), Table 6.5, p. 159.

viewed as being rather different in nature from "private" wealth' (Atkinson
and Harrison, 1978, p. 4). Among the 'conceptual problems' referred to by
Atkinson and Harrison is no doubt the fact that potential wealth taking
the form of state pension rights is never enjoyed by those individuals who
die before pensionable age.

Some of Atkinson and Harrison's results are set out in Table 3.14
(England and Wales, 1923–38) and Table 3.15 (Great Britain, 1938 and
1950–72). Up to 1954 the figures in these tables are consistent with those
in Table 3.13 in that they show a trend towards a lessening inequality in the
distribution of wealth. But while Revell showed this trend subsequently
being reversed (except for the top 1 per cent), Atkinson and Harrison

Table 3.15   Individuals' percentage shares of total wealth, Great Britain, 1938 and 1950–72

Year	Top 1%	Top 5%	Top 10%	Top 20%	Last 80%*
1938	55.0	77.2	85.4	91.6	8.4
1950	47.2	74.4	–	–	–
1951	45.9	73.8	–	–	–
1952	42.9	70.3	–	–	–
1953	43.5	71.2	–	–	–
1954	45.3	72.0	–	–	–
1955	43.8	70.8	–	–	–
1956	44.0	71.1	–	–	–
1957	42.9	68.6	–	–	–
1958	40.9	67.7	–	–	–
1959	41.8	67.9	–	–	–
1960	34.4	60.0	72.1	83.6	16.4
1961	36.5	60.8	72.1	83.6	16.4
1962	31.9	55.4	67.9	80.7	19.3
1963	–	–	–	–	–
1964	34.7	59.2	72.0	85.4	14.6
1965	33.3	58.7	72.3	85.8	14.2
1966	31.0	56.1	69.9	84.2	15.8
1967	31.5	56.4	70.5	84.0	15.1
1968	33.6	58.6	72.0	85.4	14.6
1969	31.3	56.6	68.6	84.1	15.9
1970	30.1	54.3	69.4	84.9	15.1
1971	28.8	53.0	68.3	84.8	15.2
1972	32.0	57.2	71.7	85.3	14.7

Note: * The last column has been added, on the basis of the previous column.

Source: Atkinson and Harrison (1978), Table 6.5, p. 159.

found it continuing up to 1960, possibly due to their inclusion of occupational pension rights, which became more widespread during this later period.

In Table 3.14 there is a marked difference between pre-1960 figures and the remainder; Atkinson and Harrison (1978, p. 167) commented that while it is possible 'that some half of the shift between the 1950s and the 1960s could be explained by our allowance for the wealth of the excluded population [during the former period] being too low . . . it seems unlikely that this factor can explain the whole of the apparent shift'.

For the period 1923–72 the 'main features' of these estimates are:

- a downward trend of some 0.4 per cent per annum in the share of the top 1 per cent (with a once-for-all jump between 1959 and 1960)
- no apparent acceleration in the arithmetic rate of decline in the share of the top 1 per cent
- no apparent downward trend in the share of the next 4 per cent (but a jump upwards between 1938 and 1950, and a jump downwards between 1959 and 1960).[6] (Atkinson and Harrison, 1978, p. 170)

With respect to these 'main features', however, it should be noted that the downward trend in the share of the top 1 per cent is more pronounced over the period 1950–59 than over the period 1960–72, and that the 'jump downwards' of the next 4 per cent between 1959 and 1960 was relatively small, from 26.1 per cent to 25.6 per cent in the case of Great Britain.

For the latter part of the period covered by Table 3.15, namely for each year from 1966 to 1972, Atkinson and Harrison also calculated the coefficient of variation, the relative mean deviation and the Gini coefficient. Their results are set out in Table 3.16. It is not clear from the published evidence why the coefficient of variation figures fluctuate so wildly; the partial measurement figures in Table 3.14 seem to be more consistent with the fairly stable figures for the relative mean deviation and the Gini coefficient, measures which, like the partial measurement figures, display no substantial trend over this period.

Atkinson and Harrison in addition compared their results for 1968 and 1972 with estimates they obtained using an alternative method of calculating the distribution of wealth, namely the investment income approach. While admitting that the investment income method appeared to produce results which differed somewhat from the estate multiplier method, Atkinson and Harrison noted that the former provided a wide range of estimates, depending on the assumptions made, and concluded that 'it is difficult at this stage to reject the hypothesis that the distributions are the same' (Atkinson and Harrison, 1978, p. 200).

The Atkinson and Harrison study was subsequently extended in

Table 3.16   Measures of wealth inequality, Great Britain, 1966–72

Measure	1966	1967	1968	1969	1970	1971	1972
Coefficient of variation	5.93	7.28	7.58	5.26	7.16	4.42	9.85
Relative mean deviation	1.255	1.260	1.269	1.230	1.246	1.240	1.273
Gini coefficient	0.767	0.773	0.775	0.776	0.765	0.768	0.780

Source: Atkinson and Harrison (1978), Table 5.5, p. 123.

Table 3.17   Individuals' percentage shares of total wealth, Great Britain,
*   1973–81*

Year	Top 1%	Top 5%	Top 10%	Top 20%	Last 80%*
1973	27.4	51.5	67.5	85.4	14.6
1974	22.9	48.6	65.0	83.6	16.4
1975	23.1	46.5	62.5	81.1	18.9
1976	24.6	49.0	65.4	84.0	16.0
1977	22.1	46.4	62.5	80.9	19.1
1978	22.0	45.9	62.9	81.9	18.1
1979	21.4	45.3	61.4	80.5	19.5
1980	19.6	42.8	59.8	79.9	20.1
1981	22.5	46.0	62.8	82.5	17.5

Note: * The last column has been added, on the basis of the previous column.

Source: Atkinson et al. (1989), Table 1, p. 318.

Atkinson, James P.F. Gordon and Harrison (1989) to cover the period
1973–81. The results are set out in Table 3.17. The most noticeable trend
is the almost continuous decline in the share of the top 1%, at least up to
1980, the principal gainers being the bottom 80%.

A set of consistent estimates of the distribution of wealth in the
United Kingdom, comparable with the Atkinson et al. estimates for
Great Britain but going back only to 1976, was published by the Board
of Inland Revenue. As F.J. Good (1990, p. 138) conceded with respect to
Board of Inland Revenue estimates published before 1990, 'the published
series . . . has not been on a consistent basis. This lack of consistency has
been criticised, for example, by Atkinson, Gordon and Harrison.' For the
period 1976–94, however, there are three versions of such a revised consistent series, namely Series C, comprising 'marketable wealth which includes
all assets for which a value can be immediately realised, net of liabilities'
(Stewart, 1991, p. 99); Series D, comprising 'marketable wealth plus value
of occupational pension rights' (ibid., p. 99); and Series E, comprising
'marketable wealth plus value of occupational and state pension rights'
(ibid., p. 99). The figures for Series D, which are the most clearly comparable with the estimates made by Atkinson et al., are the ones set out in Table
3.18.

Over the period for which the Board of Inland Revenue Series D figures
overlap with those of Atkinson et al., namely 1976–81, one major difference can be discerned. The figures arrived at by the Board of Inland
Revenue show a substantially lower proportion of total wealth being held
by the wealthiest 1%, 5% and 10% of the population. This difference

Table 3.18   Individuals' percentage shares of total wealth and Gini coefficient, United Kingdom, Inland Revenue Statistics, Series D (1976–94)

Year	Top 1%	Top 2%	Top 5%	Top 10%	Top 25%	Top 50%	Gini ratio
1976	18	24	34	45	67	89	0.60
1977	19	24	34	45	67	88	0.60
1978	17	23	33	45	67	88	0.59
1979	16	21	32	44	67	88	0.58
1980	15	20	31	43	67	87	0.57
1981	14	20	30	42	65	86	0.56
1982	14	19	30	42	65	86	0.56
1983	15	20	31	43	67	88	0.58
1984	14	19	29	42	66	88	0.57
1985	14	19	31	43	67	88	0.58
1986	14	19	30	43	67	88	0.58
1987	14	20	31	44	68	88	0.60
1988	13	19	30	43	66	88	0.58
1989	13	19	30	42	65	88	0.58
1990	14	19	29	41	65	89	0.58
1991	14	19	29	41	65	89	0.58
1992	14	20	30	42	66	89	0.59
1993	14	20	31	43	66	89	0.59
1994	14	20	31	43	66	89	0.59

Sources: Inland Revenue Statistics (1991), Table 11.6, p. 110 (1976–87), and Inland Revenue Statistics (1998), Table 13.6, p. 134 (1988–94).

can hardly be accounted for by their inclusion of the relatively small population of Northern Ireland, and it is not obvious how else it could be explained. But like the Atkinson et al. figures for 1976–81, the Board of Inland Revenue Series D figures for the period 1976–94 show little change over time in the distribution of wealth.

1994 was the last year for which Series D and Series E figures were calculated; the Board of Inland Revenue discontinued them because of a decline in the applicability of their assumption of long-term membership of final pension salary schemes, the Board admitting that it had been unable to find a suitable alternative assumption. In Table 3.19 figures bringing the story up to 2000 are taken from Series C. For the period 1984–95 the Series C Gini coefficient figures display a stability similar to the Series D figures for the period 1982–94, lying in the range 0.64 to 0.67, but are higher for the period 1996–2000, lying in the range 0.68 to 0.69.

Table 3.19   *Individuals' percentage shares of total wealth and Gini coefficient, United Kingdom, Inland Revenue Statistics, Series C (1984–2000)*

Year	Top 1%	Top 2%	Top 5%	Top 10%	Top 25%	Top 50%	Gini ratio
1984	18	24	35	48	71	91	0.64
1985	18	24	36	49	73	91	0.65
1986	18	24	36	50	73	90	0.64
1987	18	25	37	51	74	91	0.66
1988	17	23	36	49	71	92	0.65
1989	17	24	35	48	70	92	0.65
1990	18	24	35	47	71	93	0.64
1991	17	24	35	47	71	92	0.64
1992	18	25	38	50	73	93	0.66
1993	18	26	38	51	73	93	0.66
1994	19	27	39	52	74	93	0.67
1995	19	26	38	50	72	92	0.65
1996	20	27	40	52	74	93	0.68
1997	22	30	43	54	75	93	0.69
1998	23	30	43	55	75	94	0.69
1999*	23	30	43	55	75	94	0.69
2000*	22	29	42	54	74	94	0.69

Note: * Figures for these years are provisional, and have not been revised.

Sources: Inland Revenue Statistics (2000), Table 13.5, p. 434 (1984–96), and Inland Revenue Statistics (2002), Table 13.5 (1997–2000).

Data on the distribution of wealth in Great Britain for the first decade of the twenty-first century are reported by Her Majesty's Revenue and Customs (HMRC). These data (shown in Table 3.20) measure the wealth owned by estates passed through probate each year, covering around a third of the total British population. Over the period observed, HMRC data show a slightly greater decline in the wealth share of the wealthiest 20% than in the wealthiest 10% and a slight increase in the wealth share of the poorest 40% and 50%. The data suggest that the wealth inequality observed above for the late twentieth century in Great Britain has continued in the twenty-first century, but has not increased.

Great Britain's Office for National Statistics (ONS) has, since 2006, conducted biennial surveys of the wealth and assets of its citizens. These data, presented in Table 3.21, also show a persistent inequality in the distribution of wealth from 2006 to 2012. While the cumulative shares held

Table 3.20   Identified personal wealth shares, United Kingdom, HMRC
Table 13.8 (2001–10)

Decile	2001–03	2005–07	2008–10
Top 10%	45	44	44
Top 20%	61	59	59
Top 40%	81	79	79
Top 50%	88	86	86
Bottom 40%	7	7	8

Source: Her Majesty's Revenue and Customs (2012).

Table 3.21   Total household wealth shares, United Kingdom, HMRC,
Office of National Statistics' Wealth and Assets Surveys,
Table 3 (2001–12)

Decile	2006–08	2008–10	2010–12
Top 10%	44	44	44
Top 20%	62	62	62
Top 40%	84	84	84
Top 50%	91	90	90
Bottom 40%	5	5	5

Source: Office for National Statistics (2014).

by the wealthiest 40% and wealthiest 50% in the ONS data are larger than those in the HMRC data (and the lower percentiles' shares are accordingly lower), the wealthiest 10% and wealthiest 20% shares are broadly the same, and the data again show relatively little variation over time (see also Hills et al., 2013, chapter 2).

A particularly graphic representation of the distribution of wealth in the United Kingdom has been provided by the British geographer Danny Dorling. Figure 3.1, taken from Dorling (2014, Figure 1.3, p. 22), shows how much of the surface area of the UK would be owned by the different groups of wealth-owners if land were to be distributed in the same way as liquid wealth. The top 1% would own Wales and all of England south of a line drawn (approximately) between Carnforth and Bridlington, and the next 4% would own the remainder of England; the bottom 95% would be restricted to Scotland (the next 45%) and Northern Ireland (the poorest 50%). In sharp contrast, if wealth were equally distributed, the top 1% would have to make do with about two-thirds of Cornwall, and instead

Source: Dorling (2014).

Figure 3.1   Distribution of liquid wealth in the United Kingdom

of owning the whole of England and Wales the top 5% would be confined to Devon, Cornwall and a small piece of Somerset.

Summing up on Great Britain, inequality in the distribution of wealth appears to have declined for the five decades between 1910 and 1960, and again in the 1970s. With respect to the subsequent period, Inland Revenue Statistics Series C Gini coefficient figures imply that inequality started increasing from 1995, though Lindert (2000, p. 200) suggested that 'top-wealthholder shares of all wealth' increased from as early as 1984.

Why did these changes occur? Atkinson and Harrison (1978, p. 229) explored why in the early 1970s the share of the wealthiest 1% in total private wealth 'appeared to have been declining over the previous 50 years at an annual rate of some 0.4 per cent'. While acknowledging that their analysis of aggregate data did not provide conclusive results, Atkinson and Harrison suggested that this decline may have been due to any one or more of three factors. First, over this period, saving out of earned income by those in the bottom 99% increased because of the increased proportion of homes which were owner-occupied, the spread of occupational pension rights and the growth in the value of consumer durables. Second, there may have been exogenous factors at work, 'possibly reflecting differential rates of accumulation or changes in marriage and inheritance customs' (ibid., p. 239). Third, there was the existence of estate duties.

With respect to the 1980s and 1990s, the apparent increase in inequality in the distribution of wealth during at least the latter part of this period may have been a delayed consequence of the increase in inequality in the distribution of income beginning in 1978[7]. For the first decade of the twenty-first century, the available data suggest that wealth inequality in the UK has been relatively stable.

3.8   THE UNITED STATES

Table 3.22 shows the share of total wealth of the wealthiest 1% and the next wealthiest 4% of the population of the United States over the period 1774–2001.

Table 3.22 indicates that the rise in the wealth share of the wealthiest 5% of the population in the United States between 1983 and 2001 was largely due to the rise in the wealth share of the wealthiest 1% until 1998, but largely due to the rise in the wealth share of the next wealthiest 4% between 1998 and 2001.

We next derive further information about the distribution of wealth in the United States from not only the sources drawn on by Ohlsson et al. (2006) but also some additional sources. First, 919 probated estates

Table 3.22   *Wealth share (%) of the wealthiest 1% and the next wealthiest 4% in the United States, 1774–2001*

Year	Top 1%	Next 4%
1774	18.0	23.0
1860	21.0	28.0
1962	31.8	21.3
1969	31.1	17.7
1983	33.8	22.3
1989	37.4	21.6
1992	37.2	22.8
1995	38.5	21.8
1998	38.1	21.3
2001	33.4	25.8

Source: Ohlsson et al. (2006), Tables 1 and 2, pp. 18–23.

Table 3.23   *Individuals' percentage shares of total wealth and Gini coefficient, United States, 1774*

	Net Worth			Total Assets		
	Top 1%	Top 10%	Gini ratio	Top 1%	Top 10%	Gini ratio
All households	16.5	59.0	–	14.8	55.1	–
Free households	14.3	53.2	0.694	12.6	49.6	0.642
All adult males	16.5	58.4	–	13.2	54.3	–
Free adult males	14.2	52.5	0.688	12.4	48.7	0.632

Source: Lindert (2000), Table 3, p. 188.

provided the data for Alice Hanson Jones's estimates of the distribution of wealth in 1774 (see Jones, 1977, pp. 2131–95). Using these data, Lindert (2000, p. 188) derived a number of measures of inequality in the 1774 distribution of wealth. Lindert's figures are set out in Table 3.23.

Subsequent data relating to the distribution of wealth in the United States were provided by the census of 1860, which recorded gross real and personal estates, the latter including slaves, owned by free males aged 20 and over. This provided the basis for calculations made by Robert E. Gallman (1969), who based his estimates of the distribution of wealth on data relating to four cities and three rural areas, giving each a 'Kuznets' weighting based on mean wealth and population size (see Simon Kuznets, 1955). Two estimates were provided, '1860 A' treating slaves as property

The distribution of wealth – growing inequality?

Table 3.24   *Households' percentage shares of total wealth, United States, 1860, with projections back to 1810 and forward to 1900*

Measure	1810	1860 A	1860 B	1900 C	1900 D
Top 1%	21	24	24	26	31
Top 2%*	32	35	35	37	42
Top 3%*	40	43	42	44	49
Top 4%*	46	49	48	50	55
Top 5%*	51	54	53	55	60
Top 6%*	55	58	58	59	64
Top 7%*	59	62	62	63	67
Top 8%*	62	65	66	67	70
Top 9%*	65	68	69	70	73
Top 10%*	69	71	72	73	74
Top 20%*	–	88	88	–	–
Top 30%*	–	95	95	–	–
Top 40%*	–	98	97	–	–
Top 50%	–	100	100	–	–
Last 50%	–	0	0	–	–

Note: * Gallman's figures are presented here on a cumulative basis.

Source: Gallman (1969), Table 1, p. 6.

and '1860 B' treating slaves as potential property owners. Gallman then extrapolated back from the '1860 A' figures to 1810 by appropriate adjustment of population weights, and by similar means extrapolated the '1860 B' figures forward to 1900, '1900 D' differing from '1900 C' in that the four cities were given a Kuznets wealth weight of two instead of one. The results, set out in Table 3.24, suggest increasing inequality.

Comparing the results arrived at by Jones and Gallman, supplemented by other 'scraps' of information, J.G. Williamson and Lindert (1981, p. 56) arrived at the working hypothesis 'that wealth concentration rose over most of the period 1774–1860, with especially steep increases from the 1820s to the late 1840s'.

The United States census of 1870 enabled Lee Soltow (1975, pp. 99, 103) to compare the distribution of wealth among males over 20 in 1860 with the distribution in 1870. The 1870 census, while following the 1860 census in recording gross real and personal estate, by contrast excluded amounts of less than $100, and no longer recorded slaves as assets (slavery having been abolished in 1865). As summarised by Lindert (2000, p. 188), Soltow's results are set out in Table 3.25.

Soltow's 1860 figures for all adult males are similar to those arrived at by

*Table 3.25   Males' percentage shares in total wealth and Gini coefficient,
United States, 1860 and 1870*

	Top 1%	Top 10%	Gini ratio
1860, all adult males	30.3–35.0	74.6–79.0	–
1860, free adult males	29.0	73.0	0.832
1870, all adult males	27.0	70.0	0.833

Source: Lindert (2000), Table 3, p. 188.

Gallman. When compared with the figures for 1870, they suggest that the freeing of slaves between 1860 and 1870 reduced the share of wealth owned by both the top 1 per cent and the top 10 per cent.

A further census in 1890 'supplying data on farm and home ownership in twenty-two states' provided the basis of estimates of inequality in the distribution of net worth among families made by George K. Holmes (1893). Holmes estimated that the top 1 per cent owned 25.8 per cent of wealth, and the top 10 per cent 72.2 per cent.

For most of the twentieth century, a 'consistent series of estate tax data on individual wealth holdings ... for selected years between 1922 and 1981' (Wolff, 1996, p. 435) is the main source of information on changes in the distribution of wealth in the United States. Using the estate multiplier method, and drawing on Robert J. Lampman (1962), James D. Smith (1984, 1987) and M. Schwartz (1983), Wolff and Marcia Marley (1989) calculated for the years 1922 to 1976 and 1981 the percentage share of total assets, total net worth of individuals and total assets of households held by the top 1 per cent of wealth-holders in the United States; the threshold for tax liability was too high for calculations relating to any subsequent percentile to be made. Drawing also on household sample surveys (1962, 1983, 1989 and 1992) conducted by the Federal Reserve Board, Wolff (1996) calculated for the period 1922–92 the top 1 per cent percentage share of household marketable wealth, and of household marketable wealth augmented by pension and social security payments. Wolff's summary of the results is reproduced in Table 3.26.

Noting that the top 1 per cent shares of total assets for individuals exceed those for households, Wolff suggested the explanation that 'a married couple typically mixes a relatively high wealth spouse with a relatively less wealthy one' (Wolff, 1996, p. 436). He noted also that the increasing excess of top 1 per cent shares of marketable wealth over augmented wealth is presumably due to the increase over time in the ratio of pension and social security wealth to marketable wealth.

Table 3.26   Richest 1% percentage share of total wealth, United States, 1922–92

| Year | Individuals | | Households | | |
	Total Assets	Net Assets	Total Assets	Marketable Wealth	Augmented Wealth
1922	33.4	–	25.5	36.7	34.3
1929	37.2	–	30.7	44.2	41.1
1933	31.3	–	–	33.3	28.7
1939	38.1	–	25.3	36.4	30.2
1945	28.9	–	20.7	29.8	22.0
1949	25.7	–	18.8	27.1	20.7
1953	28.1	28.4	21.7	31.2	23.1
1958	27.0	27.7	20.0	28.8	20.4
1962	30.1	31.1	22.1	31.8	21.9
1965	31.9	33.6	23.9	34.4	23.3
1969	29.0	30.2	21.6	31.1	20.9
1972	28.6	29.8	20.2	29.1	19.0
1976	18.9	19.1	12.7	19.9	13.3
1979	–	–	–	20.5	12.9
1981	23.6	–	–	24.8	15.5
1983	–	–	–	30.9	19.0
1986	–	–	–	31.9	19.3
1989	–	–	–	35.7	21.2
1992	-	–	-	34.0	19.8

Source: Wolff (2012), Table 2, p. 50.

As Wolff (1996, p. 439) pointed out, summarising these results, the top 1 per cent shares in both series

> show a substantial increase between 1922 and 1929; a large decline from 1929 to 1933 followed by an increase between 1933 and 1939; a sharp fall between 1939 and 1949; a gradual climb from 1949 to 1965; another sharp decline from 1965 to 1976; and a substantial rise between 1979 and 1989, followed by a modest decline from 1989 to 1992.

The Federal Reserve Board household sample surveys cover more than just the share in total wealth of the top 1 per cent of households, and were an essential data source for the results set out both in Table 3.27, derived from Wolff (1994 and 2000), and in Table 3.28, which displays comparable estimates made in Saez and Zucman (2014).

The figures in Table 3.27, which draw also on Federal Reserve Flow of Funds national balance sheet data, include in the calculations of net

Table 3.27 Households' percentage shares of total wealth and Gini coefficient, United States, 1962–2010

Year	Top 1%	Top 5%*	Top 10%*	Top 20%*	Top 40%*	Top 60%*	Last 40%*	Gini ratio
1962	33.4	54.6	67.0	81.0	94.4	99.8	0.2	0.803
1969	34.4	54.7	68.7	80.7	93.5	98.4	1.5	0.811
1983	33.8	56.1	68.2	81.3	93.9	99.1	0.9	0.799
1989	37.4	59.0	70.6	83.5	95.8	100.6	–0.7	0.832
1992	37.2	60.0	71.8	83.8	95.3	99.7	0.4	0.823
1995	38.5	60.3	71.8	83.9	95.3	99.8	0.2	0.828
1998	38.1	59.4	70.9	83.4	95.3	99.8	0.2	0.822
2001	33.4	59.2	71.5	84.4	95.7	99.6	0.3	0.826
2004	34.3	58.9	71.2	84.7	96.0	99.8	0.2	0.829
2007	34.6	61.9	73.1	85.0	95.9	99.9	0.1	0.834
2010	35.4	63.1	76.7	88.9	98.3	100.9	–0.9	0.870

Note: * Wolff's figures are presented here on a cumulative basis; the third last and second last columns do not always add up to 100 because of rounding.

Source: Wolff (2012), Table 2, p. 50.

marketable wealth only the cash surrender value rather than the sum assured value of pension and life insurance plans. They indicate that inequality in the distribution of wealth in the United States, while much the same in 1983 as in 1962, increased substantially between 1983 and 1989, but remained relatively stable at the new higher level throughout the 1990s. Following the asset price meltdown of 2001, the proportion of wealth owned by the wealthiest 1% and 5% fell at the turn of the twenty-first century. The wealth share of the wealthiest 1% began climbing again shortly thereafter and, in spite of the bigger and more sustained decline in asset prices associated with the collapse of the housing market and the financial crisis of 2007–08, returned to 35.4% of total wealth by 2010, just shy of the approximately 37% or 38% shares held during the late 1980s and the 1990s. The wealthiest 5%, on the other hand, had by 2007 exceeded the previous peak share of total wealth set in 1995, and continued to increase their share further in 2010, holding 63.1% of total wealth. The wealth shares of the wealthiest 10% and 20% continued to grow steadily throughout the first decade of the twenty-first century even in the face of the financial crisis of 2007–08, and by the end of this decade the vast majority of total wealth (98.3%) was held by the wealthiest 40% of households.

Table 3.27 presents Saez and Zucman's (2014) estimates of the distribution of wealth, which reflect broadly similar trends. The more recent

Table 3.28   *Alternative estimates of households' percentage shares of total wealth and Gini coefficient, United States, 1917–2012*

Year	Top 0.01%	Top 0.1%	Top 0.5%	Top 1%	Top 5%	Top 10%	Bottom 90%
1917	9.4%	22.0%	34.8%	41.0%	67.1%	79.5%	20.5%
1918	7.6%	18.9%	31.9%	39.1%	65.3%	77.7%	22.3%
1919	6.9%	18.5%	32.4%	40.0%	67.2%	79.4%	20.6%
1920	5.1%	15.0%	28.3%	35.6%	62.7%	77.3%	22.7%
1921	4.9%	15.1%	28.6%	35.9%	63.0%	77.4%	22.6%
1922	6.0%	17.2%	31.5%	39.1%	65.2%	78.6%	21.4%
1923	5.2%	14.9%	27.9%	34.7%	63.4%	79.3%	20.7%
1924	5.6%	16.0%	29.7%	36.8%	65.2%	80.7%	19.3%
1925	6.7%	18.6%	34.6%	43.1%	70.8%	82.3%	17.7%
1926	7.5%	20.3%	36.5%	45.1%	72.4%	83.0%	17.0%
1927	8.5%	22.6%	40.3%	49.5%	73.3%	83.9%	16.1%
1928	9.8%	24.6%	42.3%	51.4%	74.1%	84.4%	15.6%
1929	10.2%	24.8%	41.7%	50.6%	74.1%	84.3%	15.7%
1930	9.0%	23.0%	40.0%	49.0%	74.7%	83.6%	16.4%
1931	8.2%	21.6%	38.8%	48.0%	73.9%	83.6%	16.4%
1932	7.5%	22.4%	39.0%	47.0%	74.3%	84.0%	16.0%
1933	7.8%	22.2%	38.6%	47.1%	74.8%	84.1%	15.9%
1934	7.4%	21.8%	39.3%	47.2%	73.5%	82.5%	17.5%
1935	7.0%	20.8%	37.7%	45.3%	71.8%	81.2%	18.8%
1936	6.5%	20.0%	37.3%	45.2%	71.9%	81.6%	18.4%
1937	6.6%	19.7%	36.6%	45.3%	68.3%	79.9%	20.1%
1938	5.8%	16.8%	32.1%	40.7%	66.2%	79.7%	20.3%
1939	5.8%	17.4%	33.2%	41.9%	67.1%	80.1%	19.9%
1940	5.2%	15.3%	29.7%	37.9%	63.9%	77.6%	22.4%
1941	4.4%	13.4%	26.9%	35.0%	62.1%	76.2%	23.8%
1942	4.1%	13.0%	26.6%	34.6%	60.4%	74.7%	25.3%
1943	3.7%	12.7%	26.5%	35.1%	61.6%	75.2%	24.8%
1944	3.8%	12.2%	25.8%	34.5%	61.6%	74.9%	25.1%
1945	3.5%	11.9%	25.5%	34.4%	62.4%	75.2%	24.8%
1946	3.4%	10.9%	23.5%	31.8%	60.9%	74.6%	25.4%
1947	3.3%	10.5%	22.3%	30.2%	59.0%	73.0%	27.0%
1948	3.2%	10.3%	22.2%	29.9%	57.6%	71.9%	28.1%
1949	3.1%	10.0%	21.6%	29.1%	56.2%	71.1%	28.9%
1950	2.8%	10.6%	22.7%	30.5%	57.3%	71.6%	28.4%
1951	3.1%	10.1%	22.1%	30.0%	57.2%	71.4%	28.6%
1952	3.1%	9.9%	21.8%	29.7%	56.6%	71.1%	28.9%
1953	2.9%	9.4%	20.7%	28.3%	55.4%	70.3%	29.7%
1954	2.9%	9.5%	21.0%	28.8%	55.1%	70.6%	29.4%
1955	3.1%	9.7%	21.0%	29.1%	55.0%	71.0%	29.0%
1956	3.2%	10.0%	21.6%	29.4%	56.0%	71.3%	28.7%
1957	3.1%	9.9%	21.5%	29.2%	57.2%	71.8%	28.2%

Table 3.28 (continued)

Year	Top 0.01%	Top 0.1%	Top 0.5%	Top 1%	Top 5%	Top 10%	Bottom 90%
1958	3.1%	9.7%	21.1%	28.9%	56.9%	71.8%	28.2%
1959	3.1%	9.8%	21.6%	29.4%	58.0%	72.5%	27.5%
1960	3.3%	10.1%	21.6%	29.4%	58.1%	72.7%	27.3%
1961	3.3%	10.0%	21.4%	29.4%	57.7%	72.9%	27.1%
1962	3.3%	10.1%	21.7%	29.6%	58.3%	73.6%	26.4%
1963	3.3%	9.9%	21.2%	29.1%	57.7%	73.1%	26.9%
1964	3.3%	9.7%	20.7%	28.5%	57.1%	72.7%	27.4%
1965	3.3%	9.9%	20.8%	28.4%	56.5%	72.2%	27.8%
1966	3.3%	10.0%	20.8%	28.3%	55.8%	71.7%	28.3%
1967	3.1%	9.4%	20.2%	27.8%	54.7%	70.8%	29.2%
1968	3.3%	10.0%	21.0%	28.6%	55.7%	70.5%	29.5%
1969	3.4%	10.0%	20.6%	27.9%	53.9%	70.1%	29.9%
1970	3.2%	9.5%	19.9%	27.6%	54.7%	70.0%	30.0%
1971	3.0%	9.2%	19.6%	27.0%	54.1%	69.9%	30.1%
1972	2.9%	8.7%	19.0%	26.5%	53.8%	69.7%	30.3%
1973	2.5%	8.0%	17.5%	24.9%	52.7%	69.1%	30.9%
1974	2.4%	8.0%	17.8%	24.9%	51.9%	68.5%	31.5%
1975	2.4%	7.6%	17.5%	24.7%	52.1%	68.2%	31.8%
1976	2.3%	7.2%	16.4%	23.5%	50.5%	67.7%	32.3%
1977	2.3%	7.3%	16.8%	23.9%	51.2%	67.2%	32.8%
1978	2.2%	7.1%	16.1%	22.9%	49.4%	66.8%	33.2%
1979	2.6%	7.9%	17.3%	24.4%	51.0%	67.4%	32.6%
1980	2.6%	8.0%	17.4%	24.3%	50.7%	67.1%	32.9%
1981	3.0%	8.8%	18.5%	25.3%	51.1%	67.0%	33.0%
1982	3.3%	9.4%	19.0%	25.7%	50.5%	65.9%	34.1%
1983	3.1%	8.9%	18.2%	24.7%	49.4%	65.0%	35.0%
1984	3.4%	9.3%	18.5%	24.8%	49.0%	64.4%	35.6%
1985	3.6%	9.7%	18.9%	25.1%	48.6%	63.7%	36.3%
1986	3.4%	9.3%	18.8%	25.1%	48.6%	63.6%	36.4%
1987	3.7%	10.2%	19.7%	26.2%	49.5%	64.3%	35.7%
1988	4.4%	11.6%	21.5%	27.9%	50.9%	65.3%	34.7%
1989	4.3%	11.5%	21.4%	27.8%	50.8%	65.2%	34.8%
1990	4.5%	11.7%	21.7%	28.1%	51.2%	65.7%	34.3%
1991	4.3%	11.2%	21.1%	27.6%	51.0%	65.5%	34.5%
1992	4.8%	12.2%	22.6%	29.2%	52.7%	67.1%	32.9%
1993	5.0%	12.5%	22.8%	29.5%	53.0%	67.5%	32.5%
1994	4.7%	12.1%	22.5%	29.2%	53.0%	67.4%	32.6%
1995	4.8%	12.3%	22.8%	29.5%	53.1%	67.6%	32.4%
1996	5.4%	13.2%	23.6%	30.3%	53.7%	68.0%	32.0%
1997	5.7%	13.9%	24.5%	31.2%	54.5%	68.6%	31.4%
1998	5.9%	14.5%	25.4%	32.3%	55.4%	69.2%	30.8%
1999	6.2%	15.0%	26.3%	33.3%	56.0%	69.5%	30.5%

Table 3.28 (continued)

Year	Top 0.01%	Top 0.1%	Top 0.5%	Top 1%	Top 5%	Top 10%	Bottom 90%
2000	6.9%	16.0%	27.3%	34.1%	56.6%	69.8%	30.2%
2001	7.0%	15.7%	26.5%	33.2%	55.8%	69.2%	30.8%
2002	6.3%	14.5%	25.2%	32.0%	55.2%	69.0%	31.0%
2003	6.5%	14.7%	25.4%	32.3%	55.5%	69.3%	30.7%
2004	7.0%	15.6%	26.7%	33.5%	56.5%	70.0%	30.0%
2005	7.4%	16.3%	27.3%	34.0%	56.5%	69.9%	30.1%
2006	7.7%	16.8%	28.1%	34.9%	57.5%	70.7%	29.3%
2007	8.5%	17.7%	29.1%	36.0%	58.6%	71.6%	28.4%
2008	9.2%	19.0%	31.0%	38.1%	61.4%	74.6%	25.4%
2009	9.6%	18.9%	30.6%	37.8%	61.5%	75.1%	24.9%
2010	10.8%	20.7%	32.4%	39.5%	62.6%	75.7%	24.3%
2011	10.1%	20.3%	32.5%	39.8%	63.0%	76.0%	24.0%
2012	11.2%	22.0%	34.5%	41.8%	64.6%	77.2%	22.8%

Note: * Figures are presented here on a cumulative basis.

Source: Wolff (2012).

increase in inequality since the asset price meltdown is demonstrated by the rising wealth share not only of the wealthiest 10%, but of the wealthiest 5%, 1%, 0.1% and 0.01% as well. From 2001 to 2012 the wealth share of each of these groups rose. The wealth holdings of the wealthiest 0.01%, 5% and 10% continued to grow during and after the financial crisis of 2007–08. The wealth shares of the wealthiest 0.1%, 0.5% and 1% saw a slight decline from 2008 to 2009, before continuing to rise again during 2009–12.

More information about the distribution of wealth is available for the seven countries discussed above than for any other country. However, a substantial amount of information is available for another four countries, namely Australia, Finland, Italy and Spain. We discuss each of these countries next.

3.9 AUSTRALIA

In the case of Australia, we start with figures emanating from the war census of 1915 conducted under the supervision of Commonwealth Statistician G.H. Knibbs, who in 1918 went on to publish *The Private Wealth of Australia and its Growth*. The 1915 census provided data on the distribution of wealth. In fact

[t]he 1915 form used by the individual in declaring net wealth was a very comprehensive statement including 16 asset items and 3 liability items. These included value questions for cash, deposits, debts owned, stock, bonds, land, buildings, furniture, interest in trust estates, leases, and other property except holdings in life insurance and friendly society policies. (Soltow, 1972, p. 129)

N. Podder and N.C. Kakwani (1976) compared these census figures of wealth in 1915 with the 1966–67 distribution. Podder and Kakwani's results (which measured household wealth, and the wealth of men, but not of women) are set out in Table 3.29.

Table 3.29   Males' (1915) and households' (1966–67) percentage shares of total wealth, and Gini coefficient, Australia, 1915 and 1966–67

Measure	1915	1966–67
Top 1%	39.46	9.26
Top 5%	66.22	24.58
Top 20%	89.71	53.51
Top 40%*	97.51	76.23
Top 60%*	99.52	91.29
Top 80%*	99.95	99.10
Last 20%	0.03	0.91
Gini coefficient	0.861	0.52

Note: * Podder and Kakwani's figures are presented here on a cumulative basis; the third last and second last rows do not add up to 100 because of rounding.

Source: Podder and Kakwani (1976), Table 14, p. 90.

The source of the Podder and Kakwani figures for 1966–67 was the asset data collected in the Australian Survey of Consumer Finances carried out jointly by Macquarie University and the University of Queensland during 1966–68. The results indicate a degree of inequality in Australia much lower than that calculated for any other country. However, Harrison (1979, p. 48) listed a number of reasons for believing that the sample survey data used by Podder and Kakwani were 'substantially unreliable', a view taken also by J.W. Nevile and N.A. Warren (1984, p. 12), who said of the Podder and Kakwani results that the 'small size and nature of the sample make them unreliable'.[8] More specifically, Harrison (1979, p. 48) judged that the Podder and Kakwani 'figures probably substantially understate the true position' with respect to the degree of inequality. Harrison's judgement finds some support in the conclusion arrived at by Peter Groenewegen

(1972, p. 105), based on estate duty figures for 1967–68, that 'at the top end of the scale about eleven per cent of the population owns nearly forty per cent of the wealth, while at the other end more than fifteen per cent of the population owns less than five per cent of the wealth'.[9]

By contrast with Podder and Kakwani, in estimating the distribution of wealth in Australia over the period 1953–69 Robert Gunton (1971, 1975) used the estate multiplier method, taking into account mortality differences according to social class and making estimates of 'excluded wealth'. Drawing *inter alia* on his Gini coefficient estimates of 0.681 in 1953 and 0.667 in 1969, Gunton concluded that '[i]nequality of wealth-holding has decreased very little over the period 1953 to 1969', adding that '[c]omparisons of Knibbs's estimate for 1915 with the later estimates show a small reduction over a long period' (Gunton, 1975, pp. ii–iii).

Harrison (1979) noted that Gunton's figures for holders of net wealth of $1 or above imply a much smaller Australian population than was actually the case at the time. In order to make comparisons with the distribution of wealth in other countries, he accordingly recalculated percentage shares by adapting the Gunton (1971) 1967–68 net wealth figures so as to apply to the actual population aged 20 and over, arriving at the results set out in Table 3.30.

In estimating the distribution of wealth in Australia in 1969–70, Phillip L. Raskall (1977) likewise used the estate multiplier method. His results are

Table 3.30   Individuals' percentage shares of total wealth, Australia, 1967–68

Top 1%	Top 5%	Top 10%	Top 25%	Top 47.5%
28.7%	56.6%	72.5%	92.1%	100.0%

Source: Harrison (1979), Table 9, p. 45.

Table 3.31   Individuals' percentage shares of total wealth, Australia, 1969–70

Top 1%	Top 5%	Top 10%	Top 20%	Top 40%	Top 60%	Top 80%	Top 20%	Gini ratio
22.0	45.5	58.5	72.2*	87.7*	95.1*	99.0*	1.0*	0.71*

Note: * Raskall's figures, presented here on a cumulative basis, have been rounded to the first decimal place; the Gini ratio has been rounded to the second decimal place.

Source: Raskall (1977), Table 10, p. 30.

set out in Table 3.31. The estimates made by Raskall portray a less unequal distribution of wealth than those made by Gunton. This is at least partly due to the more generous estimate made by Raskall of 'excluded wealth'.

In 1978 the Liberal-Country Party Government led by Malcolm Fraser fulfilled a 1977 election promise by phasing out estate duties, thereby unfortunately eliminating the data which make it possible to use the estate multiplier method to calculate the distribution of wealth. Hans Baekgaard (1997) and Simon Kelly (2001) consequently turned instead to relevant Australian Bureau of Statistics surveys. Using data from the 1986 Income Distribution Survey and the 1993–94 Household Expenditure Survey, Baekgaard arrived at distribution of wealth figures for 1986 and 1993. Baekgaard's work was supplemented by Kelly, who used data from the 1997–98 Survey of Income and Housing Costs to arrive at distribution of wealth figures for 1998. The results are set out in Table 3.32. Noting that legislative changes in 1986 and 1992 greatly increased the percentage of the population covered by occupational superannuation, Kelly concluded from the detailed wealth composition data that, but for this factor, the Gini coefficient would have been substantially greater in 1998 than in 1986.

Table 3.32 Households' percentage shares of total wealth, Australia, 1986, 1993 and 1998

	1986	1993	1998
Top 1%	11.3	12.0	12
Top 5%	30.1	29.3	30
Top 10%	44.4	43.3	45
Top 29%	63.5	62.3	65
Top 30%	76.5	75.7	78
Top 40%	86.1	85.7	87
Top 50%	93.4	92.9	93
Top 60%	98.1	97.3	97
Top 70%	99.8	99.2	99
Top 80%	100.1	99.8	100
Top 90%[a]	100.1	99.9	100
Last 10%[a]	–0.2	0	0
Gini coefficient[b]	0.64		0.64

Notes:
a   Baekgaard's and Kelly's figures are presented here on a cumulative basis; for 1986 and 1993 the second and third last rows do not add up to 100 because of rounding.
b   Gini coefficient calculations were made by Kelly.

Sources: Baekgaard (1997), Tables 3a and 3b, pp. 15–16, and Kelly (2001), Tables 8 and 9, pp. 15–16.

Data relating to the distribution of wealth in Australia subsequent to 1998 come from two sources. Figures for 2002, 2006 and 2010 can be obtained from Wilkins (2013), and are based on Household Income and Labour Dynamics (HILDA) surveys. Figures for 2003–04, 2005–06, 2009–10 and 2011–12 can be obtained from the Australian Bureau of Statistics' *Household Wealth and Wealth Distribution, Australia* (2013), and were derived from the Bureau's biennial Survey of Income and Housing. Both sets of figures, which are included in Table 3.33, suggest that between 2002 and 2009–10 the distribution of wealth as judged by the top 20% share became more unequal, but that this trend was reversed over the period 2010–12, possibly due to the global financial crisis of 2007–08, which probably had a bigger adverse effect on the more wealthy than on the less wealthy given the large decline in asset prices in the stock market but the continued rise in housing prices.

Table 3.33, in presenting data from the above and other sources, gives a rough indication of possible broad trends over time in the distribution

Table 3.33   *Wealth share (%) of the wealthiest 5%, wealthiest 10% and wealthiest 20%, and Gini coefficient, Australia, 1915–2012*

Year	Top 5%*	Top 10%*	Top 20%	Gini
1915			89.71	
1966–67			53.51	
1986			63.5	0.64
1993			62.3	
1998			65	0.64
2002			63.3	0.622
2003–04	23+*	33+*	59	
2005–06	23+	37+	61.1	
2006			64.9	0.635
2009–10	25+	38+	61.8	
2010			62.3	0.61
2011–12	25+	38+	60.8	

Note: * Figures for the wealthiest 5% and wealthiest 10% shares are estimated minima. They were derived from Table 2 of ABS Catalogue 6554.0. To estimate the minimum net worth of the wealthiest 5%, for example, it was conservatively assumed that each household in the wealthiest 5% held the minimum net worth for the corresponding net worth range. It was then assumed (also conservatively) that each household *below* the wealthiest 5% held the *maximum* net worth for *their* corresponding net worth range. The wealth share of the wealthiest 5% was measured relative to the sum of these. The same approach was adopted for the wealthiest 10%.

Sources: ABS (2013), Tables 1 and 2, Schneider (2004a), Tables 3.24 and 3.27, and Wilkins (2013), Tables B1 and 13.1.

of wealth in Australia as judged by the top 20% share (though these individual figures are calculated in such a variety of ways that inferences need to be treated with particular caution).[10] The data do seem to suggest that over the period 1915 to 1966–67, the distribution of wealth in Australia became less unequal, in conformity with the pattern for other countries. With the exception of the Gini coefficient figures for 1986 and 1998, they also suggest that the distribution of wealth as judged by both the top 20% share and the remaining Gini coefficient figures became more unequal between 1986 and 2009–10, and that this trend was reversed in the period 2010–12. On the other hand, as judged by the top 10% share the distribution remained relatively unchanged between 2009–10 and 2011–12 (possibly because the share of the next top 15% declined). A broadly similar conclusion is drawn by Alan Fenna and Alan Tapper (2015).

The picture of change in the distribution of wealth in Australia outlined above is broadly consistent with the results of a study of change in the share of the wealthiest 1%, of the wealthiest 0.5%, and of the wealthiest 0.1% of Australian households, undertaken by Pamela Katic and Andrew Leigh (2013) and reported in *Battlers and Billionaires* (Leigh, 2013). Based on inheritance tax records for the period 1915 to 1978–79, the 1987 Australian Standard of Living Study, and the HILDA surveys for 2002, 2006 and 2010, this study concluded that the share of the wealthiest 1% of Australian households fell from 34% in 1915 to a low of 6% in 1968, before rising to 10% in 1987, to 12% in 2002 and to 16% (a figure that Katic and Leigh, however, think may be too high) in 2006, before falling to 11% in 2010. It further concluded that the share of the wealthiest 0.1% of Australian households fell from 13% in 1915 to a low of 2% in 1957, where it remained with the exception of spikes in 1972 and 2006 (Katic and Leigh, p. 9) and that 'the top 0.5% explains most of the top 1% . . . movements'.

Kelly (2002, pp. 3–12), in a path-breaking study, used the National Institute of Social and Economic Modelling (NATSEM) dynamic micro-simulation model (DYNAMOD) to forecast the distribution of wealth in Australia over the period 2000 to 2030. The Gini coefficient, 0.639 in 1998, was estimated to be 0.641, 0.633, 0.660 and 0.685 in 2000, 2010, 2020 and 2030 respectively. In more detail, over the period 2000–10 an estimated fall in the share of the top 20 per cent from 64.0 per cent to 62.7 per cent is roughly balanced by an estimated fall in the share of the bottom 50 per cent from 7.0 per cent to 6.7 per cent, whereas over the period 2010–30 an estimated rise in the share of the top 20 per cent to 70.0 per cent is accompanied by an estimated fall in the share of the bottom 50 per cent to 4.9 per cent. Kelly singled out three factors as significant contributors to the forecast increase in inequality in the distribution of wealth by 2030. First, Australia was expected to have an ageing population; at least up to a point, wealth tends to increase with age. Second, the saving ratio (ratio of saving to income) of younger age cohorts was not expected to be as great as that of older age cohorts. Third, home ownership was expected to decline. Up to the present time Kelly's prophecies have not been far off the mark. Whether his Piketty-like prophecies for the next decade and a half will be fulfilled of course remains to be seen.

3.10   FINLAND

Table 3.34 sets out distribution of wealth figures for Finland that cover the period 1968–83.

Table 3.34 indicates that for the period 1968–83 there was a downward trend in the wealth share of each of the wealthiest 0.1%, wealthiest 1% and wealthiest 10% of the population of Finland. This is consistent with the experience of most other countries over this period.

Further information about the distribution of wealth in Finland is to be found in Markus Jäntti (2002), which includes estimates of the Gini coefficient for the distribution of wealth for 1987, 1994 and 1998, using data

Table 3.34   Wealth share (%) of the wealthiest 0.1%, 1% and 10%, Finland, 1968–83

Year	Top 0.1%	Top 1%	Top 10%
1968	0.1350	0.3197	0.7299
1969	0.1287	0.3261	0.7327
1970	0.1237	0.3107	0.7387
1971	0.1249	0.2916	0.7081
1972	0.1178	0.2825	0.6986
1973	0.1198	0.2732	0.6826
1974	0.1269	0.2619	0.6717
1975	0.1079	0.2392	0.6602
1976	0.0957	0.2064	0.6435
1977	0.0899	0.1923	0.6468
1978	0.0854	0.1864	0.6421
1979	0.0805	0.1767	0.6345
1980	0.0826	0.1630	0.6317
1981	0.0845	0.1755	0.6356
1982	0.0883	0.1765	0.6386
1983	0.0901	0.1757	0.6351

Source: Tuomalo and Vilmunen (1988), Table 1, p. 186.

from surveys conducted by Statistics Finland, whose calculation of net wealth did not include pension or life insurance entitlements. Jäntti concluded that over this period inequality had increased, the Gini coefficient for these years being 0.551, 0.604 and 0.615 respectively.

3.11 ITALY

In the case of Italy, while data are available on the wealthiest 1%, 5% and 10%, the observations are infrequent compared with those discussed in terms of long-run trends. Nonetheless, there are sufficient data to present some idea of the nature of wealth inequality in this country.

A background for estimates relating to inequality in Italy in the late twentieth century is to be found in estimates of the distribution of wealth relating to three points in time between 1890 and 1915, based on post-tax transfers of wealth from deceased persons, published in 1980 in an essay by Vera Zamagni. Her figures are set out in Table 3.35.

Table 3.35 Individuals' percentage shares of total wealth and Gini coefficient, Italy, 1890–91 to 1914–15

Year	Top 1%	Top 2%	Top 10%	Top 20%	Gini ratio
1890–91	48	58	78	83	0.8555
1900–02	42	53	77	82	0.8326
1914–15	41	51	78	87	0.8103

Source: Zamagni (1980), Table 3.4, p. 139.

Zamagni went on to compare her deceased-estate figures for Italy with the adult-population figures for Great Britain in 1911–13 estimated by Daniels and Campion, cited in H.F. Lydall and D.G. Tipping (1961, p. 92). She commented that, because of the direct correlation between wealth and age,

> the picture presented in Table 3.4 overstates the real concentration of wealth ownership. Keeping this in mind, a comparison with Great Britain suggests that around 1911–13 concentration of wealth was greater there than in Italy. (Zamagni, 1980, p. 139)

Estimates of the distribution of wealth in Italy in the 1980s and 1990s were produced by Andrea Brandolini, Luigi Cannari, Giovanni D'Alessio and Ivan Faiella, using data provided by the Survey of Household Income and Wealth conducted by the Bank of Italy every other year from 1987 to 1995,

Table 3.36   Households' percentage shares of total wealth and Gini
              coefficient, Italy, 1987–2000

Year	Top 1%	Top 5%	Top 10%	Top 20%	Top 40%	Top 60%	Last 40%*	Gini ratio
1987	12.4	32.0	46.3	64.4	84.2	94.5	5.6	0.620
1989	11.9	30.3	43.6	61.8	83.0	93.7	6.3	0.598
1991	9.5	26.6	40.1	58.3	80.3	92.4	7.6	0.560
1993	11.7	29.3	43.0	61.0	82.2	93.7	6.4	0.591
1995	10.8	29.2	42.6	60.2	81.2	93.1	6.9	0.581
1998	15.2	35.0	47.8	63.9	82.6	93.5	6.5	0.614
2000	17.1	36.3	48.7	64.1	82.6	93.2	6.8	0.616

Note: * Brandolini et al.'s figures are presented here on a cumulative basis; the third last
and second last columns do not always add up to 100 because of rounding.

Source: Brandolini et al. (2002), Table 7, p. 37.

and again in 1998 and 2000. In estimating the net wealth of a household,
Brandolini et al. did not include the value of pension or life insurance
plans, though they did make adjustments designed to offset biases resulting from the low response rate to the surveys. Their results are set out in
Table 3.36.

Using the Gini coefficient figures, Brandolini et al. (2002, p. 11) concluded that 'inequality showed a declining trend until 1991 and the opposite tendency in the rest of the decade'. It should also be noted, however,
that the similar Gini coefficients for 1987 and 2000 mask an increase in the
wealth share of both the top 1% and the bottom 40%, at the expense of the
rest of the population.[11] Table 3.37 (on page 71) shows the share of total
wealth (%) of the wealthiest 1%, next 4%, next 5%, next 10%, top 20%,
second 20%, third 20% and least wealthy 40% of the population of Italy
over the period 1991–2002, from which it can be seen that the wealth share
of the top 1% almost doubled from 1991 to 2002.

3.12   SPAIN

In their study of the distribution of wealth in Spain, Alvaredo and Saez
had to make do with tax data relating to taxpayers gathered into cohorts
according to their level of reported income and wealth.[12] Table 3.38 sets
out the resulting wealth share of the individuals belonging to the wealthiest
1%, wealthiest 0.5%, wealthiest 0.1% and wealthiest 0.01% in Spain over
the period 1982–2007.

Table 3.37   Wealth share (%) of the wealthiest 1%, the next wealthiest
4%, the next wealthiest 5%, the next wealthiest 10%,
wealthiest 20%, the 2nd wealthiest 20%, the 3rd wealthiest
20% and the least wealthy 40%, Italy, 1991–2002

Year	Top 1%	Next 4%	Next 5%	Next 10%	Top 20%	2nd 20%	3rd 20%	Last 40%
1991	6.2	11.9	12.3	17.4	47.9	24.5	15.2	12.4
1993	8.2	14.2	11.5	16.3	50.2	23.2	15.3	11.2
1995	8.6	14.1	11.7	17.5	52.0	22.6	14.9	10.5
1998	14.4	14.6	12.0	16.0	57.0	19.8	13.5	9.8
2000	15.5	15.4	10.5	15.2	56.6	20.5	13.1	9.8
2002	11.9	16.7	11.7	16.4	56.7	20.2	13.6	9.6

Source: Mazzaferro and Toso (2006), Table 2.

Table 3.38 indicates that the wealth share of the wealthiest 1% individuals in Spain trended downwards from 1982 to 1995, when it reached a minimum (namely 15.93%), thereafter trending upwards until 2002, when it reached a maximum (namely 20.01%), before trending downwards again. Using these figures as a measure of inequality in the distribution of wealth, we can infer that inequality in the distribution of wealth in Spain, in common with many other countries, reached a minimum during the last three decades of the twentieth century, and thereafter increased before plateauing or decreasing in the first decade of the twenty-first century. On the other hand, the wealth share of the wealthiest 0.5%, 0.1% and 0.01% individuals each continued to trend downwards after 1995. Alvarado and Saez (2009, p. 1157) suggest that the explanation for this is that over the period 1982 to 2005 'the surge in stock prices [was not] enough to compensate for the dramatic increase in real estate prices, which benefits upper (but not very top) wealth holders'. The subsequent effect of the financial crisis of 2007–08 and the collapse of the Spanish property boom is likely to have hurt those same wealth-holders.

Substantial corroboration of the results arrived at by Alvarado and Saez is provided by Duràn-Cabré and Esteller-Moré, who on the basis of the same tax figures, in order to estimate the wealthiest 1% share for the years 1983–2001, assumed not a Pareto interpolation but 'a non-increasing density for the upper brackets' (Duràn-Cabré and Esteller-Moré, 2007, p.5). The resulting pattern of change is very similar to that arrived at by Alvaredo and Saez (though the figures are about one percentage point higher until 2000, and about three percentage points higher in 2001 and 2002). As Duràn-Cabré and Esteller-Moré (2007, p. 10) put it

*Table 3.38   Wealth share (%) of the wealthiest 1%, 0.5%, 0.1% and 0.01%
in Spain, 1982–2007*

Year	Top 1%	Top .5%	Top .1%	Top .01%
1982	18.43	14.37	7.48	2.48
1983	18.07	14.00	7.39	2.57
1984	17.54	13.55	7.07	2.36
1985	17.78	13.58	6.95	2.27
1986	18.16	13.83	7.10	2.44
1987	17.71	13.38	6.71	2.21
1988	17.28	12.98	6.36	2.04
1989	16.88	12.62	6.04	1.92
1990	16.82	12.38	5.79	1.78
1991	16.12	11.73	5.39	1.59
1992	16.02	11.63	5.32	1.60
1993	16.62	11.84	5.46	1.66
1994	16.33	11.50	5.18	1.53
1995	15.93	11.20	5.00	1.47
1996	16.62	11.75	5.25	1.56
1997	17.39	12.17	5.39	1.59
1998	17.23	12.04	5.36	1.61
1999	17.19	12.27	5.31	1.59
2000	18.53	13.17	5.62	1.61
2001	18.47	13.07	5.56	1.63
2002	20.01	14.19	5.96	1.62
2003	19.44	13.43	5.45	1.47
2004	19.56	13.49	5.48	1.48
2005	18.93	13.01	5.21	1.36
2006	19.22	13.24	5.43	1.53
2007	19.65	13.52	5.58	1.62

Source: Alvaredo and Saez (2009), Table 10D.8.A.

From 1988 to 2001, we can identify two general sub-periods: 1988–1995 and 1995–2001. In the first one, the top 1%'s share goes down, although with some variations. In the second one, it goes the other way around and the share increases, especially since 2000. The overall evolution for the 1988–2001 period would suggest an increase in the share of top 1%.

3.13   COMPARATIVE STUDIES AND DATA FOR OTHER COUNTRIES

While long-run data are not readily available for all countries, in some instances there have been studies of wealth inequality over a shorter period of time, sometimes comparing two or more countries. In this section we present summaries and data from some useful examples of this work, notably Harrison (1979), Wolff (1996) and Davies and Shorrocks (2000), supplemented by Gustaffson et al. (2006), Sierminska et al. (2006a, 2006b) and Davies et al. (2011). While they do not necessarily contribute to a more detailed understanding of the trends in wealth inequality, works of this kind suggest some explanation for the variation in and contrast between wealth inequalities in different countries. They also point the way towards future primary research that might build on the foundation provided by existing studies.

We turn first to Harrison's *The Distribution of Wealth in Ten Countries*, a background paper commissioned by the British Royal Commission on the Distribution of Income and Wealth and published in 1979.[13] Harrison's selection of countries was based on the belief that, apart from the United Kingdom, there were only ten countries 'for which even vaguely reliable figures are available' (Harrison, 1979, p. 2). Harrison added the caveat that

> no attempt is made to construct an overall comparison of the degree of inequality in the distribution of wealth in the various countries. Such a comparison would lead to many false conclusions which we would not wish to encourage. (Harrison, 1979, p. 2)

Harrison nonetheless included three tables making comparisons between groups of countries, the essential features of which are reproduced in the first part of this section.

The first of Harrison's comparative tables covers the shares of total wealth owned by the wealthiest 1% in the United Kingdom and the United States, over the period 1953–72. Using figures from Table 6.5 in Atkinson and Harrison (1978), Table 1 in Smith and Franklin (1974) and Table 4 in M.K. Taussig (1976), Harrison arrived at the figures set out in Table 3.39.

Harrison commented that even allowing for overestimation of the 1953 and 1958 inequality figures for Great Britain, due to the allowance made for the wealth of the excluded population being too low, there is

Table 3.39   Richest 1% individuals' percentage share of total wealth, Great Britain and the United States, 1953–72

	1953	1958	1962	1965	1969	1972
Great Britain	43.5	40.9	31.9	33.3	31.3	32.0
United States	23.9	23.2	23.1	25.1	21.3	22.7

Source: Harrison (1979), Table 4, p. 31.

some decline in Britain over the years 1953–1972 but none in the USA. On the other hand it is clear that the decline was at an end by 1962 and from then until 1972 the USA figure stays a little over two-thirds of that for Britain. (Harrison, 1979, p. 31)

The data on long-run trends in the distribution of wealth presented in section 3.1 of this chapter also highlight the different trends in the United States and the United Kingdom, with the difference between the wealth share of the wealthiest 5% in each of these countries narrowing after 1958, and then diverging again afterwards.

In Canada, included in the second of Harrison's comparative tables, wealth at death is not recorded, and the data required for the use of the 'estate multiplier' method consequently do not exist. However, the distribution of wealth in 1956, 1959, 1964 and 1970 can be estimated by reference to the data collected in Statistics Canada's Survey of Consumer Finances for each of those years. J.R. Podoluk (1974) utilised the 1970 Survey of Consumer Finances to calculate the distribution between family units of net worth, excluding pension and insurance claims and consumer durables other than cars and houses. The results are set out in Table 3.40.

The 1970 Survey of Consumer Finances also provided the data for alternative estimates of the distribution of wealth in 1970 made by James B. Davies (1979). These are set out in Table 3.41, which includes figures not only for the distribution of wealth by household, but also for the

Table 3.40   Households' percentage shares of total wealth and Gini coefficient, Canada, 1970

Inequality measure	Percentage
Top 10% share	53.9
Top 20% share	71.6
Top 30% share	83.4
Top 40% share	91.6
Top 50% share	96.8
Top 60% share	99.6
Top 70% share	100.7*
Top 80% share	100.9*
Top 90% share	100.9*
Gini coefficient	0.724

Note: * The implied negative figure for the bottom 30% reflects an excess of liabilities over assets.

Source: Podoluk (1974), Table 6, p. 212.

Table 3.41   Households' percentage shares of total wealth, coefficient of variation, Gini coefficient and exponential index, Canada, 1970

Inequality measure	Family units	Per adult basis
Top 1% share	18.0%	17.1%
Top 5% share	39.2%	38.3%
Top 10% share	53.1%	51.9%
Top 20% share	70.1%	69.3%
Next 40% share	28.6%	29.3%
Last 40% share	0.7%	1.4%
Coefficient of variation	2.315	2.274
Gini coefficient	0.715	0.698
Exponential index	0.527	0.509

Source: Davies (1979), Table 1, p. 239.

distribution of wealth per adult unit of household. Where the figures are comparable, Davies' estimates are very close to those obtained by Podoluk.

Comparing his results with those to be found in Atkinson and Harrison (1978) for Great Britain and V. Natrella (1975) for the United States, Davies (1979, p. 239) ventured the opinion that for Canada in 1970 'top shares might be roughly of the same order of magnitude as top shares in the U.S., while apparent concentration in the upper tail is lower in both the U.S. and Canada than in the U.K'.

Noting the possibility of bias arising if response rates vary with wealth or if there is mis-reporting, and assuming on the basis of United States experience that Canadian survey response rates decline linearly with the log of wealth, Davies re-estimated his measures of inequality so as to establish likely upper and lower bounds taking these factors into account. He found that '[t]he plausible range of impacts of non-sampling error, given our basic assumptions, is surprisingly narrow. The difference between the two most extreme corrections in terms of the top shares and summary indexes does not exceed 15 percent' (Davies, 1979, p. 254).

Since Davies' work, other studies have estimated the wealth share of the wealthiest 20% of the population of Canada to have been around 69% in 1984 (Wolff 1996, Table 4) and around 63% in 1999 and 2005 (Statistics Canada, 2013).

In comparing the distribution of wealth in Canada with that in Great Britain and the United States, Harrison took the upper bound of inequality figures for Canada from Davies' then forthcoming article, and Natrella's figures for the United States. The results are set out in Table 3.42.

Table 3.42   Percentage shares of total wealth, Canada, the United States and Britain, 1969 and 1970

	Top 1%	Top 5%	Top 10%
Canada, 1970 (households)	21.6*	45.7	59.8
USA, 1969 (individuals)	25.1	43.7	53.0
Britain, 1970 (individuals)	30.1	54.3	69.4

Note: * In the published version of Davies' article, this figure appears as 21.2%.

Source: Harrison (1979), Table 6, p. 34.

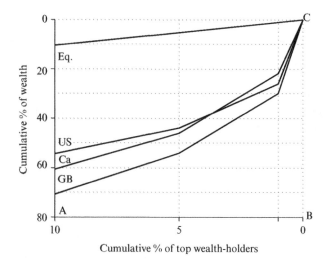

Source: Harrison (1979), Figure 1, p. 33; the horizontal axis measures from the right.

Figure 3.2   Partial wealth Lorenz curves for Great Britain, United States and Canada, 1969–70

Harrison illustrated these results with a partial Lorenz curve diagram covering the top 10 per cent of wealth-holders, reproduced here with minor changes as Figure 3.2. The Lorenz curve for Great Britain (GB) lies furthest from the line of equality (Eq.), while the curves for Canada (Ca) and the United States (US) intersect, that for the United States lying further from the line of equality for the top 1 per cent of wealth-holders, but closer for both the top 5 per cent and the top 10 per cent.

Harrison also looked at the distribution of wealth in Ireland, where the

Table 3.43　Individuals' percentage shares of total wealth, Ireland, 1965–66

Top 1%	Top 5%	Top 10%	Top 20%	Top 30%
33.7	63.0	78.1	93.2	97.4

Source: Harrison (1979), Table 16, p. 61.

estate multiplier method of measurement has been used. Patrick M. Lyons (1975) estimated the proportion of Ireland's wealth held on average over the period 1965–66 by the wealthiest 1%, wealthiest 5% and wealthiest 10% of the population aged 20 and over, assuming that the 'excluded' population had zero wealth. Harrison extended Lyons' figures to cover the wealthiest 20% and wealthiest 30% as well, the results being set out in Table 3.43.

Andres D. Chesher and Patrick C. McMahon (1976), assuming that the distribution of wealth follows a log-normal pattern, argued that the most appropriate figure for the wealth per head of the 'excluded' population in Ireland was not zero but £246, as a result of which their figures for the share of total wealth held by the wealthiest 1% and wealthiest 5% were approximately 4 and 6 percentage points respectively below those estimated by Lyons. Even taking this adjustment into account, the distribution of wealth in Ireland in 1965 appears to have been more unequal than that in other countries.

Harrison (1979) in addition compares the distribution of wealth in Australia and New Zealand. By contrast with the estimates of the distribution of wealth in Australia in 1967–68 made by Gunton, the figures for New Zealand calculated by B.H. Easton (1983) for 1956 and 1966, while also based on the 'estate multiplier' method, do not take into account either mortality differences according to social class, or the wealth held by the 'excluded population'. Using linear interpolation, Easton arrived at the figures set out in Table 3.44.

Table 3.44　Households' percentage shares of total wealth, Gini coefficient and Pareto index, New Zealand, 1956 and 1966

Year	Top 1%	Top 2%	Top 5%	Top 10%	Top 20%	Top 50%	Last 50%	Gini ratio	Pareo index
1956	25.4	40.7	48.2	63.9	79.5	98.6	1.4	0.816	1.71
1966	18.0	30.5	44.5	59.2	78.9	99.8	0.2	0.782	1.93

Source: Easton (1983), Table 73, p. 138.

Table 3.45   Individuals' shares of total wealth, New Zealand, 1966

Top 1%	Top 5%	Top 19%	Top 25%	Top 55.5%
18.2%	44.5%	60.0%	84.7%	100%

Source: Harrison (1979), Table 10, p. 45.

The decrease in the Gini coefficient indicates that inequality in the distribution of wealth was less in 1966 than it had been in 1956. Although this conclusion would appear to have to be qualified in that the figures for the bottom 50 per cent's share of total wealth show a fall between 1956 and 1966, Easton (1983, p. 138) estimated that this change was wholly accounted for by the quadrupling of the estate duty exemption limit during that period.

Using log-linear interpolation rather than Easton's linear interpolation, Harrison (1979) arrived at the figures set out in Table 3.45.

Taking into account both these figures for New Zealand and the figures for Australia which he derived from Gunton's study, Harrison commented that

> [t]he closest UK estimates to those presented here for Australia and New Zealand are the Inland Revenue/Royal Commission series B figures. In 1966 the share of the top 1% in the UK according to this source is 31.8%, rising very slightly in 1967, but not too different from the Australian figure of 28.7% when one takes account of the equalising influence of Gunton's treatment of small estates, but appreciably higher than the New Zealand estimate. (Harrison, 1979, p. 46)

Harrison added the warning, however, that 'in view of the fact that the use of the estate multiplier method in both Australia and New Zealand is at a far more rudimentary stage than in the UK, any comparison such as this must be treated very cautiously indeed' (Harrison, 1979, p. 46).

We turn now to some European countries. Harrison defended his third comparative table, involving Denmark and Sweden, on the ground that the 'basic data source in Denmark is similar to that in Sweden' (Harrison, 1979, p. 50). The figures from Harrison's table are presented in Table 3.46. Harrison's comment was that '[s]urprisingly, perhaps, in view of the fact that the Swedish survey oversamples the wealthy, the results suggest that the shares of top wealth-holders are higher in Denmark than in Sweden' (Harrison, 1979, p. 51).

We turn next to France, West Germany and Belgium. Using sample survey data collected in 1975 by CREP (*Centre de Recherche*

Table 3.46   Households' shares of total wealth, Denmark and Sweden, 1975

	Top 1%	Top 5%	Top 10%
Denmark (tax values)	25%	47%	63%
Sweden (tax values)	20%	42%	57%

Source: Harrison (1979), Table 12, p. 50.

Economique sur L'Epargne) and additional (admittedly very limited) information, with respect to France up to 1975, Adeline Daumard (1980, p. 116) concluded

> that the concentration of assets remained very high, but that there is a reduction following the First World War and, even more, after 1950. After a quarter of a century of this trend the main beneficiaries have been the owners of middle-sized fortunes, their proportion having increased considerably. But it would be inaccurate to conclude that the position of the poor has deteriorated.

After a cessation in 1964, in the late 1970s the French 'Internal Revenue Service (IRS) resumed collecting detailed information on inheritances' (Kessler and Masson, 1987, pp. 145–6), enabling A. Fouquet and D. Strauss-Kahn (1981) to estimate the distribution of wealth in 1977 using the 'estate multiplier method'. Their results, using social class mortality rates, as reported by Kessler and Masson are set out in Table 3.47.

Estimates of the distribution of wealth in France were also made by Babeau and Strauss-Kahn (1977), using the already-mentioned sample survey data collected in 1975. In the case of West Germany, estimates of the distribution of wealth in both 1969 and 1973 were made by Horst Mierheim and Lutz Wicke (1977) using sample survey data collected in each of those years, though lack of the appropriate data forced them to rank households by size of income rather than of wealth. And, in the case of Belgium, J. Walravens and P. Praet (1978) made estimates of the distribution of wealth in 1969 using the capitalised values of

Table 3.47   Individuals' shares of total wealth, France, 1977

Top 1%	Top 2%	Top 3%	Top 5%	Top 10%	Top 20%
19.1%	28.4%	35.8%	46.6%	65.5%	85.9%

Source: Kessler and Masson (1987), Table 7.4, p. 146.

Table 3.48   Households' shares of total wealth, France, 1975,
West Germany, 1973 and Belgium, 1969

	France	West Germany	Belgium
Top 1%	12.5%	18.7%	27.8%
Top 5%	36.2%	33.9%	46.7%
Top 10%	51.7%	45.3%	57.4%
Top 20%	71.0%	57.4%	70.9%
Top 30%	83.6%	66.1%	79.7%
Top 40%	91.8%	73.4%	86.1%
Top 50%	96.3%	79.2%	90.8%
Top 60%	98.3%	84.5%	94.3%
Top 70%	99.4%	88.8%	96.8%
Top 80%	99.6%	92.9%	98.5%
Top 90%	99.8%	96.6%	99.6%

Source: Harrison (1979), Tables 13, 14 and 15, pp. 55 and 57.

income figures derived from tax data, supplemented by sample survey
figures, and obtained a degree of disaggregation 'made possible by
their decision to impose the assumption of a lognormal distribution
on the aggregated data' (Harrison, 1979, p. 55). Harrison (1979) made
a number of adjustments to the Babeau and Strauss-Kahn estimates
for France, discarded the West German figures for 1969 on the ground
that absolute asset amounts were not obtained in that year, and applied
log-linear interpolation, the results, including those for Belgium, being
set out in Table 3.48.

With respect to France and Belgium, Harrison noted – but in the
absence of adequate data found impossible to explain – the fact that

> the share of the top 1% in France is quite substantially lower than the share
> of the same group in Belgium, although the implied Lorenz curves for the
> countries cross at around the top 20%. The share of the bottom 50% in France is
> therefore lower than the equivalent share in Belgium. (Harrison, 1979, pp. 56–7)

With respect to Germany, he commented

> the households are ranked by size of income, rather than by size of wealth, and
> to the extent that correlation between income and wealth is less than perfect,
> this will tend to understate the percentage shares of top wealth holders. On the
> other hand, the estimates do not exhibit the very low shares of the bottom 50%
> usually seen when consumer durables are excluded. The estimated share of the
> top 1% is higher than the figure for France, which seems strange in view of the
> fact that the CREP survey in France attempted to oversample the rich. Both

Table 3.49   Measures of inequality in the distribution of total gross or net wealth among households, France, 1986, the United States, 1983, Canada, 1984, Sweden, 1985/86 and Australia, 1986

Country	Gini ratio	Top 1%	Top 5%	Top 20%	2nd 20%	3rd 20%	4th 20%
France gross	0.71	26	43	69	19	9%	2%
U.S. gross	0.77	33	54	78	14	7%	2%
U.S. net	0.79	35	56	80	13	6%	2%
Canada net	0.69	17	38	69	20	9%	2%
Sweden HUS	–	16	31	60	–	–	–
Sweden Stat.	–	17*	37	75	–	–	–
Australia net	–	20*	41	72	21*	7*	0

Note: * These figures have been rounded.

Source: Wolff (1996), Table 4, p. 446, selected figures.

surveys however are deficient in a number of respects, so that, once again we are forced to the conclusion that little would be gained by a systematic comparison. (ibid., p. 58)

We turn next to Wolff (1996), who compares the distribution of household wealth in selected countries in the mid-1980s, using survey data. Table 3.49 reproduces the majority of his findings.

The distribution of wealth figures in the first two rows of Table 3.49 are more comparable than most because they are based on a special study designed to create equivalent databases for France (the 1986 INSEE survey) and the United States (the 1983 Survey of Consumer Finances, appropriately modified); details of the study are to be found in Kessler and Wolff (1991). They suggest a more unequal distribution of gross assets in the United States than in France, which Wolff (1996, p. 445) noted was possibly due to the fact that 'French households have a substantially higher proportion of their wealth in the form of owner-occupied housing, which is more equally distributed among the population than other assets (particularly, bonds and corporate stock)'. Wolff (1996) also reported the Gini coefficients resulting from a similar attempt to create comparable databases for 1988 between Germany (drawn from the German Socio-Economic Panel [GSOEP]) and the United States (drawn from the U.S. Panel Survey of Income Dynamics (PSID)-GSOEP Equivalent Data File). The Gini coefficients, 0.69 for Germany and 0.76 for the United States, suggest that the distribution of net worth in the United States was more unequal than that in Germany.

The figures in the third and fourth rows of Table 3.49 suggest that the distribution of net worth in the United States (calculated on the basis of the 1983 Survey of Consumer Finances) is also more unequal than that in Canada (calculated on the basis of the 1984 Survey of Consumer Finances). Adjustments to the Canadian figures to make them more comparable with the American figures, made in Davies (1993), while reducing the difference between the two countries, did not alter the basic finding.

The figures in the fifth and sixth rows of Table 3.49 are based respectively on a 1985/86 Household Market and Non-market Activities (HUS) survey, including vehicles but excluding other consumer durables, and a survey conducted at the same time by Statistics Sweden which also included vehicles but excluded other consumer durables. Noting that in these surveys the 'asset and liability coverage appears to be similar to that of the American and Canadian Surveys of Consumer Finances', Wolff (1996, p. 440) concluded:

> The concentration of wealth appears to be greater in the U.S. than in Sweden, which is consistent with the estate data comparisons. The original 1984 Canadian SCF data indicate about the same level of wealth concentration in Canada as in Sweden, though Davies' adjusted estimates show a somewhat higher concentration in Canada. (Wolff, 1996, p. 447)

The figures in the last row in Table 3.49, which are derived from the application of the income capitalisation technique to the 1986 Income Distribution Survey (IDS) in Australia reported in A.W. Dilnot (1990), exclude vehicles. Wolff (1996, p. 447) nonetheless concluded that the 'inequality of household wealth in Australia appears to be of the same order of magnitude as [in] Canada but substantially less than in the U.S.'.

Wolff (1996) also compared France and Sweden on the basis of wealth tax data, which indicate that in France in 1981 the net worth of the richest 0.45 per cent of households accounted for 9.9 per cent of the total wealth of the country, whereas in Sweden in 1978 and 1983 the net worth of the richest 0.5 per cent of households accounted respectively for 11.4 per cent and 13.0 per cent of the total wealth of the country. Although registering doubts about the comparability of the data sources, Wolff (1996, p. 447) concluded that the comparison 'does suggest that in the early 1980s wealth concentration may have been slightly higher in Sweden than in France'.

The year 2000 saw the publication of Volume 1 of the *Handbook of Income Distribution*, edited by A.B. Atkinson and F. Bourguignon, which includes a chapter on 'The Distribution of Wealth' by J.B. Davies and A.F. Shorrocks. With respect to change in wealth distribution over time, Davies and Shorrocks noted that for Sweden, while there was a 31 percentage point drop in the share of the wealthiest 10% between 1920 and 1975, this 'was almost all accounted for by the 29 point decline in the share of the top 1 percent, indeed . . . the share of those just below the top of the wealth distribution either remained constant or actually increased' (Atkinson and Bourguignon, 2000, p. 636), adding that the

> tendency for long-run changes in wealth inequality in this century to be due almost entirely to a reduction in the share at the very top of the distribution is echoed in the estate-based figures for the UK . . .and was noted by Atkinson and Harrison (1978, Chapter 6).

Table 1 in the Davies and Shorrocks chapter, derived from surveys (with the exception of Denmark and Sweden, where wealth tax records were used) compared the share of the wealthiest 1%, 5% and 10% of households, and the Gini coefficients, in ten countries around the mid-1980s. The wealthiest 5% element of this table was subsequently supplemented by Gustafsson et al. with the inclusion of figures for China based on a 1995 survey. A combination of these two tables is reproduced as Table 3.50.

In comparing wealth distributions across countries, Davies and Shorrocks (Atkinson and Bourguignon, 2000, p. 636) concluded that inequality

Table 3.50   Wealth share of the wealthiest 1%, 5% and 10% of households and Gini coefficient in 11 countries, various dates c. 1985

Country	Year	Top 1%	Top 5%	Top 10%	Gini ratio
USA	1983	35	56		0.79
France	1986	26	43		0.71
Denmark	1975	25	48	65	
Germany	1988	23			0.69
Canada	1984	17	38	51	0.69
Australia	1986	20	31 (or 41)	55	
Italy	1987		32		0.60
Korea	1988	14	31	43	0.58
Ireland	1987	10	29	43	
Japan	1984		25		0.52
Sweden	1985	11	24 (or 37)	54	0.59
China	1995			24	0.40

Sources: Atkinson and Bourguignon (2000), and Gustafsson et al. (2006), Table 8, p. 186.

appears to be lowest in Australia, Korea, Ireland, Japan and Sweden, with Gini values of 0.5–0.6 and shares of the top 1 percent of 20 percent or less. It has an intermediate value in Canada, Denmark, France and Germany, where the share of the top 1 percent ranges up to 26 percent, and appears greatest in the United States, where the Gini value is about 0.8 and the share of the top 1 percent of families exceeds 30 percent.

Next we turn to the Luxembourg Wealth Study (LWS), which was first mooted at the August 2002 conference of the International Association for Research in Income and Wealth, where 'it was apparent that data on household net worth were far behind those on income in terms of international comparability' (Sierminska et al., 2006b, pp. 375–6). The wealth distribution results of this study were reported in the paper by Sierminska et al. (2006a) in Table 9, and in its published version, namely Sierminska et al. (2006b) in Table V. These tables include *inter alia* household figures for wealthiest 10%, 5% and 1% shares and Gini coefficients for seven and five countries respectively, in 1998, 1999, 2000, 2001 or 2002; the figures from Sierminska et al. (2006b) are reproduced in Table 3.51.

Summarising the results, Sierminska et al. (2006b, p. 381) wrote that

> Table V shows that the highest Gini index is found in Sweden. The United States closely follow, and Canada comes next. Finland and Italy exhibit a more equal distribution of net worth. Finding Sweden at the top of the ranking is very surprising, as it contradicts the well-known and established evidence on income inequality – where Sweden stays at the bottom of the ranking. Part of the explanation may be the very high proportion of Swedish households which have nil or negative net worth: 32% against 23%, at most, in the other countries. In turn, this finding may reflect the fact that . . . the reference unit is in Sweden the inner family, not the household as in other countries. . . . When the share of net worth held by the top population percentiles is considered, the United States regain the lead; The [sic] richest 1% of U.S. households controls 33% of total wealth,

Table 3.51   Wealth share of the wealthiest 1%, 5% and 10% of households and Gini coefficient in five countries, various dates, c. 2000

Country	Top 1%	Top 5%	Top 10%	Gini ratio
Canada	15	37	53	0.75
Finland	13	31	45	0.68
Italy	11	29	42	0.60
Sweden	18	41	58	0.89
USA	33	58	71	0.84

Source: Sierminska et al. (2006), Table 5, p. 381.

and the next 4% controls another 25%. These proportions are far higher than in all other countries, Sweden included.[14]

Unfortunately the Luxembourg Wealth Study was subsequently discontinued. Further distribution of wealth comparisons between countries appeared in a series of publications by James B. Davies, Susanna Sandström, Anthony Shorrocks and Edward N. Wolff, culminating in the *Economic Journal* article 'The Level and Distribution of Global Household Wealth' (Davies et al., 2011). Table 5 in that article provides data relating to percentage wealth shares for various wealthiest and poorest percentages for each of no less than 20 countries, for years ranging from 1994 to 2002–03, and Table 7 includes Gini coefficients for most of the 20 countries. The figures for the wealthiest 0.1%, 0.5%, 1%, 5% and 10%, and the Gini coefficients, are reproduced in Table 3.52.

Table 3.52 Wealth share of the wealthiest 0.1%, 0.5%, 1%, 5% and 10% in 20 countries, c. 2000

Country	Year	Top 0.1%	Top 0.5%	Top 1%	Top 5%	Top 10%	Gini ratio
Australia	2002				31.0	44.9	0.622
Canada	1999					53	0.688
China	2002					41.4	0.550
Denmark	1996	11.6	22.2	28.8	56.0	76.4	
Finland	1998					42.3	
France	1994	6.3		21.3		61	0.730
Germany	1998					44.4	0.667
India	2002–03			15.7	38.3	52.9	0.669
Indonesia	1997			28.7	56.0	65.4	0.764
Ireland	1987			10.4	28.7	42.3	
Italy	2000			17.2	36.4	48.5	0.609
Japan	1999					39.3	0.547
South Korea	1988			14.0	31.0	43.1	0.579
New Zealand	2001					51.7	
Norway	2000					50.5	
Spain	2002	5.6	13.1	18.3		41.9	0.570
Sweden	2002					58.6	
Switzerland	1997	16.0	27.6	34.8	58.0	71.3	
UK	2000			23	44	56	0.697
USA	2001			32.7	57.7	69.8	0.801

Source: Davies et al. (2011), Table 5, p. 239, and Table 7, p. 246.

While stressing the differences between countries as to how the data were collected, Davies et al. (2011, p.241) nonetheless feel confident enough to state that

> Table 5 shows that estimated wealth concentration varies significantly across countries but is generally very high. Comparisons of wealth inequality often focus attention on the share of the top 1%. That statistic is reported for 11 countries, a list that excludes China, Germany and the Nordic countries apart from Denmark. Estimated shares of the top 1% range from 10.4% in Ireland to 34.8% in Switzerland, with the US towards the top end of this range at 32.7%. The share of the top 10%, which is available for all 20 countries, ranges from 39.3% in Japan to 76.4% in Denmark.

Some corroboration of the finding that the distribution of wealth is relatively equal in Japan is to be found in Wolff (1996), which reports distribution of wealth estimates for Japan based on the Family Saving Survey (FSS) and the Survey on Saving Behaviour and Motivation (SSBM), both undertaken in 1981, and the National Survey of Family Income and Expenditure (NFIE), undertaken in 1984, major consumer durables being included in each case. The resulting Gini coefficients for 1981 and 1984 were respectively 0.58 and 0.52, and the 1984 study also showed that the net worth of the richest 5 per cent of households accounted for 25 per cent of the total wealth of the country. Wolff (1996, p. 447) concluded that

> [t]he results suggest that wealth inequality is considerably lower in Japan than in the U.S. or Canada and, perhaps, Sweden as well. Bauer and Mason (1992) suggest that the low wealth concentration in Japan may be due to the extremely large weight owner-occupied housing has in the Japanese household portfolio (total real estimate comprised 85 per cent of household net worth in 1984).

3.14   CONCLUDING REMARKS

While this chapter has reported the findings of a number of studies comparing relative inequality in the distribution of wealth between two or more countries at particular points in time, we repeat that caution should be exercised in making comparisons between countries because of the wide variety of bases on which inequality is measured.

With respect to changes in inequality in the distribution of wealth over time, however, there is substantial evidence that for most countries there was a tendency for inequality in the distribution of wealth to grow up until 1913, to fall fairly continuously thereafter until about the mid-1970s, and then to grow again, at least until the global financial crisis.

Chapter 4 examines the determinants of the distribution of wealth, and Chapter 5 discusses Thomas Piketty's explanation of why over time inequality in the distribution of wealth has sometimes declined and sometimes grown.

NOTES

1. Prior to 1938 'United Kingdom' figures cover only England and Wales, and prior to 1976 only England, Wales and Scotland ('Great Britain'). For the United Kingdom a consistent set of distribution of wealth estimates goes back only to 1976.
2. Table 3.1 is derived from two tables in Ohlsson et al. showing the wealth share (%) of the wealthiest 1% and next wealthiest 4% of the population; to reduce the risk of the wood being obscured by the trees, where there are observations for three consecutive years for all countries for which there are observations, the observation for the middle year has been omitted. Observations for these omitted years are also omitted from the tables derived from Ohlsson et al. to be found in the next seven sections of this chapter. Ohlsson et al.'s tables are based on a multiplicity of sources, details of which are specified in Tables A1 and A2 in Ohlsson et al. (2006), pp. 26–7. The sources comprise Atkinson et al. (1989), Atkinson and Harrison (1978), Bjerke (1956), Dell et al. (2005), Finansdepartementet [Sweden] (1910), Inland Revenue [United Kingdom] (2006), Lindert (2000), Mohn (1873), Piketty et al. (2004), Shammas (1993), Soltow (1980), Soltow (1985), Statens Offentliga Utrednigar [Sweden] (1942), Statistics Denmark, Statistics Norway, Statistics Sweden, Wolff (1987), Wolff (2006) and Zeuthen (1928). Only in the case of France are the figures strictly comparable in the sense that they are based on a single source.
3. Table 3.2 reproduces the figures for the wealth share (%) of the wealthiest 10% in Table S10.1 in the Technical Appendix to Piketty (2014). Piketty's table is based on a multiplicity of sources, details of which are specified in Piketty's Technical Appendix. As cited there, the main sources comprise Atkinson and Harrison (1978), Atkinson et al. (1989), Kennickell (2000), Kennickell (2011), Kopczuk and Saez (2004), Lindert (2000), Piketty and Saez (2006), Waldenström (2009), Wolff (1994) and Wolff (2010). Only in the case of France are these figures strictly comparable in the sense that they are based on a single source.
4. The percentage shares for both categories actually reached a minimum, of 24.2% and 22.0%, in 1965, a year not included in Table 3.3.
5. It should be noted with respect to section 3.7 that it has been argued that all published figures relating to the distribution of wealth in Great Britain exaggerate the degree of inequality. See George Polanyi and John B. Wood (1974).
6. The figures in Atkinson and Harrison's table imply that the 'jump downwards between 1959 and 1960' should have been applied to the top 1%, not the next 4%.
7. The Gini coefficient for household income inequality in the United Kingdom 'rose by more than 30% between 1978 and 1991' (Gottschalk and Smeeding, 2000, p. 287).
8. However, Podder and Kakwani's figures for 1915 are broadly in line with those independently estimated by Nevile and Warren (1984, Table 3, p. 9).
9. Further support for Harrison's conclusion comes from Groenewegen's comment that due to a number of factors his own results 'tend to understate inequality in wealth ownership' (Groenewegen, 1972, p. 105).
10. The figures for the period 1915 to 1998 are taken from Tables 3.24, 3.26 and 3.27 above, where four primary sources are cited. The figures for 2002, 2006 and 2010 are taken from Wilkins (2013), and are based on Household Income and Labour Dynamics (HILDA) surveys. The figures for 2003–04, 2005–06, 2009–10 and 2011–12 are based on figures in the Australian Bureau of Statistics' *Household Wealth and Wealth*

Distribution, Australia (2013), which were derived from the Bureau's biennial Survey of Income and Housing. Due to the multiplicity of sources, the figures in this table are not strictly comparable.

11. The increase in the share of the top 5 per cent and the top 10 per cent, referred to by Brandolini et al., is more than accounted for by the increase in the share of the top 1 per cent.

12. According to Duràn-Cabré and Esteller-Moré (2007, pp. 4–5), in order to convert this data into information about the wealthiest 1%, wealthiest 0.5% and wealthiest 0.1% of the population, Alvaredo and Saez made use of a Pareto interpolation [what Alvaredo and Saez actually say in the published version of their paper is that they made use of a Pareto interpolation in deriving their distribution of income figures because the distribution of income among those on the highest incomes is 'very well approximated by Pareto distributions' (Alvaredo and Saez, 2009, p. 1145)].

13. Harrison's study was indebted to a number of papers presented at the CREP (*Centre de Recherche Economique sur l'Epargne*) – *INSEE (Institut Nationale de la Statistique et des Etudes Economiques*) international meeting on Wealth Accumulation and Distribution, Paris, July 1978, not all of which were subsequently published.

14. An 'inner family' is defined as 'a single adult or a couple plus dependent children' (Sierminska et al., 2006b, p. 378).

4. Determinants of the distribution of wealth

> *[E]quality of wealth is an unstable condition and, even if once established, would not endure, because of the unequal forces of thrift, ability, industry, luck and fraud, . . . inequality once established tends, by inheritance, to perpetuate itself in future generations.* (Fisher, 1912, p. 482)

Why is it that the distribution of wealth is more unequal in some countries than in others? To answer this question we shall find it useful to consider first a somewhat different one, namely, why does the amount of wealth owned by one wealth-holder, whether an individual or a household, differ from that owned by another? To answer the latter question, in turn, we need both to make some assumptions about human behaviour, and to find out what determines the amount of wealth owned by each wealth-holder.

The first section of this chapter accordingly outlines some basic assumptions about those aspects of the behaviour of wealth-holders which affect their accumulation of wealth. The second section shows how the amount of wealth owned by each wealth-holder can be explained in terms of five principal determinants. Sections 4.3 to 4.6 discuss how four of these determinants influence the degree of inequality in the distribution of wealth between wealth-holders. A final section looks at the effect on the distribution of wealth of the class, race and education distribution of a population, and then considers the relative importance of each of the determinants of the distribution of wealth.

4.1 BEHAVIOURAL ASSUMPTIONS

It is generally assumed that the well-being of an individual/household varies directly with their consumption and their leisure, and inversely with their exposure to downside risk. Other things being equal, an individual/household wishing to add to their wealth must either sacrifice some consumption so as to be able to save more out of a given income, or, if they wish to maintain their consumption, sacrifice some leisure so as to be able to earn more and hence save more. Given the sacrifice required in either case, why would an individual/household wish to hold wealth at all? The answer is as follows. First, forward-looking consumers will accumulate wealth early in life if they wish to achieve a lifetime consumption stream which involves an excess of consumption over income at some stage later in life, such as after retirement. Second, risk-averse forward-looking consumers who wish to maintain their consumption level will accumulate wealth early in life because earned income may terminate sooner than expected and death may occur later than expected. Third, forward-looking individuals/households may see their well-being as varying directly with the consumption and leisure of others, notably children and more remote descendants, in which case they will aim to have wealth to give away during their lifetime or bequeath at the end of their life; though wealth may be bequeathed even in the absence of this motive, because of death occurring earlier than expected.

Up to this point we have assumed that individuals/households are interested only in the absolute values of variables that contribute to their well-being. There is substantial evidence, however, that human behaviour is often dominated by a desire to achieve a higher social status. Following the example initially set by John Rae in *Statement of Some New Principles on the Subject of Political Economy* (1834) and Thorstein Veblen in *The Theory of the Leisure Class* (1899), Robert Frank in *Choosing the Right Pond* (1985) explored the implications of assuming that the well-being of individuals depends not only on the absolute levels of variables that contribute to their well-being, but also on how these levels compare with those achieved by others. The gist of Frank's analysis of societies made up of individuals for whom status is important is conveyed by the following thought experiment. Suppose 'that a representative group of people with no previous commitments has just emerged from a large ark in the wake of a flood that has destroyed all existing property and social arrangements' (Frank 1985, p. 114), and that in confronting the task of forming a new society or group of societies each individual is assigned the following inalienable right:

> No society shall form except by the voluntary agreement of each member to associate with every other member of that society and to abide by such rules and procedures as its members may agree to adopt. (Frank, 1985, p. 113)

If individuals receive incomes according to their abilities, which are assumed by Frank to differ significantly, the more-able individuals will look for a society in which there are at least some, and preferably many, less able people, and the less able individuals will look for a society in which there are few, if any, more-able people. The only means open to more-able people to ensure that there are less able people in their society is to pay them to join and stay. Frank concluded that '[i]f people value both status and material goods, and if they are free to form societies with whomever they wish, then transfer payments (which are equivalent to a redistributive income tax schedule) are necessary for the achievement of the most-preferred social structure' (Frank, 1985, p. 115).

In a society where people value not only material goods but also status, a forward-looking individual/household may sacrifice current consumption and leisure, accumulating wealth with a view to achieving otherwise unobtainable consumption and leisure status at some time in the future. Such behaviour is observed, for example, in migrants moving to a more affluent society; they commonly sacrifice both consumption and leisure in the years immediately following their arrival, in order for example to be able to move subsequently to a house in a suburb with higher status, purchasing what has become known as a 'positional good', a term coined by Fred Hirsch (1976) to describe a good whose value depends on its status. Of course status may alternatively be obtained merely by the possession of wealth, but since for this to happen the wealth has to be conspicuous, status on the basis of wealth alone is available only to a few, such as those whose names appear in a published list of the wealthiest (say) one hundred.

4.2 DETERMINANTS OF THE WEALTH OF A WEALTH-HOLDER

By definition the wealth of individuals at the end of a particular period of time equals the sum of their wealth at the beginning of that period and the following amounts, calculated on the basis of events occurring during that period: earned income net of taxes and transfers, minus consumption, plus the return on wealth, plus inheritances (including gifts as well as bequests). That is:

$$W_t \equiv W_{t-1} + E_t - C_t + rW_{t-1} + I_t \qquad (4.1)$$

where the subscripts $t - 1$ and t stand for two successive time periods, W for wealth at the end of the specified time period, E, C and I respectively for earned income, consumption and inheritances, and r for the rate of return on wealth (the rate of return on wealth accumulated during period t is assumed to be zero, an assumption which more closely approximates the truth the shorter is the time period chosen).

By adding up such identities for every period in an individual's life, we can derive the amount of wealth held by individuals at the end of the most recent period in their lives, assuming zero wealth at the beginning of life, namely:

$$W_t \equiv \sum_{k=1}^{t} (E_k - C_k + I_k) \prod_{j=k+1}^{t} (1 + r_j) \qquad (4.2)$$

where the first combination of symbols on the right-hand side indicates the sum over all periods, since birth, of earned income, minus consumption, plus inheritances, and the second combination indicates that wealth accumulated in each period is multiplied by one plus the interest rate applicable to that period (this identity is a reproduction of equation 2–6 in Davies and Shorrocks, 2000, p. 612; Davies and Shorrocks acknowledge an indebtedness to Meade, 1964 and 1976). From this identity it is clear that the amount of wealth possessed by an individual at any one point in time depends on five factors, namely age (t), earned income (E), savings ($E - C$), inheritances (I), and the rate of return on wealth (r).

Some economists believe that age plays a dominant role in determining the amount of wealth held by an individual at any one point in time. This belief is based on the lifecycle hypothesis regarding consumer behaviour, first expounded by Franco Modigliani and Richard Brumberg (1954), which in its basic form states that individuals accumulate wealth during their working lives with a view to funding consumption during their retirement. Other economists, by contrast, believe that inheritances play a dominant role in determining the amount of wealth held by an individual. Kessler and Masson (1988, p. 2) coined the term 'law of the 20/80' to describe the opposing views on the relative weight that should be attached to these two determinants of the amount of wealth held by an individual. Those who argue that lifecycle factors are the more important typically attach an 80 per cent weighting to them; since the publication of the findings of Laurence J. Kotlikoff and Lawrence H. Summers (1981), those who argue that bequests and gifts are the more important have likewise typically given them an 80 per cent weighting. Each view was defended at the conference on Modelling the Accumulation and Distribution of Wealth held in Paris in 1984,[1] respectively in papers presented by Modigliani and by Kotlikoff and Summers, reproduced in Kessler and Masson (1988, pp. 21–67).

In his comments on the two papers, Alan Blinder, after plumping on all points of dispute, except one, for one side or the other, concluded that following Modigliani on the treatment of consumer durables showed total wealth to be 54–70% lifecycle and 18–34% inherited, while following Kotlikoff and Summers on the treatment of consumer durables showed total wealth to be 31–47% lifecycle and 18–34% inherited, the latter leaving unanswered the question 'where does the rest come from?' (Kessler and

Masson, 1988, p. 76). One study of changes in the distribution of wealth in the United Kingdom between 1995 and 2005 found the overall effect of inheritances to be small, since the initial distribution was highly unequal and some of those who did inherit had begun the period with little or no wealth (Hills et al., 2013, p. 198). This debate, though not resolved, enables us to infer that both age and inheritances account for substantial portions of the typical individual's wealth. This conclusion is further supported by the pioneering attempt by Josiah Wedgwood (1939, p. 59) to estimate the contribution of inheritance to personal wealth in the United Kingdom before the First World War. His initial result was that for the latest generation 'the relative proportions of the total property in 1912 acquired by "saving" and inheritance are 34 *per cent* and 66 *per cent* respectively' (Wedgwood, 1939, p. 138), but taking into account a second calculation he concluded that 'the *average proportion of individual estates* acquired by inheritance and gift would be something *less* than three-fifths' (Wedgwood, 1939, p. 139, original emphasis), though not much less.

By contrast, Klevmarken's (2004) analysis of Swedish data suggests that lifecycle savings do not explain much of the variation in wealth in Sweden. The implication is that the extent to which the lifecycle hypothesis holds is likely to vary substantially between countries. Klevmarken also notes that further analyses of such matters based on the descriptive statistics of aggregate wealth data are unlikely to capture or explain the complexity of the savings decisions that are relevant to long-term wealth holdings.

The foregoing outline of the determinants of the amount of wealth held by an individual at any one point in time enables us to answer the following question: why at a particular point in time might the wealth of a hypothetical Smith be different from that of a hypothetical Jones? Any one of the following answers would provide an explanation. First, Smith has had an earned income stream different from that of Jones. Second, Smith is not the same age as Jones. Third, Smith has had a saving stream different from that of Jones. Fourth, net gifts and bequests so far received by Smith differ in amount from those received by Jones. The following sections of this chapter deal with each of these answers in turn.

4.3   EARNED INCOME

In the countries for which distribution of wealth data are available, the Gini coefficient for the distribution of income is typically about 0.3; Timothy Smeeding's updating of Luxembourg Income Study figures, for example, shows that the average figure for 21 developed countries in the mid-1990s was 0.29 (Smeeding, 2000, p. 211). By contrast, Gini coefficient figures cited in Chapter 3 for the distribution of wealth in the second half of the twentieth century range between 0.52 and 0.93, or between 0.52 and 0.83 if an outlier sample survey for Sweden is disregarded. In terms of a Lorenz curve diagram, the area measured by the Gini coefficient for the distribution of income is thus typically less than half the area measured by the Gini coefficient for the distribution of wealth; in a rough way of speaking, therefore, we can say that less than half of the inequality in the distribution of wealth is accounted for by inequality in the distribution of income.

Inequality in the distribution of income can be attributed to a number of factors, notably inequality in the distribution of either innate ability, ability acquired through education or training, access to non-human capital such as machinery or land, the taste for risk-taking, or luck. As noted in Chapter 1, however, the distribution of income is not the principal concern of this book. The subsequent sections of this chapter accordingly deal mainly with the factors which account for the fact that inequality in the distribution of wealth exceeds inequality in the distribution of income.

4.4 AGE

In a society in which for each age group both income and saving are uniform, and in which there are no inheritances and the rate of return on wealth is zero, for each age group wealth would be equally distributed, and for society as a whole the distribution of wealth would be determined by only two factors, namely the common lifetime savings pattern and the age structure of the population. If the lifetime savings pattern results in some age groups owning more wealth than others, obviously the greater the proportion of the population accounted for by the wealthier age groups, the more unequal will be the distribution of wealth. Is it true that some age groups are likely to be wealthier than others? If so, which age groups are likely to be the wealthier ones? To these questions both theoretical and empirical answers can be provided.

A theoretical answer comes in the form of the lifecycle hypothesis, to which reference has already been made. The lifecycle hypothesis assumes that individuals aim to maximise their well-being over a lifetime that includes a period of retirement. Assuming that the marginal utility of consumption diminishes as consumption increases, individuals will attempt to 'smooth' their consumption, the extreme case being that in which they attempt to consume the same amount in every year of their lives. As retirement income is typically less than working-life income, they will thus save during their working life, accumulating wealth that is subsequently run down during their retirement years. The wealth of individuals therefore depends on their age, following a pattern over time that incorporates a hump somewhere near retirement age. Consequently the mere existence of different age groups ensures that the distribution of wealth will be unequal, and the greater the proportion of the population at near-retirement age, the more unequal the distribution of wealth will be.

William Letwin (1983, Tables 1.1 and 1.2, p. 64) conducted a simulation exercise designed to calculate the effect on the distribution of wealth of the fact that a society comprises people belonging to different age groups. Assuming (for simplicity) a population aged exactly 20 or 25 or some year in between, uniform income at age 20 increasing at 4 per cent per annum, a fraction of income saved of 10 per cent, and a mortality rate of 1 per cent per annum, Letwin concluded that the share of wealth of the lowest 18.2 per cent in terms of income would be only 6.1 per cent, and that the share of wealth of the highest 21.9 per cent in terms of income would be as much as 34.8 per cent. He thus illustrated the fact that heterogeneity of age causes initial equality of income accompanied by uniform saving behaviour to translate into unequal distribution of wealth.

In its simplest form, often reproduced in textbooks, the lifecycle hypothesis assumes for each individual both constant and certain working-life income, certain dates for both retirement and death, and interest and time preference rates of zero. The more realistic form adopted by Davies and Shorrocks (2000, pp. 614–15) assumes rising but uncertain working-life income, risk-aversion, and positive interest and time preference rates. If the interest rate exceeds the rate of time preference, this version of the lifecycle hypothesis predicts that individuals 'dissave for some period when young, but then save fairly heavily in middle years and, of course, dissave in retirement' (ibid., p. 616). Is this pattern of saving, and the consequent dependence of wealth on age, supported by empirical evidence?

Before this question is answered, it is important to note that the lifecycle hypothesis cannot be adequately tested by looking at cross-section data alone. As Shorrocks (1975, p. 158) first pointed out, in a society in which for each individual wealth increases with age in a linear fashion, an increase in wealth from generation to generation causes cross-section data to indicate, erroneously, lifetime non-linear humped saving behaviour on the part of individuals. To overcome this difficulty, Shorrocks examined lifetime saving behaviour in Great Britain by ten-year cohorts, over the period 1912 to 1971, the cohort aged 26–35 in 1912 for example being aged 75–84 in 1961. His initial finding was that for the top 1, 5 and 10 per cent, the saving 'curves are approximately linear above the age of 45' (ibid., p. 159). But he amended this by adding that when the figures are corrected so as to take into account the fact that with increasing age a greater proportion of each cohort is made up of the wealthy, due to their lower mortality, 'the real purchasing power of wealth owned by individuals exhibits the hump pattern, with maximum wealth attained approximately at the normal age of retirement' (ibid., p. 161).

In some more-specific respects, however, the lifecycle hypothesis is not supported by empirical evidence, as Davies and Shorrocks (2000, p. 616) pointed out. First, even early in their working life most individuals are not net borrowers but net savers; one reason for this is that at this stage in their life individuals are unable to borrow. Second, the rise in earnings later in working life tends to be accompanied not by an increase in the saving ratio, but by a constant saving ratio, with consumption increasing by a similar proportion as income (Davies, 1979 and 1982, suggested that not only the constant saving ratio, but also net saving early in life, may be explained by the tendency of family size to increase over time). Third, consumption typically does not stay constant after retirement, but begins to decline immediately, and to decline further subsequently (Davies, 1988, suggested that this could be due to consumption competing with leisure in the case of retirees). The first two of these factors indicate that wealth increases with age less quickly than suggested by the lifecycle hypothesis, while by assuming that 'consumption after retirement' includes expenditure on maintenance of good health. The third factor indicates that wealth may decrease with age after retirement more quickly than the lifecycle hypothesis suggests.

None of this empirical evidence contradicts the basic lifecycle proposition that wealth varies with age, increasing up to the point of retirement. On the other hand, the lifecycle hypothesis predicts levels of wealth-holding greatly below those observed in practice. In his pioneering article on the relationship between wealth and age, Atkinson (1971) compared the distribution of wealth by age group in a modelled egalitarian society of individuals saving according to the lifecycle pattern on the one hand, with the actual distribution in Great Britain over the period 1963–67 on the other. His Table II (Atkinson, 1971, p. 243) assumes a society which is similar to that considered at the very beginning of this section in that it is egalitarian in every respect and there are no inheritances, but it is characterised in addition by the assumptions of a working life of 40 years, a retirement period of 10 years, a 2 per cent rate of growth of both population and earnings, and a positive rate of return on wealth. The modelled top 10 per cent share of total wealth fell within the range of 18.4 per cent, in the case of a 4 per cent rate of growth of consumption and a 3 per cent real interest rate, and 30.9 per cent in the case of a 2 per cent rate of growth of consumption and a 6 per cent real interest rate. By contrast, Inland Revenue Estate Duty figures for Great Britain over the period 1963–67 show the top 10 per cent share of total wealth to be no less than 72.7 per cent. Allowing for wealth 'missed' in the Inland Revenue Estate Duty figures, described in Chapter 3, Atkinson concluded that the top 10 per cent share of total wealth was still as high as 52.3 per cent (Atkinson, 1971, p. 252, Table VI). Assuming that the top 10 per cent share of total wealth is representative of the degree of inequality in the distribution of wealth, we can conclude that age-related factors probably account for less than half of the inequality in the distribution of wealth in Great Britain over the period 1963–67.

A study undertaken by Betsy Buttrill White (1978), comparable with Atkinson's study in that it abstracts from unequal distribution of income, similarly concluded that for the United States in the years 1953, 1959 and 1964 modelled lifecycle savings of the typical individual accounted for no more than 42 per cent of actual savings (White, 1978, p. 559), at least using assumptions which were at all realistic. And the 1981 Kotlikoff and Summers study already referred to, also abstracting from the unequal distribution of income, but distinguishing between males and females, and using a model based on a variant of this chapter's equation 4.2 in which inheritances are omitted but government transfers are added, concluded that lifecycle wealth represented at most 'only 19 percent of total 1974 U.S. wealth' (Kotlikoff and Summers, 1981, p. 722).

Because they were attempting to test the relationship between savings or wealth on the one hand, and age on the other, Atkinson, White, and Kotlikoff and Summers all abstracted from inequality in the distribution of income. Thus part of the gap they found between modelled and actual total savings or wealth could theoretically be due to the fact that in practice income is unequally distributed; for cross-section studies show that the saving ratio of those on high incomes is greater than that of those on low incomes, from which it follows that the more unequal the distribution of income is, the greater will be the aggregate amount of savings and wealth.

There is some evidence, however, that not even income distribution and age taken together completely explain the distribution of wealth. Atkinson (1971) broke down wealth distribution figures for Great Britain over the period 1963–67 by ten-year age groups, starting with the group aged between 25 and 34. Table IV (Atkinson, 1971, p. 248) shows that the top 10 per cent share of total wealth for males by ten-year age group ranged between 63.1 and 74.7 per cent, and the top 10 per cent share for females ranged between 68.8 and 92.7 per cent, compared with 72.7 per cent for the whole population. Judging by the share of the top 10 per cent, the distribution of wealth for most age groups turned out to be almost as unequal as that for the whole population; it was more unequal for the oldest age group in the case of males and the three youngest age groups in the case of females. Similarly, Atkinson's Table VI (Atkinson, 1971, p. 252), which makes adjustments to Inland Revenue figures so as to incorporate 'missing' wealth, shows that the top 10 per cent share of total wealth for males by age group ranged between a minimum of 48.0 per cent and a maximum of 65.4 per cent, compared with 52.3 per cent for the whole population, with the share for the youngest and two oldest age groups being greater than that for the whole population.

Empirical evidence thus suggests that the gap between inequality in the distribution of wealth and inequality in the distribution of income is far from being fully accounted for by the relationship between wealth and age. What other factor or factors can explain this gap? We turn first to non-uniform saving behaviour.

4.5   SAVINGS

In a society in which income is uniform, and in which there are no inheritances and the rate of return on wealth is zero, for each age group the distribution of wealth at any one point in time would depend only on the stream of past savings. In such a society there are two basic reasons why at the same age Smith (say) may have saved more in the past than Jones.

First, Smith may have saved more at each age level than Jones for life-cycle reasons. Compared with Jones, Smith may expect to retire earlier or to die later, or he may be more risk-averse and consequently save more so as to be better able to cope with unexpectedly early termination of earned income or unexpectedly late death.

Second, Smith may obtain more well-being than Jones from leaving bequests or making gifts. Now the motives of the giver of a bequest or gift can usefully be divided into two categories. First, there is what we shall call 'altruistic giving', where the well-being of the giver is enhanced by the expectation of adding to the well-being of the receiver. Second, there are what have been termed 'exchange' or 'strategic' bequests, which we shall call 'selfish giving', where the well-being of the giver is enhanced by non-pecuniary benefits provided by the receiver that would not otherwise have been forthcoming; putting it bluntly, 'be nice to your children, for they will choose your rest home', as the actress Phyllis Diller is reputed to have said.

For every giver of a bequest or gift there is of course a receiver. Another potential explanation of the unequal distribution of wealth lies in unequal receipt of bequests and gifts. To this we turn next.

4.6 INHERITANCE

In a society in which each partner comes to a marriage with the same current/prospective wealth ('class mating'), each marriage results in the same number of children, there is no tax on gifts or bequests, and parents gift or bequeath all their wealth equally among their children, and in which the characteristics of each generation replicate those of its predecessor, the distribution of wealth will remain the same from generation to generation. Another way of making this point is to say that inheritance will change the distribution of wealth if partners come to a marriage with different but less than random current/prospective wealth (the definition of 'assortative mating' in Blinder, 1973, p. 612) or there is 'random mating', where the number of children resulting from marriage varies with wealth, where there is a tax on gifts or bequests, or where wealth is only partly gifted or bequeathed to the children or divided unequally among them. We examine in turn each of these causes of change in the distribution of wealth from generation to generation, assuming in each case that none of the other causes is present.

The distribution of wealth will become less unequal to the extent that the family wealth of one spouse differs from that of the other. In this case the wealth of the newly established family will lie somewhere between the two wealth levels of the families of the spouses. Citing some data relating to the United States, Blinder (1973, p. 626) was prepared to 'hazard a guess that the correlation of wealth between men and women who marry is between 0.3 and 0.5'. If this range is representative of modern societies, assortative marriage significantly reduces inequality in the distribution of wealth.

On the other hand, the distribution of wealth will become more unequal if reproduction rates among the wealthy are lower than those among the poor, as in this case the number of the relatively poor increases relative to that of the relatively rich. Since the wealthy typically have smaller families than the poor, this is a factor which increases inequality in the distribution of wealth. On the very complicated relationship between family income and family size see Becker (1988).

Estate taxation, including taxes on the givers of gifts, reduces the amount of wealth which parents pass on to their children. Since many parents die without any wealth to bequeath, even proportional taxation of estates makes the distribution of wealth less unequal. The more progressive the estate tax, the greater is the extent to which inequality in the distribution of wealth will be reduced.

If parents do not pass on all their wealth to their children, but leave some of it to others, the effect on the distribution of wealth will of course depend on the pre-gift wealth of the recipient(s) relative to that of the children. Common sense suggests that such recipients typically have little if any wealth. If this is the case, parents not passing all their wealth on to their children will tend to reduce inequality in the distribution of wealth.

If parents pass on all their wealth to their children, but bequests and gifts are divided unequally between children, the effect on the distribution of wealth will depend on the nature of the division. In the case of primogeniture, where all wealth must be passed on to the eldest son, the distribution of wealth will become more unequal if each family has more than two children, including at least one son. On the other hand, where the ability of their children to earn income is unequal, due to their innate ability, public support or luck being unequal, altruistic parents may aim to equalise the lifetime well-being of their children (see Becker and Tomes, 1976, pp. S152–5); in this case they will give more to children whose wealth is relatively low, or likely to be, and less to children whose wealth is relatively high. Although some of this giving may take the form of providing the less-favoured children with education or training ('human capital'), it is likely that some of it will take the form of non-human wealth, and there will consequently be an offset to any tendency for the distribution of wealth to become more unequal. However, altruistic behaviour taking this form is relatively rare; 'unequal division of estates [between children] is relatively unusual in the US, and is also far from the norm in the UK' (Davies and Shorrocks, 2000, p. 622).

Blinder (1973, p. 609) cited two United States studies which throw some light on the actual distribution of inheritances. First, the *Survey of Financial Characteristics of Consumers* conducted by the Federal Reserve in 1962

> found that 57 percent of consumer units in the highest income class ($100,000 and over) had inherited assets that constituted a 'substantial' portion of their total wealth. For other income classes, this percentage never exceeded 14 percent.

Second, on the basis of data collected by the Survey Research Center in 1960, analysed by John B. Lansing and John Sonquist (1969), Blinder calculated the Gini coefficient for the distribution of inheritances to be 0.973. Since this figure is higher than any relating to the distribution of wealth, we can conclude that, if it is representative, inheritances increase inequality in the distribution of wealth.

4.7   RELATIVE IMPORTANCE OF DETERMINANTS

If a society were divided into two groups with equal distribution of wealth within each group but with per capita wealth being lower in one group than the other, that society's distribution of wealth would be less unequal the fewer the number of persons in the group with the lower mean wealth. As pointed out in Chapter 2, this can be illustrated by a rightward shift in the point D in Figure 2.4 when that diagram is used to depict a society in which some members of a population have zero wealth and the remainder have equal wealth. This result can be extended to less restrictive cases. It can be applied to a society divided into two groups with a given distribution of wealth within each group, but with one group having a lower mean wealth than the other. It can be applied also to a society divided into three or more groups with a given distribution of wealth within each group, but with some groups having a lower mean wealth than others, the conclusion in this case being that such a society's distribution of wealth would be less unequal the fewer the number of persons in the groups with below-average mean wealth.

Groupings of society by class, race and education are *prima facie* likely to result in groups whose mean wealth differs. Changes in the relative number of persons in these groups are thus likely to have an impact on the distribution of wealth. We consider in turn each of these groupings of a population, though because of paucity of relevant material the treatment will be brief.

While the sensitivity of the distribution of wealth to changes in the relative size of class groups does not appear to have been subjected to empirical investigation, it has been modelled. Wolff developed 'a two-class model of wealth distribution among individuals' (Wolff, 1988, p. 261) of the Pasinetti type,[2] the economic classes consisting of 'capitalists' and 'workers', with Wolff's model incorporating in addition the lifecycle hypothesis. Wolff concluded from this model that with an interest rate of 4 per cent and a steady-state rate of labour productivity growth of 2 per cent, decreasing the percentage of the population in the working class (including retirees) successively from 90 per cent to 80 per cent to 70 per cent reduces the coefficient from 0.980 to 0.873 and 0.771 respectively, a movement in the direction of less inequality in the distribution of wealth.

Empirical information does exist, however, on the sensitivity of the distribution of wealth to changes in the relative size of racial groups. On the basis of data provided by the United States Surveys of Consumer Finances in 1983, 1989, 1992, 1995 and 1998, Wolff (2000, Tables 7 and 8, pp. 21 and 22) calculated that as a fraction of the mean net worth of non-Hispanic whites, the mean net worth of Hispanics varied between 0.16 and 0.25, and the mean net worth of non-Hispanic African-Americans varied between 0.17 and 0.19. These figures suggest that if the proportion of the population accounted for by non-Hispanic whites had been smaller in these years, the distribution of wealth would have been more unequal.

There also exists a small amount of empirical information on the sensitivity of the distribution of wealth to changes in the relative size of groups defined according to educational achievement. Lansing and Sonquist (1969) used data from the United States Surveys of Consumer Finances in 1953 and 1962 to produce an estimate by ten-year age cohort (for example, those born in the years 1890 to 1899) over the period 1890 to 1938 of the mean net worth of each of three categories of educational achievement, namely grammar school, high school and college. They found that in both 1953 and 1962 the mean high school net worth exceeded the mean grammar school net worth for all cohorts, by more than 50 per cent for all except the 1929 cohort in 1953, and that the college mean net worth exceeded the high school mean net worth for all cohorts, by more than 50 per cent for all except the 1900 cohort in 1962.[3]

We turn now to the question of the relative importance of each of the determinants of the distribution of wealth. As indicated in the previous sections of this chapter, it does seem that inequality in the distribution of income accounts for less than half of inequality in the distribution of wealth, that age differences account for only part of the gap between inequality in the distribution of income and inequality in the distribution of wealth, and that non-uniform inheritance also makes a significant contribution to this gap. Some part of this gap is also accounted for by non-uniform saving behaviour, and by positive and non-uniform rates of return on wealth.

The effects on the distribution of wealth of changes in the relative size of groups with different mean wealth cannot be simply added to the effects already considered, for two reasons. First, changes in the relative size of groupings by class, race and education are likely to affect the distribution of wealth principally through their effects on incomes and inheritances, factors already taken into account. Second, changes in groupings by class, race and education are likely to be highly correlated, so that simply adding their effects would exaggerate their total influence.

NOTES

1. This conference was organised by the Centre d'Etude et de Recherche sur l'Epargne, les Patrimoines et les Inégalités.

2. Luigi Pasinetti (1962) is the initial source of the Pasinetti-type distribution and growth model, which was amplified in Pasinetti (1974).
3. However, Lansing and Sonquist (1969, p. 47) wrote of the 1900 cohort mean net worth figure for 1962 that it did 'not seem plausible', being too low.

5. Determinants of changes in the distribution of wealth

The fact that the return on capital is distinctly and persistently greater than the growth rate is a powerful force for a more unequal distribution of wealth.
(Piketty, 2014, p. 361)

In Chapter 3 we found that in most countries inequality in the distribution of wealth has varied substantially over time. In this chapter we build on the arguments set out in Chapter 4, which infer that inequality in the distribution of wealth is likely to increase over time if (1) the distribution of earned income becomes more unequal, (2) the age distribution of the population becomes more heavily skewed towards the elderly, (3) saving ratios become more unequal, or (4) inheritances become more unequally distributed.

To these we can add a further explanation advanced by Thomas Piketty, in his 2013 book *Le Capital au XXIsiècle* (English translation published in 2014 under the title *Capital in the Twenty-First Century*) and in other writings, an explanation discussed in the following four sections of this chapter. These sections draw heavily on Schneider (2014); although we do not pretend to provide a comprehensive appraisal of Piketty's 685-page book, a survey of the substantial literature on the book can be found in King (2016).

Piketty's arguments (like those of the classical economists and Marx before him) relate to the distribution of income (and consequently wealth) between those who receive income from assets and those who receive income from other sources, that is to say, distribution among economic 'classes' (though as Piketty says himself, his preference is to analyse distribution in terms of percentiles rather than classes). However, these arguments can be extended so as to apply also to the distribution of income and wealth between persons. This extension of Piketty's ideas forms the subject matter of section 5.4 of this chapter.

5.1 PIKETTY'S THESIS

In brief, Thomas Piketty forecasts that the return on assets capable of generating income, assets described by him interchangeably as capital or wealth (Piketty, 2014, p. 47), a return that he refers to as 'capital income' (to avoid confusion with Piketty's key concept of the 'capital-income' ratio, we shall instead refer to this as 'income from capital'), will grow much faster than what he terms 'non-capital income', notably income derived from labour. He concludes that savings from the former will eventually cause so great an inequality in the distribution of wealth that social tensions may cause capitalism to disintegrate. Piketty refers to this as 'the central contradiction of capitalism' (Piketty, 2014, p. 571).

To support this view, Piketty argues that in the very long run in a capitalist economy the annual rate of return on assets capable of generating income has been of the order of 4% to 5%, while the annual rate of growth of national income has been of the order of only 1% to 2%. Assuming that little of the return on wealth is consumed, Piketty concluded that wealth consequently grows faster than income. In turn, given minimal assumptions, the wealth of those whose income is derived from wealth will grow faster than the wealth of those whose income is derived from other sources (for proof, see Aspromourgos 2015, pp. 290–91, where, as noted in Chapter 1, it is also pointed out that a sufficient condition for an increase in inequality in the distribution of wealth over time is that the savings rate of the rich be greater than the savings rate of the poor). In turn, the wealth of those whose income is wholly or mainly derived from wealth grows faster than the wealth of those whose income is wholly or mainly derived from labour or other sources. We call this last proposition 'Piketty's thesis'.

We now provide a more detailed analysis of Piketty's thesis. Piketty defines capital as the market value of all tradable assets, comprising not only physical assets (including land and buildings) but also net financial assets (Piketty, 2014, p. 48). While in a slave-owning society ('tradable') human capital would be included, in a slave-free society human capital is by definition excluded; Weil (2015) makes the point that if Piketty had instead defined capital even more broadly, so as to include human capital, his figures for the distribution of wealth would have been less unequal. In interpreting Piketty's thesis, it is important to recognise that, for Piketty, changes in capital include changes in the price of capital, and that the return on capital includes capital gains. Those who have criticised this unconventional approach to 'capital' overlook the fact that the focus of Piketty's book is on capital not as a factor of production, but as a source of income (Piketty himself is to some extent responsible for this oversight, as he sometimes reverts to the conventional meaning of 'capital', namely a specific factor of production). 'Non-capital income', in turn, mainly takes the form of income derived from labour, but it also is defined broadly, so that income from capital and non-capital income together account for all of national income.

It is in the light of these definitions that one needs to interpret Piketty's argument with respect to a capitalist economy that if the rate of return on capital (r) exceeds the rate of growth of national income (g), the class distribution of income and wealth will over time become more and more unequal. The importance that Piketty attaches to this argument is illustrated early on in *Capital in the Twenty-First Century*, where he states that the 'fundamental inequality . . . $r > g$ . . . will play a crucial role in this book. In a sense, it sums up the overall logic of my conclusions' (p. 25).

To support his thesis with a theoretical model, Piketty introduces a 'First' and 'Second' 'Fundamental Law of Capitalism'. Piketty's First Fundamental Law of Capitalism states:

$$\alpha = r\beta, \tag{5.1}$$

which is to say α, the ratio of (annual) income from capital to (annual) national income (alternatively referred to below as the share of income from capital in national income), is equal to the (annual) rate of return on (the stock of) capital (r) multiplied by the capital-income ratio (β).

As Piketty points out, this is true by definition; it is an identity, and thus could be written as $\alpha \equiv r\beta$, as becomes crystal clear if the relationship is written in more conventional symbols as

$$P/Y \equiv P/K.K/Y, \tag{5.2}$$

where P, Y and K stand respectively for profits, income and capital.

Piketty's Second Fundamental Law of Capitalism states that in the long run

$$\beta = s/g, \tag{5.3}$$

which is to say in the long run the capital-income ratio equals the national savings rate (s) divided by the rate of growth of national income (g). This is a 'long-run' relationship in the sense that following any change in either the savings rate (and therefore in the stock of 'capital' as Piketty uses the term) or the rate of growth of national income, if there is no further change in either of these variables the capital-income ratio must eventually equal the changed ratio of s to g.

An example provided by Piketty (2014, p. 167) involves an economy where initially $s = 12\%$ and $g = 2\%$, resulting in $\beta = 600\%$ (that is, capital equal to six years of national income), but then g falls to 1.5% and stays there, as Piketty prophesies is likely to happen in the twenty-first century; in this case the slower rate of growth of national income brings about a gradual increase in the ratio of capital to income, resulting eventually in $\beta = 800\%$ (that is, capital equal to eight years of national income). This is not an identity, but an empirical proposition dependent on the facts; if during the adjustment period some capital were destroyed by war, for example, it would not be true.

5.2 DEFICIENCIES IN PIKETTY'S PRESENTATION OF HIS THESIS

The way in which Piketty presents his thesis has some deficiencies. One of these is that in focusing on a great excess of r over g, Piketty overstates his case. As far as impact on the class distribution of wealth is concerned, the relevant excess is instead the excess over g of the fraction of r not consumed. This deficiency in Piketty's argument has been highlighted most starkly by Hillinger (2014, p. 132), who postulated a case in which $r = 5\%$, $g = 3\%$ (hence $r > g$, as Piketty assumes), and the propensity to save out of profits $s_p = 40\%$, resulting in an annual increase in capital of only 2%, which is not more but less than the assumed national income growth rate. Piketty on occasion admits he has a similar reservation about his 'thesis'. For example, he states that 'if $g = 1$ percent and $r = 5$ percent, wealthy individuals will have to reinvest only one-fifth of their annual capital income to ensure that their capital will grow faster than average income' (Piketty, 2014, p. 361), though even this statement is a slight exaggeration, as strictly speaking if $s_p = 20\%$, capital will grow at the same pace as national income (and there will be no tendency towards increased inequality in wealth distribution, despite the fact that r is 5 per cent and g only 1 per cent). A comparable admission is made on page 366 of his book, where Piketty states that 'divergence [between growth in income from capital and growth in national income] is more likely to occur if the very wealthy have nothing to spend their money on and add to their capital stock'.

It further needs to be remembered that Piketty measures r before tax. Combining this with the point just made relating to the fraction of income from capital consumed, Galbraith (2014b, p. 146), denoting the tax rate on profits by t and the rate of capitalists' consumption by c_c, points out 'we could have $r > g$ but $[r(1 - t) - c_c] \leq g$', in which case capital will grow not faster but at the same rate or more slowly than national income. Galbraith's illustration assumes $r = 5\%$, $t = 0.3$ and $c_c = 0.2$, in which case $[r(1 - t) - c_c] = 0.025$, and inequality in the distribution of wealth will increase only if the rate of growth of national income is less than not 5 per cent but 2.5 per cent.

N. Gregory Mankiw makes a similar point in his contribution to the *American Economic Review* symposium on Piketty's book. Mankiw argues that 'the forces of consumption, procreation, and taxation are, and will probably continue to be, sufficient to dilute family wealth over time'. He estimates that r would need to exceed g by no less than seven percentage points to avoid such a dilution process, with heirs' consumption out of their inheritance accounting for three points, the division of family fortunes among growing numbers of heirs for another two points, and taxation of legacies and the income from capital for the remaining two points. Since US data confirm that in the long run r is approximately 5% (before tax) and g is 3%, Piketty's critical magnitude $r - g$ will in fact be no greater than two points, not the more than seven points that would be necessary for the return of 'patrimonial capitalism' that Piketty fears (Mankiw, 2015, p. 44).

In presenting his thesis, Piketty assumes that the return on capital/wealth will be of the order of this long-run trend rate of 5% in the absence of shocks that might lower that return (such as the two world wars and the Great Depression that occurred in the twentieth century) and result in a different trend over time. There are two questions that need to be answered here.

First, why in the absence of shocks should the return on capital as a factor of production always be of the order of 5%? While rejecting the neo-classical answer in terms of time preference (Piketty, 2014, pp. 358– 61), Piketty does not replace it with another. Moreover, in attempting to explain why the rate of profit should not be expected to fall with an increase in the capital-labour ratio, Piketty argues that in the long run the elasticity of substitution between capital and labour is greater than unity, which, as many have pointed out, flies in the face of all the evidence – see in particular Galbraith (2014a, 2014b) and Rowthorn (2014). Note also that severe doubt has been cast on the scientific status of all estimates of the elasticity of substitution derived from aggregate production functions (Felipe and McCombie, 2013).

Second, why should the rate of return on the many heterogeneous forms of wealth other than capital as a factor of production equal the rate of profit on the latter? Piketty does not provide an answer to this question either. Here he might have been tempted to take a leaf out of David Ricardo's book. In a letter to his friend Hutches Trower, Ricardo, assuming mobility of capital, wrote that 'it is the profits of the farmer which regulate the profits of all other trades . . .' (Ricardo, 1973, p. 104); but fortunately Piketty resisted the temptation. As Atkinson (2015, pp. 160–61) points out, it is not true that the rate of return on assets is uniform, the rate of return on financial assets being typically well below that on real assets used in production, with the real rate of return on the former sometimes actually falling below zero due to inflation. Although he does not say so explicitly, Atkinson thereby implies that the rate of return on financial assets may well be not above but below g, the rate of growth of income. Furthermore, part or all of the return on some forms of wealth, such as positional goods, namely 'goods of which it is true that for some of the members of a society part or all of the satisfaction derived from possessing them is the enhancement of social status due to the fact that such satisfaction is possible only for a minority' (Schneider, 2007, p. 62), may take a non-monetary form, the monetary return possibly being as low as zero.

In addition, as Auerbach and Hassett (2015, pp. 7–11) have pointed out, Piketty introduces an element of bias in his estimate of the rate of return on capital by describing the twentieth century as characterised by shocks, and therefore in a sense abnormal. An alternative interpretation is 'that bad things happen to capital on occasion, and that one shouldn't ignore such outcomes any more than one should count only the heads from a series of coin flips' (ibid., p. 8). Indeed, as far as the post-tax return on capital is concerned, there is a case for saying that it is the period prior to 1914, with its high rates of return, that is abnormal, because of the absence during much of that period of taxation on income; though Piketty does claim that as one of the consequences of globalisation income and wealth tax rates have declined since about 1975, and prophesies a continuation of this trend in the future.

It is worth noting that Piketty's propensity to save out of income from capital, which he denotes by s_k, plays an important role in the post-Keynesian theory of income distribution developed by two Cambridge economists, Nicholas Kaldor and Luigi Pasinetti. Kaldor assumed a simple two-class society and distinguished saving by capitalists out of profits (S_p) from saving by workers out of wage income (S_w). The two classes have different propensities to save, denoted respectively by s_p and s_w, with (unsurprisingly) $s_p > s_w$. Macroeconomic equilibrium requires that aggregate investment (I) is equal to total saving:

$$I = S_p + S_w = s_p.P + s_w.W, \tag{5.4}$$

where P denotes total profits and W total wages. In equation (5.4) causation runs from left to right, since investment is the driving force in a capitalist economy, and its magnitude is determined by capitalists' profit expectations (referred to by Keynes as their 'animal spirits'), which in turn determine the level of saving.

In the simplest possible case, where workers save nothing, so that $s_w = 0$, equation (5.4) simplifies to:

$$I = s_p.P \qquad (5.5)$$

Dividing both sides of equation (5.5) by the value of the total capital stock (K), and noting that (on the assumption of a constant capital-output ratio) the ratio I/K is equal to the rate of growth of total output, we derive the so-called 'Cambridge equation':

$$g = s_p.r \qquad (5.6)$$

Causation again runs from left to right, so that (given the capitalists' propensity to save), it is the rate of growth (g) that determines the rate of profit r. It can be seen from equation (5.6) that it is always the case that $g < r$, except in the (extremely unlikely) event that $s_p = 1$ (Kaldor, 1956). Six years after Kaldor's article was published, Luigi Pasinetti (1962) demonstrated that equation (5.6) remains valid even if workers save (so that $s_w > 0$). This means that workers' saving, and their resulting acquisition of wealth, does not alter the conclusion that *only* the capitalists' propensity to save is important (King, 2009, pp. 62–6). Piketty's analysis ignores these simple but inescapable macroeconomic relationships.

5.3   STEADY-STATE EQUILIBRIUM OR PERPETUAL DISEQUILIBRIUM?

As already noted, Piketty's thesis analyses the consequences of r exceeding g, notably, as Solow (2014) put it, 'as long as the rate of return exceeds the rate of growth, the income and wealth of the rich will grow faster than the typical income from work'; Solow added '[s]o far as I know, no one before him [Piketty] has made this connection'.

Piketty might have helped his readers understand his thesis better if he had set out the relationship between r and g in the form of a theoretical model, which we now proceed to do. If no income from capital is consumed, but all is saved and invested (a simplification that Piketty often uses but does not always draw attention to), capital will grow at the rate r. Let α_t be the value of α (the share of income from capital in national income) at time t. If in addition to capital growing at the rate r, national income grows at the rate g, then

$$\alpha_{t+1} = \alpha_t (1 + r)/(1 + g), \qquad (5.7)$$

which if $r > g$, means α_{t+1} is greater than α_t. Assuming that the values of r and g remain unchanged, it will be true in the following year that

$$\alpha_{t+2} = \alpha_t(1 + r)^2/(1 + g)^2, \qquad (5.8)$$

and it will also be true that thereafter the ratio α will continue to grow year by year at the same rate $(1 + r)/(1 + g)$.

Piketty most commonly uses examples in which $r = 5\%$ and $g = 2\%$. In this case α would increase annually by about 3% (more precisely, 1.05/1.02). Though Piketty does not mention it, an implication is that the share of income from capital in national income would double in 23.5 years; for example, if the share of income from capital in national income were initially 30%, in 23.5 years it would be 60%, and theoretically in another 23.5 years would reach (the impossible figure of) 120%. Of course, in so far as income from capital is either saved or taxed, or both, the share of income from capital in national income will grow more slowly.

At first sight there appears to be a contradiction between on the one hand Piketty's Second Fundamental Law of Capitalism, which for any given excess of r over g describes an equilibrium class distribution of wealth towards which a capitalist economy tends, and on the other hand the perpetually growing inequality in the class distribution of wealth resulting from any given excess of r over g outlined and illustrated in the previous paragraph. Piketty does not address this apparent contradiction. It can, however, be resolved in the following way. Since the savings rate for income from capital is typically higher than that for non-capital income, a continuing increase in α (the share of income from capital in national income) will cause a continual increase in the average national savings rate (s). It follows from the Second Fundamental Law of Capitalism that as a consequence β, the capital-income ratio, will also continually increase; one could say that a capitalist economy chases an equilibrium value of β that is moving (of course, if the equilibrium value of β changes at a constant rate, such an economy could alternatively be said, in a sense, to be in equilibrium).

Extending the example used in the paragraph before last, suppose that in year t the share of income from capital in national income (α) is 30%, and the national savings rate (s) is 12% (figures often used by Piketty), the rate of growth of national income (g) is 2% and the rate of growth of the share of income from capital in national income is 3% (or, again, more precisely 1.05/1.02). In this case, a 3% annual increase in the ratio of income from capital to national income will lead to a new value of α in year $t + 1$ of 1.03(30)%, that is, 30.9%; with national income growing at 2%, just to maintain the old value of α would require an increase in income from capital of 2%, and the new value of α requires a further increase in α of 3%. That is to say, income from capital in year $t + 1$ will be $(1.02)(1.03)$ times as great as income from capital at time t, or approximately 1.05 times as great, growing at an annual rate of (approximately) 5%.

Any increase in the share of income from capital in national income (α) will have consequences for both the national savings rate (s) and the capital-income ratio (β). First, as far as s is concerned, we need to make an assumption about the individual savings rates for income derived from capital on the one hand, and for non-capital income on the other. If the savings rate for non-capital income is zero (the assumption most favourable to Piketty's frequent implicit assumption that the savings rate for income from capital is high, if not 100%), the Piketty figures we have used to describe the situation in year t imply that the saving ratio for income from capital is 12%(100/30), that is 40% (Piketty does not make this calculation in his book, but does make a similar one in some lecture notes that can be accessed in the Technical Appendix to *Capital in the Twenty-First Century*, p. 37, footnote 22; the example is to be found in Lecture 6, on the twenty-second of its unnumbered pages).

Assuming that the two savings rates remain unchanged, first, an annual growth rate of income from capital of 5% implies a new national savings level in year $t + 1$ that is (1.05) times as great as in year t. Given that national income is growing at 2%, this in turn implies a new value of s in year $t + 1$ of 12%$(1.05)/(1.02)$, that is, an increase of approximately 3%, from 12% to 12.36% (theoretically the savings rate for both income classes could be 12%, in which case an increase in α would leave s unchanged, but this is an unrealistic assumption, particularly given the substantial numbers of receivers of non-capital income for whom the savings rate is likely to be zero; it would be even more unrealistic to assume that the savings rate is greater for non-capital income than for income from capital, leading to a decrease in s when α increases). Second, with $g = 2\%$, the 3% increase in s would result in an increase in β of approximately $(3/2)\%$, that is 1.5%, from 6% to 6.09%. If the example were extended, for each additional year s would increase by 3%, and β by 1.5%.

Far from resolving the apparent contradiction between his Second Fundamental Law of Capitalism and the perpetually growing inequality in the class distribution of wealth that follows logically from his 'thesis', in *Capital in the Twenty-First Century* Piketty vacillates between two alternative outcomes of an excess of r over g. On page 364, for example, he states that '[w]ith the aid of a fairly simple mathematical model, one can show that for a given structure of shocks . . . the distribution of wealth tends towards a long-run equilibrium and that the equilibrium level of inequality is an increasing function of the gap $r > g$ between the rate of return on capital and the growth rate'. On page 361, by contrast, he avers that unless a specified set of 'forces' occurs, 'the consequences of $r > g$' will be 'an indefinite inegalitarian spiral'. In his subsequent elaborations on his thesis, however, Piketty (2015a, pp. 5–6) opts for the former outcome, stating that

> for a given structure of shocks, the long-run magnitude of wealth inequality will tend to be magnified if the gap $r - g$ is higher. In other words, wealth inequality will converge towards a finite level . . . this finite inequality level will be a steeply rising function of the gap $r - g$. . . . [Though] relatively small changes in $r - g$ can generate very large changes in steady-state wealth inequality.

Likewise he specified (Piketty, 2015b, p. 68) that '. . . a larger $r > g$ gap will amplify the steady-state inequality of a wealth distribution that arises out of a given mixture of shocks', and complained (Piketty, 2015b, p. 67) that '. . . a common simplification of the main theme [of *Capital in the Twenty-First Century*] is that because the rate of return on capital r exceeds the growth rate of the economy g, the inequality of wealth is destined to increase indefinitely over time'. In the interview reported in Dolcerocca and Terzioglu (2015, unnumbered page), Piketty states that '. . . $r > g$ does not imply an infinitely rising capital share. It is perfectly compatible with a stable capital share – that is a stable capital/income ratio and stable inequality. Everything is stable except that you possibly have an enormous level of inequality.' Further, Piketty and Zucman (2015, p. 1356) accept that

> . . . if we introduce taxation into the dynamic wealth accumulation model, then one naturally needs to replace r by the after-tax rate of return $\bar{r} = (1 - r)$ ·r, where r is the equivalent comprehensive tax rate on capital income, including all taxes on both flows and stocks. That is, what matters for long-run wealth concentration is the differential $\bar{r} - g$ between the net-of-tax rate of return and the growth rate.

They go on to argue that 'a higher $r - g$ tends to magnify steady-state wealth inequalities' (p. 1343). Projecting this into the twenty-first century, they forecast that

> . . . assuming no new shock occurs, and assuming rising international tax competition to attract capital leads all forms of capital taxes to disappear in the course of the twenty-first century (arguably a plausible scenario, although obviously not the only possible one), the net-oftax (sic) rate of return $\bar{r}$ will converge to the pretax rate of return r, so that the $\bar{r} > g$ gap will again be very large in the future. Other things being equal, this force could lead to rising wealth concentration in the twenty-first century. (p. 1358)

5.4 IMPLICATIONS OF PIKETTY'S THESIS FOR THE PERSONAL DISTRIBUTION OF WEALTH

Having outlined Piketty's thesis, we are now in a position to turn to the relationship between this thesis and the personal distribution of wealth. Even though Piketty's thesis relates to the distribution of income (and consequently wealth) between those who receive income from capital and those who receive income from other sources, his 'thesis' can also be used to derive conclusions about the distribution of income and wealth between persons. In all capitalist economies some persons receive most if not all of their income from capital while others receive most if not all of their income from other sources, notably labour. Suppose, to simplify the argument, that in year t income is equally distributed between persons. Then, drawing on Piketty's most commonly used assumptions (including a rate of return on assets of 5%, an annual rate of growth of national income of 2%, and a 30–70 ratio of income from capital to non-capital income), in year $t + 1$ the income of those persons whose income is derived solely from capital will increase by 5%, while the income of those persons whose income is derived solely from labour will increase by about 1%. This is because 5% (30%) + 1% (70%) generates a national growth rate of 2.2%, which approximates 2%. Thus in year $t + 1$ the distribution of income will become unequal, an individual person's ranking by increase in income varying directly with the proportion of their income derived from capital. Removing our simplification of initial equality, if in year t the distribution of income between persons had been unequal, in year $t + 1$ it would for the just-outlined reasons have become even more unequal. Piketty's thesis thus forecasts a growing inequality in the personal distribution of income.

A more unequal distribution of income leads to a more unequal distribution of wealth unless those on relatively high incomes save a lower proportion of their income to add to their wealth than do those on relatively low incomes, which for all possible pairs of higher- and lower-income individuals is in fact hardly ever the case (unless there is steeply progressive taxation of wealth). It thus follows from Piketty's thesis that when the share of income from capital in national income increases, causing income to become more and more unequally distributed between persons, wealth also will necessarily over time become more and more unequally distributed between persons.

5.5 AN ALTERNATIVE EXPLANATION OF CHANGES IN THE CLASS DISTRIBUTION OF WEALTH

One of the reasons for the enormous impact of Piketty's explanation of changes in the class (and consequently personal) distribution of wealth is that no one had previously attempted so ambitious a combination of empirical investigation and theoretical analysis. Within a year and a half of its publication, Piketty's book had already generated a large critical literature, which at the time of writing (February 2016) shows no sign of drying up. Two of the leading mainstream journals have published symposia on the book: the *American Economic Review* in its May 2015 issue (the proceedings of a session at the annual meeting of the American Economic Association in the previous December), and its less technical stablemate the *Journal of Economic Perspectives* in the Winter 2015 issue. The heterodox *International Journal of Political Economy*, edited from Canada, also published a symposium on the book in its Fall 2014 issue, while an entire 180-page edition of the World Economic Association's online *Real-World Economics Review* was devoted to Piketty in October 2014, with 17 articles from authors on three continents; it was soon published in book form (Fullbrook and Morgan, 2014). Outside economics, the entire December issue of the *British Journal of Sociology* was given over to nine articles on the book, with authors who included an anthropologist, a geographer, a political scientist, a social policy analyst and two sociologists, in addition to three economists, one of them a self-described feminist political economist. There have also been a considerable number of (often lengthy) stand-alone review articles, ranging from the enthusiastic (Krugman, 2014; Milanovic, 2014) through the critical (Aspromourgos, 2015; Galbraith, 2014a, 2014b; Harcourt, 2015; Rowthorn, 2014) to the dismissive (McCloskey, 2014).

One of the reviewers has provided an alternative (though much less ambitious) explanation of observed changes in the personal distribution of wealth. Richard Koo (2014) argues that in industrialising Western economies, 1914 marked the end of availability of relatively inexpensive labour from rural areas, and that 1970 marked the return, first in industrialising Japan, and then in the industrialising 'Asian Tigers' and China, of relatively inexpensive labour from rural areas. In the context of the global economy of the twenty-first century, Koo believes, Piketty is right for the wrong reasons. It is increasing competition from low-wage developing countries that will 'increase inequality in the developed world until everyone in the world is gainfully employed' (Koo, 2014, p. 95). In the final analysis this is an empirical question, James Galbraith concludes, and the recent evidence does not support Piketty:

Since 2000, *declining inequality* has been observed in post neo-liberal (but still capitalist) Latin America. There is new evidence of declining inequality in China, and also in Europe after 2008, at least if one takes the continent as a whole. In the US, there has been a sawtooth pattern, closely related to the stock market, with inequality peaks in 2000, 2007 and 2013, but little trend since 2000. . . . Perhaps Piketty's Law will vanish – as quickly as it has appeared. (Galbraith, 2014b, p. 148; original emphasis)

This part of the controversy generated by *Capital* is certain to continue, in part because, as the discussion in Chapter 2 and the data in Chapter 3 suggest, measuring inequality is a challenging task, as can be interpreting the different measures available to us. Our hope is that this controversy will at least generate a more concerted effort to gather more (or more consistent) data on measures of wealth, or to at least ensure that existing measures continue to be gathered (see also Rehm and Schnetzer, 2015).

A (very) few of Piketty's critics maintain that this question is unimportant, since inequality in the distribution of wealth does not matter: a rising tide lifts all boats. This is the position of both Deirdre McCloskey (2014) and Gregory Mankiw (2015, p. 46), for whom 'wealth inequality is not a problem in itself' so long as the investment decisions of the rich result in higher standards of living for all, including the poor. This is, of course, a simple application of the Pareto principle in mainstream welfare economics. But it is denied by the great majority of the reviewers, for whom high and rising inequality in the distribution of wealth is unacceptable for many reasons (King, 2016). Piketty himself quotes the early twentieth-century radical Josiah Wedgwood (1939) on the danger posed to liberalism itself by patrimonial capitalism, which means that 'political democracies that do not democratize their economic systems are inherently unstable' (Piketty, 2014, p. 508, cited by Aspromourgos, 2015, p. 304). Thus there is a strong case for considering criteria by which alternative wealth distributions might be ranked, and to this we now turn.

6. Ranking alternative distributions of wealth

[A]re there not economists who, not content with exaggerating the applicability of laissez-faire, laissez-passer to industry, even extend it to the completely extraneous question of property? (Léon Walras, [1874] 1954, p. 257)

The arguments in Chapters 4 and 5 imply that the distribution of wealth in a society will change if there is a change in any one of five factors, namely the distribution of earned income, age structure, the propensity to save, bequest behaviour, or the rate of return on wealth. If one or more of these changes takes place, how can we determine whether the old or the new distribution of wealth should be given the higher ranking?

It might appear that one could simply select a value of some measure of inequality, which in the case of the Gini coefficient would be nearer to zero the more egalitarian one's views, and rank alternative distributions of wealth according to how closely they approximate to that value. However, there are two fundamental problems associated with this approach, a measurement problem and a distributive justice problem, neither of which can be resolved without reference to ethical values.

First, there are many possible ways of measuring distribution (see Chapter 2), and any two measures will in some circumstances yield a different answer to the question of whether a given change in distribution increases or decreases inequality, as Atkinson (1970, pp. 252–7) demonstrated in the case of five of the measures most commonly used. The reason for such lack of consistency is that each measure actually depends on a unique set of implicit assumptions about social welfare. This is the basis of Atkinson's conclusion that 'degree[s] of inequality cannot, in general, be compared without introducing [ethical] values about distribution' (Atkinson 1970, p. 66).[1] By analogy with Kenneth Arrow's well-known social choice theorem, discussed below, we call this 'Atkinson's general impossibility theorem'.

The impossibility of ranking alternative distributions of wealth without reference to ethical values poses a fundamental problem. It has long been widely accepted that one cannot derive an 'ought' statement from an 'is' statement, a proposition first advanced by David Hume, and sometimes referred to as 'Hume's Law'. It follows from this that statements involving values (or 'ends') do not belong to the category of the empirically verifiable, or more strictly (following Karl Popper) to the category of the empirically falsifiable. Note, however, that the attitude of philosophers towards Hume's Law varies according to their interpretation of it, and not all agree with it. It was basically because statements involving ends are non-falsifiable that Lionel Robbins declared such statements to be non-scientific, and consequently outside the boundaries of economic science as he defined it, namely 'the study of human behaviour as a relationship between ends and scarce means that have alternative uses' (Robbins, 1932, p. 16).

On the other hand Robbins did not exclude statements involving ends from what he called 'political economy' (see Robbins, 1976, pp. 2–3), and he later departed from his early extreme position that if we disagree about ends 'there is no room for argument' (Robbins, 1932, p. 134); his excursions into the political economy of the arts (see, for example, Robbins, 1963) attest to this.

The 'room for argument' comes about in part because 'prescriptive conclusions can be drawn from factual premises *among others*' (Sen, 1970, p. 61), a proposition (it should be noted) that does not violate Hume's Law. Thus an argument using facts may resolve a disagreement over ends; for example, having previously believed that the distribution of wealth should be more equal, Smith may change his mind if confronted by Jones with evidence that a more equal distribution of wealth would reduce the aggregate amount of wealth available for distribution. Sen used the label 'non-basic' to describe those individual value judgements which are capable of being changed by reference to facts. He also argued that, just as empirical propositions are ultimately non-verifiable, so no individual value judgement can ever be conclusively shown to be non-basic; it is always the case that some future-discovered fact might influence a value judgement that the holder currently believes to be 'basic'. An example is to be found in the belief that societies should be communist, once held but subsequently abandoned by many in the light of empirical evidence, for example by Arthur Koestler as a consequence of his experiences in the Spanish Civil War.

While reference to facts may resolve some differences of opinion over ethical values, however, there will almost certainly be remaining differences of opinion. This is the source of the second fundamental problem associated with ranking alternative distributions of wealth. Individuals in a society each have a set of values by which they are consciously or sub-consciously guided, and in many societies this set of values differs widely between individuals. These values include not only those which relate to personal behaviour, labelled 'personal preferences' by Ronald Dworkin (1981a, p. 192), but also some which relate to the individual's view of what society ought to be like, labelled by Dworkin as belonging either to the category of 'impersonal preferences', namely 'preferences about things other than their own or other people's lives' (Dworkin, 1981a, p. 192), or to the category of 'political preferences'. The last include, explicitly or implicitly, a view on what Aristotle named distributive justice, namely 'how a society or group should allocate [i.e., distribute] its scarce resources or product among individuals with competing needs or claims' (Roemer, 1996, p. 1).

Each individual's opinion on the distribution of wealth is likely to follow from such an overall view of what society should be like. It is useful to follow Jonathon Wolff (1991, p. 3) in assigning such views to one of three categories, namely single-value, hierarchical plural-value, or conflict plural-value. By a 'single-value' view of society Wolff meant judging society by one criterion only, by a 'hierarchical plural-value' view he meant judging society by multiple criteria, each weighted according to its place in a hierarchy, and by 'conflict plural-value' he meant judging society by multiple unweighted criteria. Conservative, libertarian, utilitarian and egalitarian views, for example, belong to the first of these categories, the Rawlsian view to the second, and the view expressed by Isaiah Berlin in the paper discussed in section 6.4 of this chapter to the third. Selecting these views of society as the most widely held, we briefly summarise canonical expositions of each in successive sections of the chapter, citing along the way sources on which the reader may draw for a more complete account. Since none of these views of society enjoys universal approval, reference is made in each case to some of the principal objections which have been raised, those objections especially relevant to the application of each view to distributional issues being given priority. The subsequent section of this chapter discusses the means by which divided opinions in a society can be transformed into social choice, and a final section draws on the preceding ones to arrive at some conclusions.

6.1 THE CONSERVATIVE VIEW OF SOCIETY

The conservative view of society, classic expositions of which are to be found in the writings of Edmund Burke and Michael Oakeshott, is based on the idea that the best societies are those in which there is continuity between the past, the present and the future. Thinking in pre-Darwinian (pre-mutation) terms, Burke ([1790] 1989, pp. 83–4) drew a parallel between the course of human societies and that of nature, writing that the idea of inheritance furnishes a sure principle of conservation, and a sure principle of transmission; without at all excluding a principle of improvement. It leaves acquisition free; but it secures what it acquires. Whatever advantages are obtained by a state proceeding on these maxims, are locked fast as in a sort of family settlement; . . . By a constitutional policy, working after the pattern of nature, we receive, we hold, we transmit our government and our privileges.

With respect to the specific question of the distribution of wealth, Burke's view was that in a government, private property must be

out of all proportion, predominant in the representation. It must be represented too in great masses of accumulation, or it is not rightly protected. The characteristic essence of property, formed out of the combined principles of its acquisition and conservation, is to be *unequal*. The great masses [of property] therefore which excite envy, and tempt rapacity, must be put out of the possibility of danger. Then they form a natural rampart about the lesser properties in all their gradations. (Burke, [1790] 1989, p. 102)

Burke's case for a substantially unequal distribution of wealth is thus not merely that what has been inherited from the past should be conserved, but that unless there is unequal distribution the whole institution of private property will be endangered.

In his description of political activity Oakeshott ([1951] 1962, p. 127) drew a parallel not with nature but with men sailing

a boundless and bottomless sea; there is neither harbour for shelter nor floor for anchorage, neither starting-place nor appointed destination. The enterprise is to keep afloat on an even keel; the sea is both friend and enemy; and the seamanship consists in using the resources of a traditional manner of behaviour in order to make a friend of every hostile occasion.

Oakeshott added with respect to this traditional manner of behaviour that though it

is flimsy and elusive, it is not without identity, and what makes it a possible object of knowledge is the fact that all its parts do not change at the same time and that the changes it undergoes are potential within it. Its principle is a principle of *continuity*; authority is diffused between past, present, and future; between the old, the new, and what is to come. (Oakeshott, [1951] 1962, p. 128)

While less explicit than Burke on the distribution of wealth, Oakeshott did state with respect to those of conservative disposition first that they find acceptable only changes which are small and slow, changes which are large or rapid involving too great a risk of loss of the valuable characteristics inherited by current society, and second that they regard the role of government as merely to act as arbiter when the interests of persons collide, this latter being capable of being elaborated on to show why they place 'so high a value upon the complicated set of arrangements we call "the institution of private property"' (Oakeshott, [1956] 1962, p. 191).

While not necessarily taking a conservative view of society as a whole, many neoclassical economists of the present day align themselves with conservatives when it comes to the question of distribution. Initial responsibility for this lies with one of the founders of neoclassical economics, namely William Stanley Jevons, a utilitarian who ruled out interpersonal comparisons of pleasures and pains on the ground that '[e]very mind is . . . inscrutable to every other mind, and no common denominator of feeling seems to be possible' (Jevons, [1871] 1957, p. 14). While Jevons's view on this question was rejected by such relatively early neoclassical economists as Alfred Marshall and A.C. Pigou, since the 1930s most neoclassical economists have followed Jevons in not being prepared to make interpersonal comparisons. For this reason they refuse to recommend any change if it is impossible to make someone better off without making at least one person worse off, thereby ruling out any redistribution of wealth (or income for that matter). Thus with respect to distribution the current mainstream-economist view of society coincides with the conservative view, supporting the status quo.

It is sometimes implied, particularly in the works of neoclassical economists, that such maintenance of the status quo is in some sense 'value free'. But we know from Hume's Law that the 'is-ness' of an economy cannot imply an 'ought-ness'; advocacy of maintenance of the current state of society is no less value-laden than advocacy of change.

A basic argument against the conservative view of society was neatly expressed by Friedrich Hayek in the Postscript to *The Constitution of Liberty*, entitled 'Why I Am Not a Conservative', in the following words:

> by its very nature it cannot offer an alternative to the direction in which we are moving. It may succeed by its resistance to current tendencies in slowing down undesirable developments, but since it does not indicate another direction, it cannot prevent their continuance. (Hayek, 1960, p. 398)

Most critics of the conservative view of society have in common two beliefs: first that the 'concept of tradition gives a poor picture indeed of the amount of inventiveness, innovation, and conscious dexterity which is necessary for any state to survive at all' (Crick, [1962] 1982, p. 122), and second that there are universal criteria by which societies can be judged. They differ, however, on what these universal criteria are. We look first at the criteria favoured by Hayek, now commonly referred to as the libertarian view of society.[2]

6.2   THE LIBERTARIAN VIEW OF SOCIETY

Although the term 'libertarian' was once applied to left-wing thinkers such as syndicalists and anarchists who advocated a very high degree of equality along with a reduced role for government, since the 1970s it has come to be applied instead to those who advocate a reduced government role because they support free markets. The free-market libertarian view of society is to be found most forcefully presented in Robert Nozick (1974). Nozick took as his starting point the writings of John Locke, who argued that since every man has a property in his own person, whatsoever

> he removes out of the State that Nature hath provided, and left it in, he hath mixed his *Labour* with, and joyned to it something that is his own, and thereby makes it his *Property*. It being by him removed from the common state Nature placed it in, it hath by this *Labour* something annexed to it, that excludes the common right of other Men. (Locke, [1690] 1960, p. 306)

Adding the assumption that individuals have natural rights, in the sense of entitlement to non-interference by others, and to life, liberty and property, Nozick advocated a minimal state. He rejected what he called 'end-result' principles of distributive justice such as utilitarianism, which are based solely on distributive outcomes, on the grounds that they wrongly assume the existence of a 'social pot' coming like manna from heaven; rectifying this mistake involves recognising that 'whether a distribution is just depends on how it came about' (Nozick, 1974, p. 153). He argued instead for a 'historical' principle which he named the 'entitlement' theory, which, by contrast with end-result principles, results in a just distribution that is not 'patterned', but unplanned.

According to the entitlement theory, 'the holdings of a person are just if he is entitled to them by the principles of justice in acquisition and transfer, or by the principle of rectification of injustice (as specified by the first two principles)' (ibid., p. 153). 'Justice in acquisition' refers to the idea that in certain circumstances it may be just to appropriate unowned property 'from nature'; Nozick however did not specify what these circumstances are, going only so far as to lay down a proviso designed to rule out compatibility of justice in acquisition with 'a catastrophic situation'. This is the proviso that appropriation of an unowned object by one person does not result in anyone else 'no longer being able to use freely (without appropriation) what he previously could' (ibid., p. 176). The proviso is relevant in some cases of monopoly; for example, 'a person may not appropriate the only water hole in a desert and charge what he will' (ibid., p. 180). 'Justice in transfer' is defined as voluntary exchange of one justly acquired object for another justly acquired object. Nozick summarised the entitle-ment conception as follows:

> From each according to what he chooses to do, to each according to what he makes for himself (perhaps with contracted-for aid of others) and what others choose to give him or what they've been given previously (under this maxim) and haven't yet expended or transferred. (ibid., p. 160)

The libertarian view of society thus endorses the existing distribution of wealth, with the sole exception that redistribution is justified where its purpose is to rectify past, or 'historical', injustice (see Lyons, 1977; Waldron, 1992; Patton, 2005).

Libertarians oppose those who see liberty as power to do what one wants. This view of liberty

> inevitably leads to the identification of liberty with wealth; and this makes it possible to exploit all the appeal which the word 'liberty' carries in the support for a demand for the redistribution of wealth. (Hayek, 1960, p. 17)

In Hayek's view, however, liberty and wealth 'are both good things which most of us desire and although we often need both to obtain what we wish, they still remain different' (Hayek, 1960, p. 17). Courtiers, for example, may have great wealth but have very little liberty to do what they would like to do, while poor artisans, shepherds, farmers or even peasants may have a great deal of liberty to decide how they are going to live their lives.

There have been several critiques of the libertarian view, including later reflections and revisions by Nozick himself (1989) regarding inherit-ance transfer. One prominent critique is offered by Robert Frank (1985), who demonstrated that the entitlement theory is open to objection even within a libertarian framework if individuals attach importance to their relative standing in society. In this case higher-standing individuals will be prepared to part with some of their 'justly acquired objects' in order to persuade lower-standing individuals to join, or remain in, their society. The benefits of such a heterogeneous society, however, cannot be withheld from any higher-standing individual who does not pay, and

> [h]igh standing in the social hierarchy is thus no different from any other public good. In order for people to have the amount of it that they really want, it may [will?] be necessary to act collectively. (Frank, 1985, p. 118)

Frank drew the conclusion that the importance individuals attach to their relative standing would lead to redistributive taxation even in a libertarian society.

Egalitarian critics of the libertarian view of society, while not ruling out the idea that individuals have rights, reject the libertarian view that these rights include absolute 'justly-acquired' property and inheritance rights. Utilitarian critics, on the other hand, reject altogether the idea that individuals have rights. They also argue that there may be relatively little happiness in a libertarian society. It is to the utilitarian view that we now turn.

6.3   THE UTILITARIAN VIEW OF SOCIETY

The utilitarian view of society is most commonly associated with Jeremy Bentham and John Stuart Mill. Bentham was a 'hedonist' utilitarian who believed that every action should be aimed at achieving the greatest happiness of the greatest number,[3] 'hedonist' being reflected in his view that '[p]rejudice apart, the game of push-pin is of equal value with the arts and sciences of music and poetry' (Bentham, [1825] 1838, Vol. II, p. 253). For Bentham, only the consequences of our actions are relevant to their moral status. He was a consistent and thoroughgoing consequentialist who dismissed any idea that individuals possess *rights* to anything (including property): 'Natural rights, nonsense; natural and imprescriptible rights, rhetorical nonsense, elevated nonsense, nonsense going on stilts' (cited by Ryan, 2012, p. 695).

According to John Stuart Mill, Bentham also stated that in calculating the greatest happiness of the greatest number, '[e]veryone [is] to count for one and nobody for more than one' (Mill, [1838] 1969, p. 257). The closest approximation to this dictum so far discovered in Bentham's writings is the following:

> Given two operations, the effect of one is to provide each of ten persons with a single portion of happiness; the effect of the other is to provide each of five persons with two similar portions. The respective merits of the two operations are exactly equal; there is no reason to prefer one to the other. (Bentham, [1788] 1963, pp. 449–50)[4]

This statement implies that while the happiness of one person is not to be given greater importance than that of another, the distribution of happiness between persons is irrelevant except as a means to the achievement of the greatest happiness of the greatest number.

By contrast with Bentham, John Stuart Mill was not a 'hedonist' but an 'ideal' utilitarian, one who believed that some pleasures should be ranked more highly than others. In his judgement it is 'better to be Socrates dissatisfied than a fool satisfied' (Mill, [1861] 1969, p. 212), implying that the value of knowledge and ideas and the pleasures they provide should take priority over other pursuits.

Unlike Jevons, the founder of neoclassical economics, twentieth-century utilitarians such as John C. Harsanyi and J.J.C. (Jack) Smart followed Bentham in being prepared to compare the happiness of one individual with that of another. Harsanyi, for example, argued that 'interpersonal comparisons of utility are not value judgements based on some ethical or political postulates but are rather factual propositions based on certain principles of inductive logic' (Harsanyi, 1955, pp. 319–20). Individuals may make these comparisons either according to their 'subjective preferences', which describe the individual's preferences as they actually are, or according to their 'ethical preferences', which are 'impersonal' in the sense that they are based on the assumption that the individual has an equal chance of obtaining any social position, from the highest to the lowest, or at least disregards any knowledge he has to the contrary.[5] Harsanyi went on to conclude that in the absence of an objective criterion for making interpersonal comparisons, if an individual's impersonal preferences are to be rational they 'must define a cardinal social welfare function equal to the [weighted] arithmetic mean of the utilities [as judged by the individual] of all individuals in the society' (Harsanyi, 1955, p. 316). Thus an individual's social welfare function takes the form:

$$W = \Sigma \, a_i U_i \qquad (6.1)$$

where U_i is the utility of the ith individual and a_i is the weighting attached to the utility of that individual.

Harsanyi said little on how individual social welfare functions so defined can be aggregated into collective social welfare functions. He relied principally on the hope, forlorn many would say, that a combination of advances in 'psychological laws' which contribute to our factual knowledge, and increasing agreement on 'individualistic ethics' that precludes one individual from judging the preferences of another, will lead individuals closer to adopting identical social welfare functions.[6]

Harsanyi's views belong to the 'rule utilitarian' school, according to which the greatest happiness of the greatest number is to be achieved by following a rule or rules. By contrast, Smart's writings endorse 'act utilitarianism', the view that each action should be judged according to the contribution it makes towards achieving the greatest happiness of the greatest number. Utilitarianism being a single-value view of what society should be like, it is not surprising to find Smart (1978, p. 104) writing that

[a] utilitarian would compromise his utilitarianism if he allowed principles of justice which might conflict with the maximisation of happiness (or more

generally of goodness, should he be an 'ideal' utilitarian). He is concerned with the maximisation of happiness and not with the distribution of it. Nevertheless he may well deduce from his ethical principle that certain ways of distributing the means to happiness (e.g. money, food, housing) are more conducive to the general good than others. . . . He will consider whether the legal institutions and customary sanctions which operate in particular societies are more or less conducive to the utilitarian end than are other possible institutions and customs.

This passage from Smart supports the rejection by Robin Barrow (1991, pp. 97–104) of the proposition advanced by Alasdair MacIntyre that 'utilitarianism is necessarily interpreted in terms of dominant beliefs and attitudes' (MacIntyre, 1964, p. 4). Rather, 'a utilitarian is quite at liberty to make a radical criticism (on moral grounds) of his society' (Barrow, 1991, p. 101), and in consequence utilitarianism is likely to be rejected by conservatives.

Utilitarianism is also unacceptable to egalitarians, who would find it impossible to agree with Smart's contention that with respect to the question of what a society should be like, distribution is relevant only as a means to an end. The egalitarian's objection has been highlighted as follows by Sen. If Individual A derives twice as much utility from any given level of income as Individual B, because (say) B is 'a cripple', 'the rule of maximising the sum-utility of the two would require that person A be given a higher income than B' (Sen, [1973] 1997, p. 17). But while utility is maximised, handicapped person B is further disadvantaged by being allocated a lower level of income. It was the apparently inequitable (unfair) nature of this outcome which led Sen to state that, with respect to choosing between alternative distributions, 'utilitarianism is indeed a non-starter' (Sen, [1973] 1997, p. 18). It is to the egalitarian view of society that we turn next.

6.4   THE EGALITARIAN VIEW OF SOCIETY

The egalitarian view of society found its classic expression in R.H. Tawney (1931), though the meaning to be attached to 'equality' has been explored in greater depth, notably by Dworkin (1981a, 1981b) and Sen (1973, [1980] 1982, 1984, 1987, 1992, 1993, 2001, 2009). Tawney ([1931] 1952, pp. 35–6) put forward the view that while

[m]en differ profoundly as individuals in capacity and character, they are equally entitled as human beings to consideration and respect, and . . . the well-being of a society is likely to be increased if it so plans its organization that whether their powers are great or small, all its members may be equally enabled to make the best of such powers as they possess.

Tawney believed that contemporary social and economic inequality, in Britain in particular, both rendered it impossible for most individuals to make the best of the powers they possessed, and precluded a national sense of community, of 'fraternity'. Drawing a parallel with the equality before the law that underpins political liberty, he argued that economic liberty likewise needs to be underpinned by at least a minimum degree of economic equality; in the economic as well as other spheres, 'freedom for the pike is death for the minnows' (Tawney, [1931] 1952, p. 182).

Fifty years after Tawney's *Equality* was published, Dworkin (1981a, 1981b) highlighted the distinction between equality of welfare, or the well-being resulting at least in part from access to resources, on the one hand, and equality of resources, or the inputs on which well-being depends, on the other. He rejected the former as the egalitarian goal, arguing that it would advantage those with expensive tastes such as champagne at the expense of those with 'cheap tastes', the latter being illustrated by Sen's examples of the battered slave, and the 'tamed' housewife who has been conditioned to accept a subservient status. Instead Dworkin endorsed equality of resources as the egalitarian goal.[7] Suppose, he suggested, that

> a number of shipwreck survivors are washed up on a desert island which has abundant resources and no native population, and any likely rescue is many years away. These immigrants accept the principle that no one is antecedently entitled to any of these resources, but that they shall instead be divided equally among them. (Dworkin, 1981b, p. 285)

He then proposed that subsequent lifetime inequality of resources resulting from unequal degrees of unavoidable bad luck ('brute luck') be reduced by a compulsory insurance scheme based on the average expectation of brute luck, and that subsequent lifetime inequality of resources resulting from unequal abilities be reduced by an income tax calculated according to what the average 'immigrant' would be prepared to pay to insure against a low income.

Roemer (1996, p. 263) categorised Dworkin's views as involving a fundamental distinction between 'involuntary' and 'voluntary' inequality, arguing that according to Dworkin

> distributive justice consists in a restricted kind of utilitarianism: persons should be rendered equal in condition insofar as their condition results from circumstances over which they cannot be held responsible, but differences in condition are admissible when those differences are due to actions/beliefs for which they are responsible. (Roemer, 1996, p. 263)

Thus inequality of resources is not justifiable, for example, in the case of persons with different degrees of handicap, but is justifiable in the case of persons with different degrees of extravagancy in tastes.

Sen too rejected equality of welfare as the egalitarian objective, instead making his starting point the resources available to an individual. More specifically, in works starting with his 1979 Tanner lecture entitled 'Equality of What?' he argued for equality of capabilities; by capability he meant the 'doings' and 'beings' within reach of an individual, these doings and beings being referred to as functionings. Equality of capabilities, however, requires some inequality of resources, as in order to have access to the same capability a person who is handicapped, for example, will generally require greater resources than one who is not. Further, equality of capabilities would result in inequality of happiness, as it would enable a battered slave or a 'tamed' housewife to achieve a level of happiness initially not dreamt of. In addition, Sen sought to incorporate in the concept of capability the available breadth of choice, stating that 'the capability approach, broadly defined, is not concerned only with checking what set of bundles of functionings one could choose from, but also with seeing the functionings themselves in a suitably rich way as reflecting the relevant aspects of freedom' (Sen, 1987, pp. 37–8).

Given that wealth is among the resources available to persons, the egalitarian view of society, at least as articulated by Tawney, Dworkin and Sen, is obviously directly applicable to the question of the distribution of wealth. However, the egalitarian view does not necessarily lead to the conclusion that wealth itself should be equally distributed. Rather it leads to the view that wealth should be distributed sufficiently equally for the achievement of equality in capability, or its equivalent.

The egalitarian view of society was criticised by Berlin, in his paper on 'Equality' (1956). Berlin objected to what he saw as the egalitarian presumption that '[a] society in which every member holds an equal quantity of property needs no special justification; only a society in which property is unequal needs it' (Berlin, 1956, p. 304). Taking a conflict plural-value view, he argued in support of his objection that

> when the pursuit of equality comes into conflict with other human aims, be they what they may – such as the desire for happiness or pleasure, or for justice or virtue, or colour and variety in a society for its own sake, or for liberty of choice as an end in itself, or for the fuller development of all human faculties, it is only the most fanatical egalitarian that will demand that such conflicts invariably be decided in favour of equality alone, with relative disregard of the other 'values' concerned. (ibid., p. 319)

Of these other values, he saw 'colour and variety in a society' as particularly threatened by the egalitarian view of society, which he argued stems from a desire for total uniformity.[8] As we have seen, however, some egali-tarians, notably Sen, have been at pains to protect 'colour and variety in society'. Further, a fundamental difficulty with a conflict plural-value view such as that of Berlin, as Wolff (1991, p. 3) pointed out, is that it does not explain how conflicts between values are to be resolved.

6.5 RAWLSIAN DISTRIBUTIVE JUSTICE

In his extension of Kantian ideas in *A Theory of Justice* (1971), John Rawls argued that the principles of justice are those which would be chosen in an initial situation that is fair, defined as a situation in which no one knows which position in society they will subsequently occupy; given this 'veil of ignorance' anyone could turn out, for example, to be the richest or the poorest. Adopting a hierarchical plural-value stance, Rawls concluded that in this situation the principle of justice to which priority would be given would be: 'each person is to have an equal right to the most extensive basic liberty compatible with a similar liberty for others' (Rawls, 1971, p. 60). A second principle of justice that would be adopted would be the proposition that economic and social inequalities are to be arranged so that, subject to them being 'attached to offices and positions open to all under conditions of fair equality' (ibid., p. 302), they are 'to the greatest benefit of the least advantaged' (ibid.).

Rawls named the second principle the 'difference principle'. In order to make the difference principle workable, Rawls supplemented it by stipulat-ing that 'benefit' is to be measured in terms of a weighted index of those 'things that every rational man is presumed to want' (Rawls, 1971, p. 62), which he called 'primary goods', and defined as comprising rights and liberties, powers and opportunities, income and wealth.[9] If the remaining characteristics of a society are given, the question of what distribution of wealth is just can thus be answered by Rawls' second principle of justice.[10]

Rawls' difference principle is alternatively known as the 'maximin' prin-ciple, on the ground that it maximises the primary goods index of the least advantaged ('minimum') economic class. This emphasis on primary goods demonstrates that Rawls shares with Dworkin and Sen the view that it is equality of resources which is important. He explicitly rejects the 'equality of welfare' approach of utilitarianism, notably on the ground that desires for goods other than primary goods vary so much among individuals that it is not possible to make the interpersonal comparisons required by the utilitarian philosophy.

One of the grounds on which Rawls' derivation of his second principle of justice has been criticised is that it implicitly assumes, without providing justification for the assumption, that the principles-of-justice choosers are either risk-averse or pessimistic as to their future position in society. Rawls' second principle of justice has also been criticised for attaching too much importance to the least well-off, in that it takes no account of the magnitude of the aggregate gains and losses involved in moving from one social state to another. Thus it would support moving from social state A to social state B if the least-advantaged economic class thereby becomes very slightly better-off, even if every other economic class is grossly worse-off, or even if the degree of inequality between every other economic class increases; as Sen succinctly put it, between the least-advantaged and others '[t]here is *no* trade-off' (Sen, 1970, p. 139). Rawls' second principle of justice would support, for example, a change from a social state A characterized by a (4, 46, 48, 50, 52) distribution of 200 units of wealth among five economic classes, to a social state B characterised by a (12, 19, 21, 23, 25) distribution of 100 units of wealth.

An alternative to Rawls' second principle of justice which is not subject to this criticism is to be found in Sen's 'weak equity axiom' (see Sen, [1973] 1997, pp. 18–20). Applied to the distribution of wealth, this is the axiom that in the distribution of a given total of wealth, for each pair of individuals the optimal solution must give a higher level of wealth to the individual who gets a lower level of well-being for each level of individual wealth. Assuming a handicapped person gets a lower level of well-being for each level of individual wealth than a person who is not handicapped, for example, the weak equity axiom requires that the handicapped person have the higher level of wealth. As Sen pointed out, in the absence of any specification as to how much higher the level of wealth must be, this is a rather mild requirement. On the other hand, ordering well-being per unit of wealth for every pair of individuals presents a practical measurement problem far greater than that posed by Rawls' second principle of justice, which only requires the measurement of the well-being of the least well-off.

A third criticism, expounded in depth by Wylie Bradford (2000), is that Rawls is inconsistent in excluding from the question of justice the specification of property rights over the means of production, instead relegating determination of these to the customs and traditions of the society concerned. In particular, Bradford argued that Rawls fails to demonstrate that the right to participate in the management of production is any less basic a liberty than the primary goods which he lists. Bradford's argument, to put it in a nutshell, is that well-being depends not only on distribution, but also on both job satisfaction and a perception that productive effort is appropriately rewarded, and that Rawls ignores these aspects of well-being.

6.6 USING INDIVIDUAL VALUES TO RANK DISTRIBUTIONS

If we are to translate individual values into social choice, we need what Sen (1970, pp. 22–3) called 'collective choice rules'. Only one such rule would be necessary in a society in which there was unanimity on values: social choices must precisely reflect individual values. Even in this case, however, it cannot be said that social choices are 'value-free'. As Sen pointed out, it is a *non sequitur* to state that 'if everyone agrees on a value judgement it is not a value judgement at all, but is perfectly "objective"' (Sen, 1970, p. 57); this follows from Hume's law. Atkinson's general impossibility theorem thus holds even in the case of unanimity on values.

In general, however, in any society, each of conservative, libertarian, utilitarian, egalitarian and Rawlsian views is likely to be held by some individuals. In this case, finding collective choice rules which result in social preferences that reflect individual values is more complex. The first to tackle this problem comprehensively was Kenneth Arrow (1951), whose initially-named 'general possibility theorem' demonstrated that even if all that is required is a social ordering that is transitive, reflexive and complete, the task of deriving social preferences which reflect individual values is impossible if it has to be undertaken within the constraints of four apparently perfectly reasonable conditions (hence the common renaming of it as Arrow's 'general impossibility theorem'). For an ordering to be transitive, if x is at least as good as y, and y is at least as good as z, then x must be at least as good as z, in which case transitivity is said to apply; for it to be reflexive x must be at least as good as itself; and for it to be complete either x is regarded as at least as good as y or y is regarded as at least as good as x or x and y are regarded indifferently.

We follow Sen (1970, pp. 37–8) in labelling the four above-mentioned apparently perfectly reasonable conditions respectively 'unrestricted domain', 'weak Pareto principle', 'independence of irrelevant alternatives', and 'nondictatorship'. The condition of unrestricted domain stipulates that collective choice rules must work for any logically possible set of individual orderings. The weak Pareto principle requires that the rules are such that if everyone prefers x to y, then society prefers x to y.[11] The condition of independence of irrelevant alternatives stipulates that, for any given set of alternatives, the social ordering must depend on the rankings by individuals of those alternatives alone, and not on their ranking of other 'irrelevant' alternatives. Finally, the condition of nondictatorship rules out the possibility that an individual exists of whom it is true that whenever he or she prefers x to y society also prefers x to y, regardless of the preferences of others.[12]

The negative implications of Arrow's general impossibility theorem can be overcome only by relaxing one or more of the assumptions on which it is based. For example, the theorem no longer applies if the social ordering is only required to be quasi-transitive, that is to say, the social ordering obeys the rule that if x is preferred to y, and y to z, then x is preferred to z, in which case quasi-transitivity is said to apply. Given that quasi-transitivity differs from transitivity only in that it does not cover 'at least as good as' cases, relaxing the requirements for social ordering to this extent would seem to be reasonable, given the fact that social orderings can then be derived from individual values.

Assuming quasi-transitivity, Sen ([1973] 1997, p. 10) added the condition of anonymity, namely that the social ordering depends only on the combination of preferences held by members of a group, not on who holds them. Adding this further 'apparently perfectly reasonable condition' enabled Sen (ibid., pp. 10–12) to demonstrate that distributional judgements cannot play any part in this method of deriving a social ordering, and to conclude that the framework of analysis has to be broadened to include interpersonal comparisons, '[d]espite the widespread allergy to interpersonal comparisons among professional economists' (ibid., p. 14). He went on to argue:

> [i]f I say 'I would prefer to be person A rather than person B in this situation', I am indulging in an interpersonal comparison. While we do not really have the opportunity (or perhaps the misfortune, as the case may be) of in fact becoming A or B, we can think quite systematically about such a choice, and indeed we seem to make such comparisons frequently. (ibid., p. 14)

Sen's 'exercise of the imagination' has much in common with Rawls' 'veil of ignorance'. Assuming that Sen's individual is not lying about his preferences, for self-interested motives, in both cases the judgements made are disinterested.

One way of applying disinterested judgements to the question of the distribution of wealth is to make use of Atkinson's concept of 'inequality-aversion'. Atkinson derived this concept in the following way. Having concluded, as noted earlier in this chapter, that it is not possible (except in the case of non-intersecting Lorenz curves) to rank alternative distributions by degree of inequality without introducing ethical values, he proposed the explicit use of a social welfare function which is assumed to have the characteristics of being both additively separable and symmetric. An additively separable social welfare function is a function in which one individual's well-being does not depend on that of any other individual, and a symmetric social welfare function is one that remains unaffected if the situation of any two individuals is reversed, for example by assigning to each individual the wealth level previously enjoyed by the other (by implication, individual well-being functions are assumed to be identical). Given these two somewhat restrictive assumptions, alternative distributions of wealth-derived well-being would be ranked according to the value of the integral

$$\int_0^{\bar{w}} \Omega(w)f(w)dw \qquad (6.2)$$

where, for levels of wealth (w) between zero and $\bar{w}$, $\Omega(w)$ describes how individual well-being varies with wealth (we have substituted 'W', representing 'well-being', for Atkinson's 'U', representing 'utility', in order to broaden the concept of individual well-being beyond utility, enabling it to be extended, for example, to Sen's concept of capability); $f(w)$ is the function determining the probability of w taking on a specific value; and dw represents the rate of change of wealth levels. The meaning of this integral can be illustrated by reference to Figure 2.1 (p. 15 above). If the horizontal axis of this diagram were used to measure not individual wealth but individual well-being, the value of the integral would be measured by the size of the area below the probability density line.

Atkinson added the relatively uncontroversial assumption that individual well-being functions are increasing and concave, which is to say (where well-being is an increasing function of wealth) that individual well-being increases with each unit increase in wealth but at a constant or decreasing rate.[13] This assumption is a sufficient condition for us to conclude in the case of two non-intersecting wealth Lorenz curves that the curve closer to the line of complete equality represents not only greater equality in the distribution of wealth, but also (*ceteris paribus*) greater social welfare. It also enables us to rank distributions in the case of two intersecting Lorenz curves. But if agreement on the actual numbers to be used in the ranking process is needed, mathematics requires that the measure of inequality used be invariant with respect to linear transformations of the individual well-being function.

To obtain such a measure of inequality, Atkinson first improved on the analysis to be found in Hugh Dalton (1920) by introducing the concept of the 'equally distributed equivalent' level of income (y_{EDE}), defined as 'the level of income per head which if equally distributed would give the same level of social welfare as the present distribution' (Atkinson, 1970, p. 250). Following Atkinson, but applying this concept to wealth, we can measure inequality in the distribution of wealth-induced well-being (I) as follows:

$$I = 1 - w_{EDE}/\mu \qquad (6.3)$$

where μ is the mean of the actual distribution of wealth and, by analogy with y_{EDE}, w_{EDE} is the 'equally distributed equivalent' level of wealth, that is to say the level of wealth per head which if equally distributed would give the same level of social welfare as the present distribution. If wealth were equally distributed w_{EDE} would equal μ, and the value of I would consequently be zero, reflecting the absence of inequality in the distribution of wealth-induced well-being. If all wealth were held by one person, wealth-induced well-being would be zero for all but that person, and wealth-induced social welfare would consequently approach zero, causing w_{EDE} in turn to approach zero and I to approach 1, reflecting the maximum degree of inequality in the distribution of wealth-induced well-being. A value of I equal to (say) 0.2 implies that the equally distributed equivalent level of wealth per head is only 0.8 of the actual wealth per head; in this case, redistributing wealth so that all persons hold the same wealth would increase social welfare, provided that any loss of wealth resulting from such factors as the disincentive effects of the redistribution does not exceed 20 per cent of initial wealth. In Chapter 8 we discuss whether or not such disincentive effects are likely to occur.

As it stands, this measure of inequality does not have the desirable property of being unaffected by changes in per capita levels of wealth. For a measure of inequality to have this property, it is a mathematical requirement that individual well-being functions be homothetic. Satisfaction of this requirement, in the case of discrete distributions, such as that of the wealth of a population comprising a finite number of persons, requires that:

$$I = 1 - \left[\sum_i \left(\frac{w_i}{\mu} \right)^{1-\varepsilon} f(w_i) \right]^{1/(1-\varepsilon)} \tag{6.4}$$

where the second term on the right-hand side restricts the expression w_{EDE}/μ in equation (6.3) to a specific form, with w_i standing for the wealth of the ith person, and ε measuring what Atkinson labelled 'inequality-aversion'.[14] The only variable in this equation which depends on ethical values is ε. This is inadequately described by the term inequality-aversion because, as Atkinson himself noted, it actually indicates the relative weight attached to redistribution at the lower end of the scale as compared with redistribution at the upper end; a more helpful label for ε is 'relative poverty-aversion'. When applied to the distribution of wealth a value of ε equal to zero implies a linear wealth-derived social welfare function, where wealth transfers have the same effect on I no matter where on the wealth scale they take place, while as ε approaches infinity I ceases to become responsive to transfers of wealth except those at the very bottom of the wealth scale, and thus reflects Rawlsian values. An intermediate value of ε equal to 1 implies, according to equation (6.4), that in a two-person society, social welfare will be unaffected if $1 is taken from the wealthier person and 50 cents given to the less wealthy person [the remaining 50 cents 'being lost in the process – e.g. in administering the transfer' (Atkinson, 1973, p. 67)]. A value of ε equal to 2 implies that social welfare will be unaffected if $1 is taken from the wealthier person and 25 cents given to the less wealthy person.

For a given distribution of wealth, any value assigned to ε will generate a unique value of w_{EDE}/μ, and therefore a unique value of *I*. In the case of two non-intersecting wealth Lorenz curves, one curve will always have a lower value of *I* than the other, regardless of the value of ε. However, one of two intersecting Lorenz curves will have a lower *I* for some values of ε and a higher *I* for other values of ε. For example, in Figure 2.3 *I* will be lower for the Lorenz curve AEC if the value of ε is high enough, but lower for the Lorenz curve ADC if the value of ε is low enough. Which of the two societies represented by these wealth Lorenz curves is ranked as having the higher wealth-derived social welfare clearly depends on the value assigned to ε.

In a dictatorial society the value of ε, and therefore of *I*, would be determined by the dictator. How can the value of ε be determined, however, in a democratic society? Given that each individual will have their particular degree of relative asset-poverty-aversion, this value of ε can be fed into their view of the factors on which social welfare depends, or in other words into their individual social welfare function. In turn, the social ordering derived from individual social welfare functions incorporating ε will reflect *inter alia* individual attitudes towards the distribution of wealth.

6.7 CONCLUDING REMARKS

In Chapter 3 we established that in those societies for which relevant information exists, the distribution of wealth is always highly unequal. In Chapters 4 and 5 we examined the factors which determine how unequal this distribution will be and those which determine how the distribution changes over time, and in this chapter we have discussed how unequal this distribution should be according to each of several fundamental views of society. With the exception of the conservative view of society, all of these views lead to the conclusion that there are circumstances under which the existing distribution of wealth should be changed. Utilitarians see a change in the distribution of wealth as one means by which the sum of human happiness can be increased. Libertarian followers of Nozick admit that where wealth has been unjustly acquired in the past, it should be returned to the rightful owners, or their descendants. Most, if not all, egalitarians believe that the distribution of wealth over the whole of society should be more equal than it is, or ever has been. Rawlsians would support a redistribution of wealth which increased the well-being of the least well-off, provided that it did not adversely affect human liberty.

While there is widespread agreement that the distribution of wealth should be changed, however, views about how extensive this change should be will obviously be diverse. Thus before the distribution of wealth in a democratic society can be determined, individual views have to be translated into a social ordering. But 'why should distributive justice be so intimately linked to the preferences of individuals?' (Roemer, 1996, p. 37). The answer is, unless there emerges a philosopher king who is able to convert everyone to believing in the one view of distributive justice, deriving social choice from individual values is the best that we can do.

NOTES

1. For endorsement of Atkinson's conclusion, see Charles Blackorby and David Donaldson (1978), and Rodney Maddock et al. (1984, pp. 3–9).
2. While preferring to call himself an 'Old Whig', Hayek admitted that 'libertarian' might be the best replacement for the increasingly ambiguous term 'liberal' (Hayek, 1960, p. 408).
3. The phrase 'the greatest happiness of the greatest number' was first coined, however, by Frances Hutcheson, teacher of Adam Smith.
4. See also the comparable statements by Bentham, cited in Mill ([1838] 1969, p. 515).
5. Without actually coining the term, Harsanyi thereby anticipated Rawls' concept of the veil of ignorance, to which reference is made in section 6.5. Harsanyi, in turn, was anticipated by W. Vickrey (1945, p. 329).
6. This idea has sparked considerable interest by those whom one might call the growing body of explicitly utilitarian welfare economists, who task themselves with identifying and justifying social welfare functions that concern the ethical nature of distributions (see Hammond, 1991, and Fleurbaey and Hammond, 2004).
7. 'Primary goods' are discussed more extensively in Rawls (1982) than in Rawls (1971).
8. This has long been a popular critique of egalitarianism. Nozick, for example, argued that egalitarianism would have the unintended consequence of exacerbating envy, by reducing the range of comparative values on which persons establish self-esteem. Non-egalitarian societies are more diverse and thus enhance an individual's chance of finding dimensions to their lives that other people also believe to be important, along which the individual does reasonably well.
9. The strong Pareto principle, so named because it produces an ordering even when all individuals except one are indifferent between (say) x and y, states that if at least one individual prefers x to y, and every individual regards x as at least as good as y, then society must prefer x to y.
10. There also exists a more recent and radical version of Rawls' *Theory of Justice* as a property-owning democracy (one that disappears in his later work) – see Chambers (2012, p. 28).
11. For a non-mathematical summary and critique of Arrow's general impossibility theorem, see Sen (1970, pp. 37–40).
12. Sen ([1973] 1997, pp. 38–9) pointed out that within a utilitarian framework, to avoid the conclusion that the (say) income distributions (10, 0) and (5, 5) are equally good, it is necessary to assume that individual well-being functions are strictly concave, which is to say that they increase at a decreasing rate.

13. The inspiration for, and mathematical derivation of, Atkinson's concept of 'inequality aversion' came from literature relating to risk-aversion by decision-makers in the presence of uncertainty. See Atkinson (1970, p. 245).

14. This view appears to have provoked a large and expanding literature on resource egalitarianism based on ideas of solidarity, community or responsibility (see Kolm, 2008; Cohen, 2009; Fleurbaey, 2008; Fleurbaey and Maniquet, 2009; and Roemer, 2012).

7. How to change the distribution of wealth

The philosophers have only interpreted the world; the point, however, is to change it. (Marx, [1845] 1976, p. 8)

As noted in Chapter 6, with the exception of the conservative view, all views of society lead to the conclusion that there are circumstances under which the existing distribution of wealth should be changed. In this chapter we accordingly examine the means by which wealth can be redistributed.

In order to simplify the argument, we assume that the objective in a society in which the means of production are privately owned, referred to henceforth as a capitalist society, is to make the characteristically highly unequal distribution of wealth less unequal, though in most cases the argument could be applied in reverse if the objective were to make the distribution of wealth more unequal. Where the means of production are communally owned, however, we assume the objective to be replacement of communal by private ownership, with change in the distribution of income derived from the means of production being one of several consequences.

The distribution of wealth in a capitalist society can be made less unequal by taxation, at least in the short run. Wealth-redistributing taxes may be levied directly, first by the taxation of wealth-holders, and second by the taxation of wealth when it is transferred, through a tax on either the giver or the receiver of gifts *inter vivos*, a tax on deceased estates or a tax on inheritances. Wealth-redistributing taxes may alternatively be levied indirectly, affecting saving out of income, a prime source of increases in wealth; saving can be redistributed by means of either a progressive income tax system or a progressive tax on saving.

Much of the well-being flowing from possession of wealth is attributable to the income derived from wealth. If the objective is a more equal distribution of well-being, therefore, redistribution of the income derived from wealth can be regarded as an alternative to redistribution of wealth itself. A more equal distribution of the income derived from wealth is likely to result from replacement of capitalism by some form of communal ownership of the means of production generating income. Communal ownership may take the form of assets being owned either by a community as a whole, or by a sub-section of a community, such as the workers in a particular firm.

Where communal ownership already exists, it may be replaced by capitalism. This is likely to result in a more unequal distribution of the income derived from wealth. However, this result may not follow, at least for a time, if private property is introduced through the issue to all citizens of an equal number of vouchers (alternatively known as coupons) representing a title to wealth.

After examining in turn each of these means of changing the distribution of wealth, or of the income derived from wealth, we discuss political obstacles to the redistribution of wealth and ways in which they might be overcome.

7.1 TAXATION OF WEALTH-HOLDERS

An annual wealth tax may be levied in proportion to total wealth. Suppose for the time being that any resulting revenue is spent by the government in a way which does not affect the distribution of wealth (this assumption is dropped later). In this case, although the distribution of wealth among wealth-holders is unaffected, inequality between wealth-holders and those with negative or zero wealth is reduced. Of course, a progressive tax on wealth, where there is a tax-free threshold and/or the marginal tax rate increases as wealth increases, makes the distribution of wealth less unequal for all. Alternatively, a tax may be levied on some component or components of wealth. A tax may be levied for example on land, or on houses including or excluding the family home, or on financial assets, or on capital gains. In this case, while inequality between wealth-holders and those with negative or zero wealth is reduced, the effect on the distribution of wealth among wealth-holders will depend on the degree of inequality in the distribution of the taxed component(s) compared with that of those components which are not taxed.

In the late twentieth century, Wolff (1995, p. 35) reported, 11 of the 24 Organisation for Economic Co-operation and Development (OECD) countries taxed wealth-holders annually in conjunction with tax on income, and another two had done so in the past. Of these countries, all exempted some components of wealth (including pension rights and pension-type annuities) from the tax base, and all set a tax-free threshold. In some cases the tax was proportional, in others it was progressive. The maximum tax rate, the marginal tax rate in Sweden for wealth above $140,000, was, however, only 3 per cent.[1]

Wolff (1995, pp. 41–50) estimated the consequences for the United States of introducing either the German, the Swedish or the Swiss wealth tax. Noting that the United States income tax system is itself progressive with respect to wealth, 'tax rates on income rising from 7.2 percent for the lowest wealth class (under \$25,000) to 17.2 percent for the richest (\$1,000,000 or more)' (ibid., p. 46), Wolff concluded that in the United States wealth tax rates

> measured as a percentage of income would rise from zero for the lowest wealth class to 5.7 percent for the highest under the German tax system; from zero to 25.5 percent under the Swedish system; and from zero to 3.2 percent under the Swiss system. (ibid., 1995, p. 46)

Wolff noted also that the introduction of a wealth tax would redistribute wealth from the elderly to the young, from families to the unmarried, and from whites to blacks.

The degree of inequality in the distribution of wealth could alternatively be reduced by taxing not total wealth but increases in wealth. If increases in wealth were solely due to the return on wealth, and the rate of return were uniform, a proportional tax on increases in wealth would not reduce inequality in the distribution of wealth among wealth-holders, though it would reduce inequality between wealth-holders and those with zero or negative wealth. However, if the rate of return on wealth varies directly with the amount of wealth, which as noted in Chapter 4 is commonly the case, a proportional tax on increases in wealth will cause inequality between wealth-holders to be less than it otherwise would be. A progressive tax on increases in wealth would clearly reduce inequality in the distribution of wealth, except in the highly unlikely case that all are wealth-holders and there is a strong inverse correlation between the amount of wealth on the one hand and increases in wealth on the other. Alternatively, inequality in the distribution of wealth would be reduced if the rate of return on the wealth of the less wealthy were increased by measures such as 'profit-sharing schemes, investment trusts specially devised for spreading risks for small savings invested in risky but high-yielding assets, [and] arrangements for the purchase by instalments of their houses by tenants of publicly owned buildings' (Meade, 1976, p. 201).

A principal source of increases in wealth is saving. A proportional tax on saving is thus likely to reduce inequality in the distribution of wealth in a society some of whose members do not save, and a progressive tax on saving is likely to reduce inequality in the distribution of wealth even if everyone saves. A tax on saving was advocated over a century ago by A.F. Mummery and J.A. Hobson (1889, p. 205), albeit as a remedy for underconsumption, namely a ratio of consumption to output too low to generate full employment.[2]

Alternatively, savings might be exempted from taxation altogether. This would involve the replacement of the existing income tax by a progressive consumption tax, as advocated by John Stuart Mill, Alfred Marshall, A.C. Pigou and Irving Fisher, and also by Nicholas Kaldor (1955). Writing in the context of post-war austerity, Kaldor was concerned above all with the injustice of a system that allowed the wealthy to maintain high levels of expenditure on consumer goods by reducing their wealth (dis-saving), an option that was not open to those without significant wealth. More recently the case for an expenditure tax has been made by Robert Frank (2011), on the rather different grounds that it would reduce the harm done by the futile and wasteful 'expenditure arms races' that occur when households and individuals attempt to maintain or enhance their social status by outlaying more on conspicuous consumption goods than their neighbours. This, Frank argues, is a zero-sum game, exactly like an arms race between two or more super-powers, and it has damaging social and environmental consequences. Once again, it is clear that the highly unequal opportunities for dis-saving that are offered by a highly unequal distribution of wealth need to be taken very seriously.

Another important source of increases in wealth is capital gains, which occur when an asset increases in value above the cost of its acquisition. As of 1990, 15 OECD countries reduced the rate at which wealth would otherwise be accumulated by imposing a tax on capital gains realised on asset sales, most commonly by treating capital gains as a component of taxable income. By reducing inequality in the accumulation of wealth, a tax on realised capital gains is likely also to reduce inequality in the distribution of wealth.

If it were the case that the distribution of wealth was equal for every age group, with inequality being entirely explained by the desire of each individual to accumulate wealth during their working life for the sole purpose of maintaining consumption levels after retirement, even egalitarians might oppose the taxation of wealth-holders, accepting that inequality in the distribution of wealth between different age groups does not involve distributive injustice. While in practice inequality in the distribution of wealth is far from entirely explained by lifecycle considerations, as noted in Chapter 4, it is indeed partly explained by them. A government could take this into account by setting the tax-free threshold according to age, making the threshold high until (say) the average retirement age, and lower thereafter. This would enable wealth-holders to be taxed with minimal impact on their lifetime consumption plans. Given the widespread acceptance of the lifecycle hypothesis regarding consumer behaviour, and the fact that an age-related tax on wealth-holders was proposed by Meade as early as 1976 (see Meade, 1976, p. 109), it is somewhat surprising that no government has so far implemented such a tax. A possible explanation is the political power of the retired, though this does not seem very plausible.

Increased taxation of wealth is commonly seen as one way in which the distribution of income can be made less unequal (see for example Wolff, 1995, pp. 47–50, where the simulated introduction in the United States of a Swedish wealth tax reduced the Gini coefficient for income net of both income and wealth taxes from 0.50 to 0.48). It is also true, however, that increased taxation of income is one way in which the distribution of wealth can be made less unequal. Given that saving is a principal source of increases in wealth, and that saving is a function of after-tax income, the distribution of wealth can be changed indirectly through a change in the taxation of income. *Ceteris paribus*, the more equal the distribution of after-tax income, the more equal will be the level of saving, and hence the more equal the accumulation of wealth. Increasing the degree of progression in an income tax structure is thus likely to reduce the degree of inequality in the distribution of wealth. By contrast with a tax on wealth, on increases in wealth or on saving, a tax on income has the advantage that, in principle at least, it does not distort a household's choice between consumption and saving.[3] Moreover, if a government desired to reduce the inequality of the distribution of income as well as of wealth, it could achieve both objectives using the one instrument of increased progressivity in the income tax structure.

A tax on wealth will increase the revenue flowing from taxation provided that wealth-generation is not too responsive to taxation, or more precisely, provided that the tax elasticity of wealth-generation is less than one. Where this is so, if the tax proceeds are divided among those with negative or zero wealth, a tax on wealth is likely to reduce inequality in the distribution of wealth in two ways. It would be certain to have dual consequences if the recipients were for a time barred from using their newly acquired wealth for consumption purposes. The government might, for example, make it a condition of receipt of a portion of the tax proceeds that until (say) retirement the recipient continued to hold the wealth, being permitted only to change the form in which it was held; since acceptance of the wealth transfer would be voluntary, even a libertarian might not object to such a stipulation. The cash received could thus be used to buy bonds or equities, or a house, or to contribute to a superannuation scheme, but not (until retirement) to buy consumer goods.

Alternatively, the proceeds from a tax on wealth could be used to fund the 'KidSave' scheme proposed in the United States by Senator Robert Kerrey in 1997. Under the KidSave scheme every American child would be guaranteed $1,000 at birth plus $500 for each of the first five years of life, to be invested until retirement under the auspices of Social Security, with parents and then grown children being able to opt for high-, medium- or low-risk funds. While at an 8.5 per cent compound interest rate of return this would result in every American at age 65 having wealth amounting to at least $720,000, available to fund their retirement and/or leave inheritances to their children (see Collins, Leondar-Wright and Sklar, 1999, pp. 62–3 and 93), it is totally unrealistic to expect such a high rate of return in real terms, and an 8.5 per cent nominal rate of return has no real significance unless the expected inflation rate is specified. Nonetheless, provided the rate of return substantially exceeded the inflation rate, this would result in every American having a significant amount of wealth at the time of retirement. A scheme similar to KidSave, but requiring a contribution by parents and accessible for wealth-enhancing purposes at age 18, labelled Nest-Egg Accounts, was a few years later proposed in Australia by the then Labour Party Opposition front-bencher, subsequently Opposition Leader, Mark Latham. Funding a KidSave or Nest-Egg Accounts scheme by means of a tax on wealth also, by contrast with funding it in a way which of itself left the distribution of wealth unaffected, would have a dual effect on the distribution of wealth.

A similar measure is among the 15 policy proposals made by Anthony Atkinson (2015, pp. 302–4). His 'Proposal 6' is for a 'capital endowment' or 'minimum inheritance' to be paid by the state to all citizens on reaching adulthood. Most of Atkinson's recommendations concern the redistribution of income, but two more are directly relevant to the distribution of wealth. 'Proposal 10' is that receipts from inheritance and gifts *inter vivos* should be taxed under a progressive lifetime capital receipts tax, and 'Proposal 11' calls for a proportional or progressive property tax based on up-to-date property assessments, which would restore the local government rating system in Britain that was abolished by the Thatcher government in the late 1980s. Atkinson does not advocate a tax on total wealth, listing this only as an 'idea to pursue', along with several other tax reforms.

Instruments available for redistributing wealth are not confined to those which involve the taxation of wealth-holders. An alternative is taxation of wealth transfers. The distribution of wealth can be influenced by taxing either transferors, thereby reducing the amount they can transfer, or transferees, thereby reducing the amount they receive. This instrument of change in the distribution of wealth is dealt with in the next section of this chapter.

7.2 TAXATION OF WEALTH TRANSFERS

It is very often the case that a wealth-holder has at some stage been the transferee in a transfer of wealth. The fraction of the amount given actually received by a transferee depends on the tax regime. Transferors, for example, may be subject to either a gift tax on wealth they pass on during their lifetime, or to an estate tax on the wealth they leave at the time of death, or both. This would of course be inconsistent with the libertarian position on the absolute right to inherit – 'from each as they choose, to each as they are chosen' (Nozick, 1974, p. 160) – though it should be noted that in his later work Nozick retreated from his earlier uncompromising position and revised his views on the ethics of inheritance (Lacey, 2001, pp. 73, 96).[4]

Likewise, transferees may be subject either to a gift tax on gifts received during the lifetime of the giver, or to an inheritance tax on a bequest willed by a deceased person, or both. With respect to inheritance, John Stuart Mill ([1848], 1965, pp. 218 and 225) ventured the opinion that 'although the right of bequest, or gift after death, forms part of the idea of private property, the right of inheritance, as distinct from bequest, does not', concluding that 'what anyone should be permitted to acquire, by bequest or inheritance', should be limited to the means of a comfortable independence. By contrast with a tax on gifts given or an estate tax, in any case, from an egalitarian point of view a tax on gifts received or an inheritance tax has the advantage that it can take into account the wealth of each transferee.[5] For example, as Meade (1976, p. 202) pointed out, with a progressive inheritance tax including a tax-free threshold

> a wealthy man could avoid all tax by leaving his property in small amounts to a number of persons who were themselves not at all wealthy. The incentive to redistribute property by gift or bequest would be at a maximum.

As Meade added, a

> variant of this scheme is an Accession Duty where the rate of tax rises not according to the total wealth of the recipient but according to the total amount he has already received up to date by way of gift or inheritance. Such a variant penalises the wealth received by gift or inheritance but not wealth accumulated by the recipient from his own effort and savings. (ibid., p. 202, footnote 5)

As of 1990, 22 of the 24 OECD countries had a tax on wealth transfers, Australia and Canada being the only exceptions. In the case of three countries it was only the transferor who was taxed, subject to different tax thresholds, and characterised by progressive marginal tax rate structures ranging from 3 per cent at one extreme to 60 per cent at the other, the exception in the latter case being New Zealand, which had a proportional tax rate of 40 per cent on deceased estates. (The New Zealand estate tax rate was subsequently reduced to zero and the tax itself was repealed in

1999 (Duff, 2005).) In the case of 17 countries it was only the transferee who was taxed, again subject to different tax thresholds and marginal tax rate structures, both of these commonly depending on the relationship of the transferee to the transferor (Italy had both an estate tax and an inheritance tax.) In the United States there have been repeated attempts to repeal the federal estate tax (Graetz and Shapiro, 2005), though at the time of writing opponents of the tax have succeeded only in raising the threshold at which it becomes payable.

Taxation of wealth transfers will increase revenue from taxation, provided that introducing the tax does not eliminate wealth transfers, or more precisely, provided that the tax elasticity of wealth transfers is less than infinite. Accordingly taxation of wealth transfers is likely to reduce inequality in the distribution of wealth, and if the tax proceeds are divided among those with negative or zero wealth it will have a dual effect.

7.3 COMMUNAL OWNERSHIP OF WEALTH

Human societies have not always been characterised by private ownership of wealth. In tribal societies wealth, comprising 'farmlands, pastures, hunting or fishing territories' (Sahlins, 1972, p. 93), commonly belonged to the tribal chief. The tribal chief had the duty of allocating use of these resources among the families who made up the tribe, though in allotting resources he was subject to various conventions, such as the convention that every family was to have access to some resources. Even houses might be communally owned, being reallocated for example on the death of a family member. Because resources were not privately owned, products were not privately owned either; they were 'pooled', their distribution among members of the tribe, that is to say the distribution of income derived from wealth, also being a matter of convention. In such societies, while the distribution of income derived from wealth is determined by a combination of custom and command, the question of how wealth is to be distributed does not arise.

While very few societies governed by custom and command exist today, communal ownership of wealth can alternatively involve distributional decision-making by the members of the community collectively. In this case the income derived from wealth is shared by all, instead of being claimed exclusively by the wealth-holder, as is the case in capitalist societies. Such communal ownership can take a number of forms.

One form of communal ownership is a producer co-operative, defined by Derek C. Jones (1980, p. 142) as an autonomous enterprise in which the initial structure and organisation is such that: (a) many workers (usually by individual ownership of stock) are members of the firm; (b) worker-members participate in the enterprise's control and management; (c) control is usually on the basis of one-member-one-vote . . . ; and (d) worker-members share in the net income (surplus) and capital is paid a fixed and limited return.

All of these criteria are satisfied by the Mondragon producer co-operatives in the Basque region of Spain, the first of which was established in 1956; their characteristics are described in some detail in Jones (1980, un-numbered table, p. 149). Now as Jaroslav Vanek (1970, p. 2) pointed out, the members of a producer co-operative 'enjoy collectively the *usufruct* of the assets of the enterprise but not full ownership, in the sense that they can neither destroy the assets nor sell them and distribute the proceeds as income'. Since the share of the *usufruct* received by each member is determined by democratic vote, the distribution of the *usufruct* need not be equal. Even if it were equal within each producer co-operative, in an economy in which all enterprises were producer co-operatives there would only be an equal distribution of the *usufruct* among all members of the society if there were 'easy entry of competitors or a well-functioning market in firm memberships' (Putterman, Roemer and Silvestre, 1998, p. 886). If at least one of these two conditions is satisfied, the resulting equal distribution of the *usufruct* among members of the society could be regarded, from the point of view of distribution of well-being, as the communal counterpart of a capitalist society in which wealth is equally distributed.

Alternatively, a communal ownership counterpart of a capitalist society in which wealth is equally distributed may take the form of all capital and land being owned by a local government which is required to distribute the income derived from wealth equally among the local citizenry. As in the case of a producer co-operative society, equal distribution of the income derived from wealth among citizens of all localities would only occur if the firms in each locality were open to competition, such as has occurred in China (see ibid., p. 886).

Third, a communal ownership equivalent of a capitalist society in which wealth is distributed equally may take the form of all capital and land being owned by a central government which is required to distribute the income derived from wealth equally among all its citizens. Attempts to establish such a distributional arrangement in any society larger than a tribe have been so short-lived that we may question whether such a system is compatible with human nature. For example, while central government ownership of capital and land was in place in the communist Union of Soviet Socialist Republics (USSR) for most of the 75 years of its existence, between 1917 and 1991, from 1931, at Joseph Stalin's instigation, wages became highly unequal, and when 'perks' are taken into account the distribution of income was even more unequal (see Nove, 1992, p. 211).

Elements of communal ownership may coexist with private property. In France, for example, since 1554 the produce remaining after harvest belongs not to the property-owner, but to the first to glean it (examples are to be found in the 2000 Agnes Varda film *Les glaneurs et la glaneuse*).

7.4   DISTRIBUTION BY ISSUE OF VOUCHERS

In the 1990s, governments in Russia and Eastern European countries decided to replace communal with private ownership of wealth. They were thus faced with the question of how wealth was to be distributed among individuals/households. In most cases the issue of vouchers entitling their holders to wealth played some part.

The theoretical underpinnings of wealth voucher systems were outlined in *Privatization in Eastern Europe: Is the State Withering Away?* (1994), written by Roman Frydman and Andrzej Rapaczynski, the authors of a 1990 paper which provided the basis for the voucher system introduced in Poland. The voucher system introduced at the same time in Czechoslovakia, as it then was, differed from the Polish system in that it did not make any provision for each privatised enterprise to have at least one large stakeholder, and it is the Czechoslovakian version which appears to have provided the basis for the voucher system succinctly outlined in Roemer (1994b), though Roemer's system differs fundamentally from the Czechoslovakian one in that it prohibits the exchange of vouchers for money.

Roemer envisaged an economy comprising citizens, public firms, mutual funds and the state treasury, in which on reaching adult age all citizens would receive from the government an equal amount of coupons. In Roemer's coupon economy only coupons can be used to buy shares in mutual funds, which alone can buy shares in public firms, using these coupons. Coupons are thus the currency in which prices of shares in both mutual funds and public firms are denominated. Money enters the picture only in transactions involving public firms and the state treasury, public firms selling coupons to raise investment funds, and buying coupons from the state treasury when they accumulate more money than they require for investment purposes. A citizen or mutual fund holding a share in a mutual fund or public firm respectively is entitled to a proportionate share in profits. On the other hand, citizens are prohibited from making *inter vivos* gifts of mutual fund shares, and at the time of death their mutual fund shares must be sold and the resulting coupons returned to the state treasury. Roemer's coupon economy is characterised by a relatively equal distribution of wealth. As Roemer (1994b, p. 462) put it, because

> shares can be purchased only with coupons and coupons cannot be sold by citizens for money, rich citizens will not generally own more shares than will poor citizens except insofar as they are better informed about investment opportunities. This effect is mollified by the requirement to purchase mutual funds [shares], not the shares of individual firms. Of course, some citizens will end up holding relatively valuable portfolios of mutual funds, but those cannot be bequeathed to children.

In the society described by Roemer, coupons, though not exchangeable for money, are marketable. Individuals/households would thus enjoy not only a relatively equal distribution of wealth, but also many of the benefits of wealth itself, as opposed to just the income derived from wealth. Unfortunately Roemer made no reference to the benefits of wealth itself when setting out his Table A1 (Roemer, 1994a, pp. 136–7), which shows that the ratio between the 'dividend per adult' resulting from redistribution of the wealth of the non-financial corporate sector of the United States economy through distribution to adults of coupons entitling each to an equal share on the one hand, and the median income of black males (used as a proxy for the poverty level) on the other, while as high as approximately 0.25 in 1950, fell to approximately 0.025 in 1989.

By contrast with Roemer's system, the voucher scheme introduced in Russia in 1992 allowed shares and other assets to be alternatively purchased with cash, permitted vouchers to be sold for cash, and gave preference to enterprise insiders (see Frydman et al., 1993, p. 66). Although almost all Russians collected their vouchers, the resulting distribution of state-owned wealth, as vouchers were used over the subsequent two years to purchase shares in state enterprises, was predictably highly unequal (see Brady, 1999, pp. 71–85).

7.5 POLITICAL OBSTACLES AND THEIR REMOVAL

> [I]f equalization of the distribution of wealth is possible through the electoral process, and if it is in the interest of the large majority of people (as would appear to be the case since median wealth is far below mean wealth in all capitalist democracies), why is it not implemented through political action by rational citizens? (Putterman et al., 1998, p. 892)

Putterman et al. suggested six answers to this question. First, voters believe that reducing inequality in the distribution of wealth would reduce the aggregate amount of wealth to such an extent that each would have less wealth than before – a view examined in detail in Chapter 8. Second, although current voters believe that redistribution of wealth would result in a steady state in which most future voters are better off, they are not prepared to pay the transition costs, which would be particularly high if the redistribution took place in only one or a few countries and resulted in emigration of capital and ability, also a view which is examined in Chapter 8. Third, government decisions are determined not by the will of the majority but by small interest groups, because their activities are less handicapped by the presence of 'free rider' members than are those of large interest groups. Fourth, the cost of informing oneself about how the economy works is greater than the expected beneficial effect of one's vote: hence rational ignorance. Moreover, the media, which influence the beliefs of voters, are owned and closely controlled by large capitalist interests that benefit from convincing voters that egalitarian political projects are self-defeating (Putterman et al., 1998, p. 893).

As Piketty (1995) pointed out, however, each voter's beliefs may alternatively be formed by personal experience, a majority voting against a redistribution of wealth in a society where most voters believe that their income, and consequently wealth, depends mainly on their effort and very little on luck. Fifth, voters with low wealth may wish to leave open the possibility that one day they or their descendants may become relatively wealthy, an attitude which it is perfectly rational for each to take even though it is impossible for all to achieve this goal; in Australia, during the election campaign in 2001, such individuals became known as 'aspirational voters'. As a result, voters may be reluctant to vote in ways which might constrain what they hope will be their wealthier future selves or descendants. Sixth, while the position of the median voter is crucial in a single-issue two-party democracy, in practice many democracies are multi-party, and even in two-party democracies redistribution of wealth is only one of many political issues and may well be dominated by one or more of the other issues (this last case is analysed in Roemer, 1998).

Recent research examining popular perceptions of levels of inequality also has implications for the challenges faced in implementing policies to change inequality (in either direction). These examples focus on income inequality, but they have important implications for the nature of political constraints in changing inequality in the distribution of wealth and, if similar results hold for perceived levels of wealth inequality, the implications would apply to wealth inequality as well. In two studies examining perceived levels of wealth inequality in the United States and in Australia, Norton and Ariely (2011) and Norton et al. (2014) conducted surveys to determine the level of inequality people believed to exist in their country

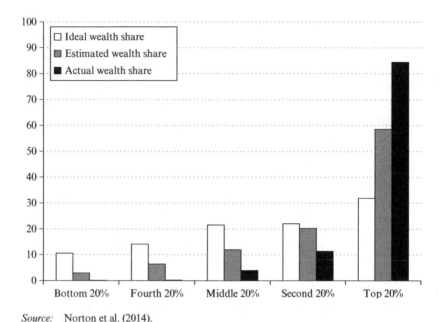

Source: Norton et al. (2014).

Figure 7.1   Ideal, estimated and actual distribution of wealth in the United States, by quintile

and the level of inequality they thought to be desirable in their country. In both countries, survey subjects perceived the level of inequality to be worse than desired. When compared with the *actual* level of inequality in these countries, however, subjects' perceptions also *underestimated* the extent of inequality in their countries, as shown in Figures 7.1 and 7.2.

One implication of these studies is that a population will underestimate the degree of redistribution required in order to reach its ideal level of inequality. In this case, a population's preferences for policies that redistribute wealth will be insufficient to achieve the level of inequality that is considered ideal. This suggests that even in an ideal-type representative political system, in the absence of any other practical or political constraints, this misperception alone will frustrate efforts to achieve the popularly desired level of inequality. However, one recent study of relevant political conflicts in 19 countries between 1816 and 2000 found that it was mass mobilisation for war, and not the coming of universal suffrage, that proved crucial in the introduction of inheritance taxation (Scheve and Stasavage, 2012). Evidently the politics of wealth equalisation is a complicated business.

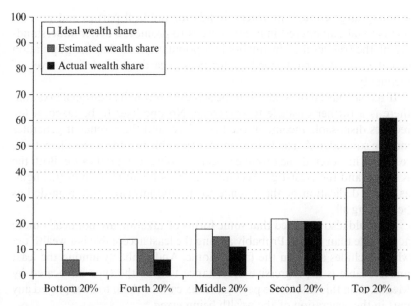

Source: Norton et al. (2014).

Figure 7.2 Ideal, estimated and actual distribution of wealth in Australia, by quintile

Overcoming these political obstacles would clearly be a mammoth task. Here are a few suggestions. First, anticipating the subject matter of Chapter 8, inform voters that reducing inequality in the distribution of wealth sometimes increases the aggregate amount of wealth rather than reduces it, and that while this might be the case less often if the initial distribution of wealth were relatively equal, it is likely to be quite often the case given the current degree of inequality in the distribution of wealth. Second, redistribute wealth slowly enough for the transition costs to be shared over more than one generation. Third, inform voters of the extent of inequality in the distribution of wealth, in the hope that egalitarian interest groups will form. Fourth, increase funding of public institutions involved in the advancement or dissemination of knowledge without fear or favour, such as universities, the British Broadcasting Corporation and the Australian Broadcasting Corporation. Fifth, inform voters that the probability of someone who is relatively poor becoming relatively wealthy is very low; if voters are convinced, only risk-lovers will remain in favour of the current inequality in the distribution of wealth. If some or all of these measures were taken, redistribution of wealth might become an issue looming large enough in voters' minds for political parties and governments to take an interest in it. Sixth, work to promote a better understanding of the true level of inequality in a population, so that the population can develop better-informed preferences regarding its desired level of inequality.

If redistribution of wealth is to be achieved through additional taxation, there is a further obstacle to overcome. No one likes to be taxed; a tax reduces disposable income in the first place, and the revenue it generates may be squandered. The reduction in disposable income is less likely to be resented, however, if the revenue is seen as going to a good cause. Both the KidSave and the Nest-Egg Accounts schemes might be seen in this light, as might dedication of the revenue to specific infrastructure regarded as benefitting all.

It should also be noted that some forms of taxation are politically more acceptable than others. Probably among the least acceptable is a wealth tax which includes a tax on the family home. And probably among the least unacceptable is a progressive inheritance tax, of the type advocated by Meade, as in this case those paying the tax cannot claim to have played any part in the generation of the wealth being taxed.[6]

NOTES

1. Wolff's source is the Organisation for Economic Co-operation and Development, *Taxation of Net Wealth, Capital Transfers and Capital Gains of Individuals* (1988). The OECD (2001, p. 34) included a paragraph on wealth taxes conveying *inter alia* the information that the number of OECD countries levying a net wealth tax was currently ten, a net decrease of one compared with the state of affairs described in OECD (1988).
2. For a comprehensive account of underconsumption, see Schneider (1987).
3. In practice an income tax may distort the choice between consumption and saving, to an extent dependent on the way in which income is defined, as Nicholas Kaldor argued when proposing an expenditure tax (Thirlwall, 1987, pp. 120–29).
4. While Josiah Wedgwood devoted an entire chapter to 'The Justification of Inheritance' (Wedgwood, 1939, chapter VIII), the issue has, rather surprisingly, been neglected by many later authorities. The two-volume, 1,462-page *Encyclopedia of Ethics*, for example, has no entry on the ethics of inheritance, and there are only two references to 'inheritance' in the 99-page index (Becker and Becker, 1992). Two recent texts on economics and ethics ignore the question altogether (Beckerman, 2011; Hausman and McPherson, 2006).
5. Note, however, Harry G. Johnson's contention with respect to wealth transfer taxes that 'due to the state's greed for revenue, the tax is usually based on the amount left by the testator rather than the amounts received by the heirs' (Johnson, 1975, p. 17).
6. For a comprehensive discussion of how to change distribution, focusing on the redistribution of income, see Boadway and Keen (2000).

8. Equality versus affluence?

> *Every policy which one might adopt in order to influence the distribution of . . .*
> *properties will have other effects and, in particular, will affect the efficiency of*
> *the economic system.* (Meade, 1976, p. 189)

The wealth of individuals, and hence their well-being, depends not only on the fraction of the social cake of wealth they possess, but also on the size of that cake. And the size of that cake, that is to say the amount of aggregate wealth available for distribution, depends *inter alia* on the distribution of wealth, for reasons explored in this chapter. But does its size increase or decrease when the distribution of wealth becomes (say) less unequal? The question to be examined, in other words, is whether greater equality in the distribution of wealth can be achieved only at the expense of affluence, or whether instead greater equality in the distribution of wealth would itself increase affluence.

Discussion of the interconnection between the amount of aggregate wealth available for distribution and one of the determinants of the distribution of wealth, namely the distribution of inherited wealth, goes back as far as 1776. In *The Wealth of Nations* ([1776] 1976, pp. 385–6), Adam Smith argued that both primogeniture (where a deceased estate must pass to the first-born male) and entail (where the division of a deceased estate between descendants is strictly laid down in perpetuity) result in large properties whose relatively few owners devote themselves to 'ornament', precluding the alternative of land improvement, which is likely to occur where there are numerous small proprietors. In other words, Adam Smith believed that if the amount of wealth in the aggregate, generated by devoting revenue to saving rather than consumption, is to be maximised, inequality in the distribution of inherited wealth, at least of the landed variety, must be limited.

Adam Smith's near-contemporary and interpreter to the French, Jean-Charles-Leonard Simonde de Sismondi ([1824] 1957, p. 36), came to a similar conclusion, as the following passage indicates:

> Let all laws be abolished which interfere with the division of inheritance and which, by favouring the formation or preservation of large fortunes, prevent capital or land from being distributed in small lots among those who do manual labour.

Sismondi's reasoning, however, was somewhat different from that of Adam Smith, his view being that a less unequal distribution of inherited wealth would result in 'unproductive' consumption (of luxuries) by the rich (Adam Smith's 'ornament') being replaced by consumption (of necessities) by those who are not rich, which would be 'productive' in the sense that it provided sustenance for further productive activity.

By contrast J.R. McCulloch, while arguing that individuals should not be required to follow any fixed rule in the division of their property among their children, observed that even primogeniture has its advantages in that the attempt on the part of the other classes 'to emulate the splendour of the richest landlords' (McCulloch, [1825] 1995, p. 272) will act as a powerful incentive to their industry and enterprise. However, John Stuart Mill came to a different conclusion:

> No doubt, persons have occasionally exerted themselves more strenuously to acquire a fortune from the hope of founding a family in perpetuity; but the mischiefs to society of such perpetuities outweigh the value of this incentive to exertion, and the incentives in the case of those who have the opportunity of making large fortunes are strong enough without it. (Mill, [1848] 1965, p. 233)

By 'mischiefs to society' Mill meant injustice, as the following passage indicates:

> Unless a strong case of social utility can be made out for primogeniture, it stands sufficiently condemned by the general principles of justice; being a broad distinction in the treatment of one person and another, grounded solely on an accident. There is no need, therefore to make out any case of economical evil against primogeniture. (Mill, [1848] 1965, p. 892)

He added that such an economic case could nonetheless be made, arguing that the owners of large estates inherited by primogeniture not only typically spend so much supporting both their siblings and their own luxurious way of life that there is nothing left for land improvement, but also are typically reluctant to sell any part of the land to those who could improve it because this would diminish the 'splendour' of the family.

Drawing heavily on Mill, Josiah Wedgwood concluded that 'the ethical arguments in favour of claims to inherit, whether under will or the laws of succession, are extraordinarily weak in the case of near relatives and non-existent in the case of distant relatives and strangers' (Wedgwood 1939, p. 207).

We look next at speculation on the interconnection between the distribution of wealth and the total amount of aggregate wealth available for distribution, which goes back at least as far as 1802. Adopting a hierarchical plural-value stance, Bentham argued that while with respect to the distribution of wealth between two individuals '[t]*he more nearly the actual proportion approaches to equality, the greater will be the total mass of happiness*' (Bentham, [1802] 1962, p. 305; original emphasis), '[e]quality ought not to be favoured, except in cases in which it does not injure security' (Bentham, [1802] 1962, p. 303); by 'security' Bentham meant protection of private property by law, a necessary condition for the private accumulation of wealth. Possibly influenced by Bentham, the otherwise egalitarian 'Ricardian socialist' William Thompson (1824, p. 91; original emphasis) similarly concluded:

> *Wherever equality does not lessen production*, it should be the sole object pursued. Wherever it decreases really useful production (that which is attended with preponderant good to producers,) it saps its own existence, and should cease.

Edwin Cannan (1905, pp. 367–8) took the further step of making a judgement as to whether any reduction in the degree of inequality, both in his own time and in the future, would 'sap its own existence', speculating along the following lines:

> The economist regards the existing inequality of distribution as in itself extremely wasteful, but sees that it must in the main be retained for the present, because it provides both the motive force and the regulator for the existing system of production; and, even if it were practicable, it would not be worth while to make and introduce the ideal of distribution if it led to a considerable fall in production per head. The existing inequality, regarded broadly, is, in fact, a necessary evil. But there are many good reasons to suppose that it is greater than is necessary, and for hope, at any rate, that it may in the course of time be largely reduced, if not altogether abolished, without any appreciable injury (or even advantage) to production.

Seventy years later Arthur Okun took a more pessimistic view, in a book to which he gave the title *Equality and Efficiency: The Big Trade-Off* (1975). Okun's position is neatly summed up by his 'leaky bucket experiment', in which he asks the reader how much 'leakage' in the form of inefficiency they would accept in exchange for a given reduction in income inequality; the existence of a 'leakage' is simply taken for granted. The view that there is a negative relationship between the degree of economic equality and economic efficiency, endorsed by the social-democratic Okun, became a relatively unquestioned part of mainstream economics until the last decade of the twentieth century, when during the decades before and after the turn of the century a number of articles on the matter were published (see in particular Bénabou, 1996; Barro, 2000, pp. 5–8; and Voitchofsky, 2009, pp. 275–6).

Theoretical reasons put forward during that period for believing that inequality and economic growth are negatively related include the arguments that where there is relatively great inequality, (1) credit market imperfections particularly affecting the poor will reduce their ability to contribute to economic growth, (2) remedial transfer payments and the associated tax finance will distort economic decisions, as will lobbying activities by the rich to prevent such redistribution, and (3) sociopolitical unrest will reduce productivity. Theoretical reasons put forward for believing that inequality and economic growth are positively related include the arguments that where there is relatively great inequality, (1) large set-up costs will be easier to meet, (2) even though they may wish to do so, the poor will lack the resources, such as education, needed to disrupt economic activity effectively, and (3) assuming the savings rate of the rich is greater than that of the poor, more investment funding will be available (which is the opposite of the underconsumption argument referred to in Chapter 7). The net effect of these negative and positive factors will of course depend on their relative strengths.

8.1   EMPIRICAL EVIDENCE

As far as the empirical investigations are concerned, to the best of our knowledge, there has so far been none that has looked at the relationship between inequality in the distribution of wealth and economic efficiency. One study, however, has examined the relationship between the distribution not only of income but also of human capital on the one hand and economic growth on the other; the remaining studies have investigated the relationship between inequality in the distribution of income and economic growth. We next provide a brief account of these studies, in the belief that this will give some indication of what to expect when a study of the relationship between the distribution of wealth and affluence, as indicated for example by economic growth, is at last undertaken.

Empirical studies undertaken by Alesina and Rodrik (1994) and by Persson and Tabellini (1994) both concluded that there is a negative relationship between inequality and economic growth. Using comprehensive income inequality figures for 112 countries published by Deininger and Squire in 1996, Li et al. (1998) found to the contrary that all tests show a negative correlation between the distribution of income and economic growth, though they admitted that in some cases the correlation was not significant, and cautioned against concluding that the direction of causation was from distribution to growth.

Deineger and Squire's figures for the 84 countries for which he thought them sufficiently reliable were also used by Robert Barro, who in 2000 published a wide-ranging article whose initial finding was that there is no correlation between inequality and either economic growth or the investment that leads to it. When Barro delved deeper, however, by dividing the 84 countries into the categories of poorer and richer, he found that there was a negative correlation for poor countries and a positive correlation for rich countries. He speculated that a reason for this might be the credit-market constraints faced by the less-well-off in poor countries.

The study including distribution of human capital as one of the variables was undertaken by Castello-Climent (2010), who followed Barro in drawing attention to the fact that a generalisation for a group of countries may not apply to sub-groups of countries, or indeed individual countries. In particular, Castello-Climent found that the relationship between inequality in the distribution of human capital and economic growth was negative for low- and middle-wealth countries, but uncorrelated for advanced countries. He also found that the relationship between inequality in income distribution and economic growth was negative for low- and middle-income countries, uncorrelated for continental European countries, and positive for advanced Anglo-Saxon countries, Japan and South Korea.

A study by Voitchovsky (2009) similarly drew attention to the fact that a generalisation applying to a whole society may not apply to individual members or sub-groups of it. Voitchovsky found a positive relationship between inequality in the distribution of income and economic growth in the case of the wealthier members of a society, but a negative relationship in the case of the poorer members of society, the outcome for a society as a whole thus depending on the net outcome of these opposing factors.

An IMF paper by Ostry et al. (2014) investigated the sustained impact on economic growth of measures taken to reduce inequality in the distribution of income. The paper concluded that in some cases these measures actually increased economic growth, in other cases made no difference to economic growth, but in no cases reduced economic growth. In sum, such empirical evidence as exists does not support the view that there is a positive relationship between inequality in the distribution of income and economic growth; if anything, it suggests the opposite.

In the remainder of this chapter we add our own theoretical treatment of the relationship between the distribution of wealth and affluence to the arguments outlined earlier, by considering first a society with a given endowment of labour and natural resources in which, to start with, we also take as given, first the division of income between saving and consumption, and second the division of time between work and leisure and hence the number of hours devoted to work. The aggregate wealth of such a society at any point in time depends principally on the efficiency with which inputs have in the past been turned into outputs. The greater the output per unit of input in the past, the greater will be the past aggregate annual output distributed as income and consequently the past annual aggregate saving contributing to current wealth.

Once the assumption of a given division of income between saving and consumption is dropped, aggregate wealth may vary directly also with the fraction of income devoted to saving, though not necessarily. If individuals save, they increase their wealth. However, as John Maynard Keynes pointed out in *The General Theory of Employment, Interest and Money*, to assume that it is also true that if a society saves, it too increases its wealth, is to commit the fallacy of composition, namely that what is true of each part must be true of the whole. In macroeconomic equilibrium, aggregate saving equals aggregate investment demand. If the saving ratio increases, aggregate investment demand may or may not increase sufficiently to match the planned increase in saving. If it does increase sufficiently, national income will rise to the extent necessary to ensure that the planned increase in saving is realised. If it does not, planned saving will exceed investment demand, the consequent deficiency of aggregate demand will cause the equilibrium level of income to fall, and realised saving will fall short of planned saving. Thus an increase in planned saving will only result in an equal increase in wealth if it is matched by an equal increase in investment demand (Keynes, 1936, chapter 3). This proviso needs to be borne in mind whenever the relationship between saving and aggregate wealth is under discussion.

If the assumption of a given division of time between work and leisure is dropped, the aggregate wealth of our society will also vary directly with the fraction of time devoted to work, at least up to the point where the marginal product of labour ceases to be positive.

Now in any society efficiency, the saving–consumption decision and the work–leisure decision may depend on the distribution of wealth. A less unequal distribution of wealth, for example, might result in either less efficiency, or less income being devoted to saving, or less time being devoted to work, the outcome being a smaller amount of aggregate wealth. If this were the case a policymaker of egalitarian inclinations would be forced to weigh the perceived benefit of a reduction in the inequality of wealth distribution against the consequent reduction in aggregate wealth.

In the remaining sections of this chapter we explore the interconnections between the distribution of wealth on the one hand and efficiency, the saving–consumption decision, and the work–leisure decision on the other. In the immediately following sections of the chapter, we abstract from the complications arising from the fact that each modern economy is open

in the sense that it has interactions with other economies. A subsequent
section of the chapter re-examines the aforementioned interconnections in
an open economy context.

8.2 EFFICIENCY, RISK AND DISTRIBUTION OF PRIVATE PROPERTY

The way in which wealth is distributed in a society may affect the efficiency of its resource allocation. What is meant by 'efficiency'? An
economy is generally said to be efficient if it is impossible to make anyone
better off without making at least one person worse off. Such a situation
is also known as 'Pareto-efficient', following its original description by
Vilfredo Pareto. If an economy is not Pareto-efficient, by contrast, it is
possible to reallocate resources in such a way that the gainers can compensate the losers and still be better off than before; though unlike some
later exponents of the 'compensation principle' such as Kaldor (1939)
and (debatably) J.R. Hicks (1939), Pareto himself refused to approve such
resource reallocation unless compensation was actually paid (see Kemp,
2001, pp. 209–11).

It is useful to distinguish between 'static' and 'dynamic' efficiency.
Ceteris paribus, a necessary condition for 'static efficiency' in an economy
with given resources is that, for a given level of leisure, gross domestic
product (GDP) be maximised, as otherwise someone could become better
off without anyone becoming worse off. And a necessary condition for
'dynamic efficiency' is that for a given level of consumption as well as
leisure, the rate of growth of GDP be maximised. An economy can thus
be said to have become more efficient if with given resources and given
leisure, GDP increases or, for any given level of consumption as well, the
rate of growth of GDP increases.

Efficiency may depend on the distribution of wealth where there is a
'principal–agent relationship', a term which 'has come to be used in economics to refer to situations in which one individual (the agent) acts on
behalf of another (the principal) and is supposed to advance the principal's
goals' (Milgrom and Roberts, 1992, p. 170). An example of such inter-
dependence is to be found in a 1984 article by Carl Shapiro and Joseph
E. Stiglitz. Shapiro and Stiglitz considered the principal–agent relationship
involved where workers act on behalf of, and are supposed to advance
the goals of, their employer. In this situation each worker has an incentive to become a 'free rider', that is, to put in less effort than everyone else
but enjoy the same wage. Free-riding workers are labelled by Shapiro and
Stiglitz as 'shirkers' if they put in insufficient effort for it to be profitable

for the firm to continue to employ them (because their contribution to the firm's product is less than the wage rate). Shapiro and Stiglitz assumed that it is not profitable for the firm to devote sufficient resources to discover which of its workers are shirkers (monitoring costs are too high), and as a result a shirker faces only a less than 100 per cent probability of being identified as a shirker and consequently fired. In the Shapiro and Stiglitz economy, further, the unemployed receive a given unemployment benefit rate which is below the wage rate paid by any firm. Assuming workers to be risk-neutral, in these circumstances the number of shirkers will vary inversely with the gap between the wage rate and the unemployment benefit rate, this gap being a measure of the penalty for being caught shirking. As it is not profitable for a firm to employ a shirker, each firm will pay a wage rate sufficiently high to deter shirking. And this wage rate must be above that which equates demand and supply in the labour market, because if no one is unemployed there is no deterrent to shirking. Hence the demand for labour will fall short of its supply.

Now if the government taxes pure profits, defined as any excess of price over average cost (including interest and the going compensation for risk-taking), and uses the proceeds to subsidise wages, it will be profitable for firms to employ more workers, and national income will rise. Hence, for any given saving ratio, aggregate wealth will rise. Thus assuming that those who receive profits are more wealthy than those who earn wages, this redistribution of income in a less unequal direction increases the level of aggregate wealth.

Noting that '[w]hile it would increase aggregate output (net of effort costs), such a tax policy would *not* constitute a Pareto improvement, since profits would fall', Shapiro and Stiglitz concluded with respect to the pre-tax situation that:

> the equilibrium is Pareto optimal in this case, even though it fails to maximise net national product. We thus have the unusual result that the Pareto optimality of the equilibrium depends on the distribution of wealth. (Shapiro and Stiglitz, 1984, p. 440)

Although Shapiro and Stiglitz referred here to the distribution of wealth, the tax policy they considered actually involves a redistribution of income. Similar consequences would follow, however, from a wages subsidy funded by a tax on, and consequently redistribution of, wealth.

When the Shapiro and Stiglitz example is varied to incorporate a tax on wealth instead of on profits, it illustrates a fundamental point made by Stiglitz (1994, p. 48), namely that while a situation may be Pareto-efficient, a redistribution of wealth could result in another Pareto-efficient situation combined with an increase in national output. More specifically, the example shows that while inefficiency resulting from a principal–agent problem may not be removable given the existing distribution of wealth, it may be removable if wealth is redistributed. Reduction of inefficiency, in turn, makes it possible for aggregate wealth to be increased.

The Shapiro and Stiglitz economy is an example of an economic system in which at least one of the necessary conditions for market forces to generate Pareto-efficiency may not be satisfied. These conditions comprise information being fixed in the sense that it is 'unaffected by any action taken by any individual, any price, or any variable affected by the collective action of individuals in the market' (Stiglitz, 1994, p. 29), and the existence of a complete set of markets providing insurance against risk. Where these conditions are not satisfied 'the actions of individuals have externality-like effects on others, which they fail to take into account' (ibid., p. 29), and because the government has powers of compulsion that the private sector does not, 'there are interventions by the government that could be unambiguously welfare improving' (ibid., p. 29). As Stiglitz noted, the existence of such interventions, arising solely out of powers of compulsion, does not depend on the government having more information than the private sector.

In an economy where economies of scale are present, there is a further connection between efficiency and the distribution of wealth. In those industries where economies of scale exist, large firms are more efficient than small ones. Large firms may have many shareholders. If there are many shareholders in a firm and they all own the same number of shares, it is probable that they will have little influence on the decisions made by the firm's managers. When the principal–agent relationship takes this form, the outcome may be a firm operating inefficiently, for reasons neatly summarised by James A. Brickley, Clifford W. Smith and Jerold L. Zimmerman (1996, pp. 131–2) as follows:

> At least four sources of conflict arise between shareholders and managers: (1) Choice of effort – additional effort by the manager generally increases the value of the firm, but additional effort can reduce the utility of the manager. (2) Differential risk exposure – managers typically have substantial levels of human capital and personal wealth invested in the firm. This large investment can make managers overly risk-averse from the standpoint of the shareholders who typically hold only a small fraction of their wealth in any one firm. For example, managers might forgo profitable projects because they do not want to bear the risk. (3) Differential horizons – the manager's claim on the corporation is generally limited to her tenure with the firm. The corporation, on the other hand, has an indefinite life, and stockholder claims are tradable claims on the entire future stream of residual cash flows. Managers, therefore, have incentives to place lower values on cash flows occurring beyond their horizon than is implied by

the market values of these cash flows. (4) Free-cash-flow problems – a manager might be reluctant to reduce the size of the firm by paying cash out of the firm (for example as dividends) even if the firm has no profitable investment projects. Rather the manager might prefer to empire-build.

This tendency of manager-agents to disregard the interests of owner-principals has been referred to by Demsetz (1995) as the 'control problem'. One might think that this problem is best solved by having firms with a single owner, who is in a better position to force managers to run the firm efficiently than multiple owners would be. But, as Demsetz pointed out, this would expose each owner to excessive firm-specific risk. On the other hand, major shareholders will not be able to control the operations of a firm if their monitoring time is spread too thinly, and they will therefore use their wealth to buy shares in a limited number of firms. Using the 'working assumption that capital markets in the United States have provided us with a rough estimate of the noninstitutional ownership structure required to establish effective control of large firms', Demsetz (1995, p. 46) concluded that the minimum percentage of shares in a large firm held by the five largest non-institutional shareholders should be 10 per cent between them. Thus for large firms to operate efficiently, a society needs a minimum number of people who are wealthy enough to own 2 per cent of several large firms. For any given amount of aggregate wealth, the more large firms there are, the greater the inequality in the distribution of wealth required if these firms are to operate efficiently.

These considerations led Demsetz to the conclusion that '[e]xtreme inequality *and* extreme equality in wealth distribution both reduce the degree to which effective control can be maintained' (ibid., p. 45). Extreme inequality would result in the time and expertise of the few major share-holders being too widely spread for them to be able to exercise effective control over each firm. On the other hand, if for example in the United States in 1976 wealth had been distributed across families equally, each group of five families would have had only $50,000 to invest, whereas in fact in the firm representing the average of the largest 500 corporations, the five major shareholders invested a total of more than $100 million. Demsetz calculated that for the five largest shareholders to have invested $100 million in each of the largest 500 firms, with no one holding shares in more than one firm, 0.004 per cent of families would have had to have owned 8.33 per cent of the nation's wealth.

Let us take the argument a step further than Demsetz did by assuming specifically that, to reduce firm-specific risk, wealthy shareholders put their eggs not in just one basket but, using a conservative estimate, in four. In this case, to satisfy Demsetz's criterion for efficiency, 8.33 per cent of the nation's wealth would have had to be owned by a quarter of the number of the nation's families estimated by Demsetz, namely 0.001 per cent.

It is interesting to compare this estimate of the concentration of wealth necessary to satisfy Demsetz's criterion for efficiency in 1976 with the Wolff and Marley (1989, p. 784) actual figures for 1981, showing that about 20 per cent of United States wealth was owned by 0.08 per cent of families, figures which suggest it is doubtful whether as much as 8.33 per cent of national wealth was held by only 0.001 per cent of families. The implication is that the distribution of wealth in the United States at that time was possibly insufficiently unequal to satisfy Demsetz's criterion for efficiency.

It might appear that the control problem does not exist where a substantial fraction of a production firm's shares are held by institutional investment funds. In this case, however, the problem reappears in the form of shareholder control of the managers of the funds. Demsetz argued that the control problem is solved only in the case of open-end mutual funds because, unlike production companies and closed-end funds, an open-end mutual fund is obliged to return the full amount invested by a member on request. And even in this case

> [a]lthough the ability of investors to reclaim funds from an open-end investment fund ameliorates the diffuse investor agency problem that otherwise would arise, it is not clear by just how much. The problem of controlling the fund's management is more effectively dealt with if capital is provided in a concentrated fashion to the fund itself, for this strengthens incentives to monitor and discipline the fund management. Such concentration, however, would make the fund less effective in coping with the wealth distribution problem that has brought it into the present discussion. (Demsetz, 1995, p. 53)

Demsetz went on to acknowledge that the distribution of wealth on the one hand, and efficiency on the other, are connected not only through the control problem, but also in other ways. The distribution of wealth affects the distribution of investment in human capital, Demsetz concluding again that extremes should be avoided. Equal distribution would spread investment in human capital too thinly, and extreme inequality in distribution would result in some latent talent not being realised. Echoing Roemer's reference to a very unequal distribution of wealth as a 'public bad', but providing a somewhat different interpretation of the idea, Demsetz added that '[t]he distribution of wealth also affects the political stability of a nation, and this has important consequences for the productivity of an enterprise' (ibid., p. 47). The implication here presumably is that in the interests of political stability there is a degree of inequality beyond which a nation should not go. In this last context, however, it may be the degree not of inequality but of polarisation – that is, concentration at the two extremes – that is the more relevant (see Esteban and Ray, 1994).

As already noted in Chapter 7, when private ownership of wealth replaces communal ownership it may take the form of wealth-holding by voucher. Where vouchers are distributed equally among the population there is a risk that the number of shareholders in any one firm will be so numerous that owners will be unable to ensure that the managers run the firm efficiently. It is for this reason that the Roemer coupon economy outlined in Chapter 7 incorporates financial intermediaries which act on behalf of many citizens, but are themselves sufficiently few in number for them to be able to monitor the managers of the firms in which they hold shares. Putterman (1996), however, expressed doubts as to whether the Roemer coupon economy would be as efficient as a private property economy in which the title to wealth is money. His argument was that Roemer's

> proposal entails shifting large firms to a 100 per cent leverage basis, making the shareholder a residual claimant but not a supplier of equity. Creditors have reason to shun such leverage and may have to be compensated with higher returns and/or control rights. The first possibility means a diminution in the size of profits, which are the sole object of redistribution in the proposal. Giving too much control right to creditors could actually drive expected dividends and thus share prices to zero, eliminating both the redistributive benefits of the proposal and its retention of an informationally useful share price feature. Socially desirable risk taking would also be reduced. If shareholders retain effective control, on the other hand, the leveraged feature of firms could induce what might be socially *excessive* risk taking. (Putterman, 1996, p. 150)

As Putterman, Roemer and Silvestre (1998, p. 891) wryly noted, if these 'challenges are correct, the attractiveness of Roemer's proposal declines'.

8.3   EFFICIENCY AND COMMUNAL OWNERSHIP

As already noted in Chapter 7, while the distribution of wealth among wealth-holders can be made less unequal by means of taxation, alternatively the distribution of income derived from wealth can be made less unequal by replacing private ownership of capital and land by communal ownership, with the communal agent being required to distribute profits and rent in an egalitarian way. The question examined here is whether such a replacement of private by communal ownership would reduce the amount of wealth in the aggregate, or alternatively perhaps increase it.

Suppose first that all enterprises in an economy are producer co-operatives. Connell Fanning and David O'Mahony (1983, p. 17) argued that

[t]here is no particular need in a worker-directed enterprise to devise incentive schemes for the purpose of encouraging effort. This is automatically achieved by the very nature of such a firm because, given the income-distribution arrangements, the whole work force has a common interest which approximates more nearly to self-employment than to the employee situation in conventional firms.

However, how nearly the interest of each worker in a producer co-operative approximates to self-employment is likely to vary inversely with the size of the co-operative; the larger the co-operative, the easier it is likely to be for a worker to get away with becoming a free rider, sharing equally in the co-operative's output but putting in less effort than everyone else, thereby reducing the co-operative's efficiency. As Alchian and Demsetz (1972, p. 786) put it, '[i]ncentives to shirk are positively related to the optimal size of the team under an equal profit-sharing scheme'.

There is also the question of whether a producer co-operative can be hierarchical and specialised enough to match the efficiency of a privately owned firm. It is not clear that the answer to this question is in the negative. As John P. Bonin and Putterman (1987, pp. 55–6) put it,

> assuming that a certain amount of hierarchy and specialization in decision-making is conducive to more efficient enterprise operations, we cannot rule out the adoption of hierarchical forms by self-managed firms, provided that ultimate control resides in the working body, as opposed to an owner-manager, financial shareholders or the state. . . . If detailed participation in decision-making is not desired, for whatever reason, delegation remains consistent with the principle of ultimate democratic control by the workforce.

It can, however, be argued that producer co-operatives are likely to be dynamically inefficient, in the sense that investment would be sub-optimal, because each worker would have no incentive to invest in projects intended to yield profits beyond the time of their expected working life. Of course the firm might resort to debt finance. But under limited liability workers might in this case be tempted to take excessive risks with lenders' funds. If this were the only permitted source of finance, 'the lender-agency problem would lead to a higher interest rate' (Putterman et al., 1998, p. 886), and although the interest rate would be lower the more shares in the firm were owned by workers, this would be 'at the cost of nondiversification of their human and physical asset portfolios' (ibid., p. 886). As Putterman et al. summarised it, '[r]isk-aversion and liquidity problems could thus explain the limited incidence of pure worker ownership in existing market economies' (ibid., p. 887).

Note, however, that the source of all these problems is resort to debt finance, and that there is an alternative source of finance by which producer co-operatives can be made dynamically efficient, namely the establishment of a revolving fund. In this case a target sum having been agreed on, each year in addition to members receiving a dividend 'a surplus is paid into the revolving fund and the members given dated certificates stating their claim on the dividend which would have been theirs if the retained surplus had been paid out' (Smith, 1983, p. 102). Once the target sum has been achieved, 'the general meeting still declares a dividend to be placed in the fund, but a similar amount is paid out to those who subscribed in the first year' (ibid., p. 102). Thus with a revolving fund, members of a producer co-operative each have a vested interest in the success of the co-operative extending beyond their working life.

Suppose alternatively that all capital and land is owned by a government which is required

> to distribute a nation's profits in a roughly egalitarian manner in the population, through expenditure of profits of state firms by the public treasury, or perhaps by the distribution of dividends directly to citizens. The question is whether either of these two forms of profit distribution can be accomplished by a property form in which good incentives exist for monitoring firm management. (Putterman et al., 1998, p. 889)

We look first at local government ownership. One form of local government ownership is exemplified in late twentieth-century China, where 'township and village enterprises are not corporations, but are owned entirely by the local municipality, which solves the monitoring problem, as local government has every incentive to monitor management' (ibid., p. 889). In this case, however, municipal governments might be tempted to devote to the public sector more of the revenue they receive than efficiency or equity dictates. This problem would not occur in an alternative form of local government ownership involving tradable shares in firms, with restrictions on the amount of shares a local government could hold in firms within its own municipality. But, in this case, 'local governments would presumably have diversified portfolios in the firms of other localities, and the incentive to monitor firms by such municipal units would presumably be slight' (ibid., p. 889).

Central government ownership of firms, too, is likely to involve inadequate monitoring of 'agent' managers by citizen 'principals'. A 'citizen who nominally co-owns a national portfolio of assets has little incentive to monitor their performances and prospects' (ibid., p. 885), since to have an effect on management decision-making any one citizen would have to put in sufficient effort to form an influential coalition of citizens. A more likely outcome is that 'the resources citizens invest in monitoring and attempting to influence politicians vary closely with their prospective gains and losses' (ibid., p. 885), causing inefficiency because 'the potential gains to an involved minority are concentrated while, due to an equal distribution of profits, the potential losses to the less-affected majority are diluted by large numbers' (ibid., p. 885).

No neat conclusion seems to follow. While some co-operatives may be more efficient than the typical capitalist enterprise, others may be less so.

8.4 WEALTH DISTRIBUTION AND THE SAVING–CONSUMPTION CHOICE

Consider a society consisting of well-being-maximisers in which the well-being of each pair of parents is an increasing function first of their lifetime consumption and that of their children, and second of their leisure. Suppose that the work–leisure choice is given for both parents and children, an assumption we retain for the remainder of this section of the chapter. In this society an attempt to decrease inequality in the distribution of wealth by increasing the tax rate on bequests will reduce the well-being accruing to parents from saving, because each dollar saved to provide a bequest will not enable their children to increase their consumption by as much as before. Each pair of parents will therefore save less and consume more. Assuming that aggregate demand and hence national income does not rise as a result of the increased consumption, and that the increased tax revenue (if any) is used in a way that does not affect aggregate wealth, each pair of parents will accumulate less wealth, and the aggregate amount of wealth in the society will fall.

The above is a greatly simplified version of an intra-generational simulation model devised by Davies (1982), who adapted a model developed by Blinder (1974). Davies attempted to make his model realistic by wherever possible using data relating to the Canadian economy (over the period 1964–71) to set parameter values. One of the conclusions that follows from his model is that if, in an attempt to reduce inequality in the distribution of wealth, bequests (including gifts *inter vivos*, presumably) had been taxed not at the existing Canadian rate of 9.7 per cent but at 100 per cent, aggregate wealth in Canada would have dropped over the period 1964–71 by 42 per cent (this figure is implied by Table 1, Davies, 1982, p. 489).[1] Of course if Davies had calculated the effect on aggregate wealth of a less dramatic increase in the tax rate on bequests, say to 20 per cent, the decline in wealth might have turned out to be quite small. Nonetheless, given the assumptions of his model, any increase in the tax on bequests would necessarily have resulted in a lower amount of aggregate wealth.

The Davies model describes the effect on aggregate wealth of the taxation of wealth transfers. Assuming the work–leisure choice to be given, the effect on the saving–consumption choice and hence aggregate wealth will be the same regardless of whether the tax is imposed on the transferor or the transferee.

Suppose alternatively a society in which the government sets out to reduce inequality in the distribution of wealth by increasing taxes on wealth-holders, through increasing tax rates on wealth, or on increases in wealth, or on saving. Those persons whose well-being depends solely on absolute levels of consumption will respond because of both income and substitution effects. The income effect will take the form of less saving as well as less consumption, and the substitution effect of an increase in any of these tax rates will take the form of less saving and more consumption. With respect to saving, the overall effect will unambiguously be a decline, and hence there will be less accumulation of wealth, at least if the reduction in saving does not lead to an increase in aggregate demand, and hence in national income. This conclusion holds even if we relax the assumption that the well-being of all depends solely on absolute levels of consumption and leisure, and assume instead that the well-being of some ('target savers') is maximised when they achieve a target accumulation of wealth; in their case the proportion of income saved will increase so as to achieve the same accumulation of wealth as before. Given that not all are target-savers, however, in the aggregate there is bound to be some reduction in the accumulation of wealth.

One might guess that the wealth-tax elasticity of saving is quite low below a certain threshold, but substantial above it, in which case it would be particularly helpful to know where the threshold lies. While this information is not currently available, we do know that most developed countries levy a tax on wealth, with marginal tax rates on wealth as high as 3 per cent. Since governments do not usually kill the goose that lays the golden egg, we may conclude that taxes on wealth with marginal tax rates of this order probably do not significantly reduce the amount of aggregate wealth.

8.5   WEALTH DISTRIBUTION AND THE WORK– LEISURE CHOICE

The Davies model outlined in the previous section of this chapter can be extended to illustrate some of the interconnections between the distribution of wealth, the work–leisure choice and the amount of aggregate wealth, by dropping Davies' assumption that the work–leisure choice for both parents and children is given. As Robbins (1930, pp. 123–6) demonstrated, where the income received by workers is taxed, the amount of effort workers exert will fall if 'the elasticity of demand for income in terms of effort is greater than unity' (ibid., p. 123), that is to say, if the income effect of the tax (workers reduce both income and leisure, due to being worse off as a result of the lower post-tax reward for each unit of effort) is outweighed by the substitution effect (workers substitute leisure for effort, due to the lower cost of leisure in terms of post-tax reward for each unit of effort); conversely, the amount of work they do will rise if the income effect of the tax outweighs its substitution effect.[2] Thus the consequences of an increase in tax rates on wealth transfers will depend on whether the income or the substitution effect is the greater.

Parents for whom the substitution effect is the greater will not only save less, but also work less and enjoy more leisure, since continuing to work for the same number of hours as previously would now subtract from their well-being. Not only will these parents save a smaller proportion of each dollar of income, they will now also have less income out of which to save. However, once they reach working age the children of these parents, with less wealth coming from bequests, will work more than they would otherwise have done, at the expense of leisure, and with a given saving ratio they will consequently save more. Hence, taking the two generations into account, it is not clear *a priori* whether aggregate wealth will fall or rise.

Parents for whom the income effect is the greater, on the other hand, though also saving less, will work more at the expense of leisure, as continuing to work for only the same number of hours as previously would result in less well-being than was now possible. While these parents save a smaller proportion of each dollar of income, they will now have more income out of which to save, leaving the net effect on saving uncertain. Once they reach working age the children of those parents whose net saving increases, with more wealth coming from bequests, will work less than they would otherwise have done, enjoying more leisure, and with a given saving ratio they will consequently save less. Again, taking the two generations into account, it is not clear *a priori* whether aggregate wealth will rise or fall.

Suppose alternatively that a government wishing to decrease the inequality of wealth distribution, and noting that an important determinant of the distribution of wealth is the distribution of income, increases income tax rates, leaving families with a lower after-tax return from work. Well-being-maximisers will respond because of both income and substitution effects. The income effect will take the form of less after-tax income and less leisure, and the substitution effect will take the form of less income as a result of working less and enjoying more leisure. Assuming the proportion of after-tax income saved is unaffected, there will be less saving, and hence less accumulation of wealth. The proportion of after-tax income saved will, however, be affected in the case of those whose well-being is maximised when they achieve a target level of wealth; in their case the proportion of after-tax income saved will increase so as to achieve the same accumulation of wealth as before. Once again, unless all fall into this category, there is bound in the aggregate to be some reduction in the accumulation of wealth.

A tendency since around 1980 to reduce maximum marginal income tax rates from levels which in some countries exceeded 50 per cent could perhaps be taken as an indication that governments have come to believe that such high marginal tax rates cause GDP, and hence saving and wealth accumulation, to be lower than it otherwise would be.

A pertinent example of the interconnection between the distribution of wealth and the choice between work and leisure is to be found in share-cropping (alternatively known as *métayage*), a not uncommon arrangement both in Europe in past centuries and in developing countries at the present time. Sharecropping involves two classes, those who own land and those who do not, with tenant-farmers sharing the proceeds of their work with the landlord. As in the case of an employer of workers, sharecropping too involves a principal–agent relationship, the tenant-farmer acting on behalf of, and being supposed to advance the goals of, the landlord.

If the income effect of tenant-farmers receiving less than 100 per cent of what they produce is outweighed by the substitution effect, in the absence of either effective monitoring, or a sufficiently attractive contract, tenant-farmers will put in less effort than would be the case if they were entitled to the entire product. As Pranab Bardhan, Samuel Bowles and Herbert Gintis demonstrated (2000, pp. 561–7),

> [i]f risk neutral tenants are not wealth constrained, or if output does not depend strongly on tenant effort, the landlord will be able to devise a contract securing a Pareto efficient level of tenant effort, even where tenant effort is not verifiable.

However, first, tenant-farmers *are* commonly wealth-constrained. In principle, wealth-constrained tenants who work the land could sign an appropriate bond, 'providing employers with assurances not only concerning work performance but also labor turnover; with adequate assurances employers will have greater incentives to provide training, and this will enhance economic efficiency' (Stiglitz, 1994, p. 49). But this would not be possible in practice, because the potential of tenant-farmers and other 'workers to put up bonds for good performance is affected by their initial wealth' (ibid., p. 49), and neither borrowing nor payment of rent at the end of the production period would be an adequate substitute for a bond, as 'in both cases incentive (moral hazard) problems arise from the possibility of default' (ibid., p. 49). Nor would landlords find an insurer willing to insure them against tenant-farmer default, at least at a cost they would be prepared to pay.

Second, output commonly depends strongly on tenant-farmer effort. It follows that there are two circumstances under which 'a transfer of wealth to asset poor tenants may be productivity enhancing, even if the amount transferred is insufficient to permit the tenant to become the owner' (Bardhan et al., 2000, p. 561). Thus in the case of a sharecropping economy where tenant-farmers' elasticity of demand for income in terms of effort is greater than unity, the government could increase the total amount produced by effecting a redistribution of wealth toward tenant-farmers. In the limiting case everyone would own the land that they worked. This would make it possible for farmers to keep more of what they produced than before, even if the government guaranteed the landlords and their descendants the same amount of product as before. There would be an improvement in Paretian terms, given that the landlords and their descendants would be no worse off than before and that any sacrifice of leisure made by the farmers in the process of producing more would be voluntary, reflecting an increase in their well-being. A less stringent interpretation of Pareto improvement would require the government to compensate only those who were landlords before the redistribution, not their descendants as well. In either case, however, there would be Pareto improvement only if there were 'feasible means of recovering the costs of the redistribution from the recipients without destroying the incentive effects upon which the gains depend' (ibid., p. 596).

However, while a changeover from sharecropping to land ownership by farmers might result in greater efficiency, even in this case the well-being of the former sharecroppers would not necessarily increase, because the farmers would now bear all the risks associated with production, including for example that of crop failure. For risk-averse persons, whom we may assume to make up the majority, well-being varies inversely with risk. In this case a well-being-maximiser is confronted by a trade-off between wealth and risk-avoidance.

At first sight sharecropping may not seem to be relevant to a modern economy. However, much of the analysis of sharecropping can be extended to franchising. For in the case of an industry in which franchises exist, such as the fast-food industry, output may fall if in addition to a one-off franchise fee the franchisor imposes a royalty rate on the franchisee's sales; it will fall if the franchisee's elasticity of demand for income in terms of effort is greater than unity, though by threatening withdrawal of the franchise, franchisors with low monitoring costs may be able to ensure that their franchisees' output does not fall below a certain minimum level. If output does fall, the fall will be bigger the greater the royalty rate.

Nonetheless royalties are typically imposed (see Lafontaine, 1992, p. 265). One reason for this is that one or both parties to a franchise contract are risk-averse. In the case of a contract with a uniform royalty rate, 'the optimal royalty rate will increase as the amount of risk increases if the franchisor is less risk averse than the franchisee' (ibid., p. 265), an assumption argued by Lafontaine to be realistic given the relatively high proportion of a franchisee's capital typically invested in the one business (though franchisees may not be risk-averse *per se*, just currently lacking the capital to become franchisors, but hoping to acquire it).

Asymmetric access to capital has relevant implications not only in the case of franchising but also where the following conditions hold:

> (i) the level of risk assumed by a producer is private information and hence cannot be contracted for by a lender; (ii) any loan contract has a limited liability provision so that the promise to repay a loan may be unenforceable; and (iii) there is a minimum project size. (Bardhan et al., 2000, p. 548)

Bardhan et al. (2000, p. 545) demonstrated that in these circumstances 'because inferior projects will be funded and superior projects not implemented when some agents have limited wealth, a redistribution of assets may be productivity enhancing'.

So far in this chapter we have adopted the economists' standard assumption that people simply aim to maximise the absolute values of variables that contribute to their well-being. As already noted in Chapter 4, however, there is substantial evidence that sometimes, or even often, individuals' actions are also based on a desire to achieve a higher social rank. To simplify analysis of the consequences of such behaviour, let us initially assume a society in which achieving a higher social rank is the only motivation behind human behaviour, and in which the social rank of individuals is determined only by first the gap between their consumption and that of others, and second the gap between their leisure and that of others. While if such a society is characterised also by a given work–leisure choice, a policy designed to redistribute wealth would not have any obvious consequences for the accumulation of wealth; if the work–leisure choice is instead variable, the accumulation of wealth may be affected.

In such a status-based society, a wealth tax levied on higher-wealth persons (who because of their consequent loss of wealth are hereafter described as 'losers') in excess of that required for the society to form in the first place and subsequently survive, the proceeds being transferred to those with lower wealth (hereafter described as 'winners') would have the following consequences. The lower after-tax wealth of the losers would reduce the unearned component of their income, and with an unchanged saving ratio this would cause them both to consume less and to save less. Assuming the initial levels of consumption and leisure of the losers to be optimal in the sense that the combination resulted in their achieving the highest social rank available to them, losers would then seek to earn more income by sacrificing some of their leisure, their purpose being to recover some of their lost consumption. Losers' output would thus increase, and losers would recover some of their lost saving. Gainers, by contrast, would increase their leisure by sacrificing some of their now-supplemented income, thereby offsetting some of the increase in their consumption resulting from the receipt of additional transfer payments. Gainers' output would thus decrease, and they would lose some of their augmented saving. Thus by contrast with a society in which individuals are motivated only by absolute levels of desired variables, in a status-driven society it is not clear that an increase in wealth taxes will reduce the level of aggregate wealth, the increased output and hence saving of losers having to be weighed against the decreased output and hence saving of gainers.

Assuming that transferors (for example parents) believe the consumption of transferees (for example children) as well as their own consumption confers status, similar consequences would follow also from the introduction of a tax on wealth transfers. It would again be a matter of the increased output of losers being weighed against the decreased output of winners.

The introduction of an income tax more progressive than that required for a society to avoid losing lower-status members to a lower-status society would have consequences similar to those already spelled out in the case of a tax on wealth, as would the introduction of a progressive tax on saving.

In, sum, however, it is more realistic to assume that persons are motivated by both absolute and relative levels of consumption and leisure. In this case the effect of a redistribution of wealth on the amount of aggregate wealth becomes difficult to assess.

A further point worth noting is that a redistribution of income or wealth in the direction of less inequality is likely to be resented by those whose income or wealth becomes lower relative to what it was before, and it can be argued that resistance on the part of this group is likely to be sufficiently disruptive to reduce GDP, hence reducing the amount of saving available for the accumulation of wealth.

8.6   APPLICATION OF THE ANALYSIS TO AN OPEN ECONOMY

In the case of an open economy, by contrast with a closed economy, there is an ambiguity as to the meaning of the distribution of wealth, since the term may refer to either distribution between residents or distribution between citizens. Since taxation is the most important means by which wealth can be redistributed, and since taxes are commonly levied according to residence rather than citizenship, we adopt the former definition.

In an open economy, increasing the taxation of wealth may result in the most wealthy residents emigrating. If there is a positive correlation between the most wealthy and the most productive people, emigration will cause per capita gross national output and income to be less than it otherwise would be, and assuming the saving ratio to be given, aggregate wealth will decline.[3] Alternatively, the most wealthy residents may shift their wealth to a country with lower taxes on wealth in a way which results in their wealth being taxed only in the lower-tax country, allowing them to retain more wealth to generate income. In so far as this wealth was destined to be used productively wherever it was situated, this would lower domestic employment and the income derived from it.

Of course the above conclusions relating to shifting of wealth do not apply to the same extent if the domestic government has in place legislation which affects movements of wealth from one country to another. A proposal providing an example of such legislation is the 'Tobin tax',[4] a tax applied to transactions involving international currency exchanges. In the extreme case, movement of wealth out of the country could be prohibited altogether. If any such legislation exists, increasing the taxation of wealth would result in less loss of wealth, if any. While some opportunities of generating wealth in foreign countries might be forgone as a result of the legislation, some losses of wealth due to the adverse economic effects of unpredictable capital flows between countries might be avoided. And although the introduction of such legislation might lead some of the wealthy to emigrate, the effect on the country's per capita wealth would depend on whether those who emigrate would have generated wealth in excess of the mean if they had stayed; it would be presumptuous to assume that they would have, particularly in the case of those whose wealth was inherited. The probability of loss of wealth would of course be smaller the greater the number of other countries which introduced similar legislation at the same time.

In *Capital in the Twenty-First Century*, Thomas Piketty advocated the introduction of a progressive global wealth tax (Piketty, 2014, pp. 515–39). Several of his critics rejected this proposal, and his support for very high marginal rates of income taxation, as being politically unrealistic. Thus James Galbraith describes the global wealth tax as 'utopian' and 'futile', since any such tax would simply be evaded (Galbraith, 2014a, p. 81). Piketty himself conceded as much, but nevertheless insisted on raising the issue. After all, 'all human progress begins with contemplation of the unprecedented' (Aspromourgos, 2015, p. 303).

Implementation of a global wealth tax would certainly require strong measures to be taken against tax evasion. Gabriel Zucman estimates that at least 8% of global household wealth is hidden in tax havens – some $7.6 trillion in 2014 (Zucman, 2015, p. 43). He calls for strong measures to be taken against the worst culprits: Luxembourg should be expelled from the European Union, and Switzerland subjected to a 30% across-the-board tariff on its manufactured exports, unless their governments crack down on tax avoidance by foreign nationals and transnational companies (ibid., chapter 4). Zucman provides an elaborate account of Google's tax-shifting strategy, which goes far beyond old-fashioned transfer pricing, and estimates that two-thirds or more of the ten-point decline in the effective corporate tax rate in the United States between 1998 and 2013 can be attributed to 'increased tax avoidance in low-tax countries' (Zucman, 2014, p. 133). Transnational companies should, he argues, be taxed not according to their declared profits but on a formula that combines sales, capital and employment (Zucman, 2015, p. 110). This has elements of a global wealth tax, in a slightly different form.

8.7   CONCLUDING REMARKS

Let us take a closed economy first. Given not only the possibility of involuntary unemployment, but also the existence of both income and substitution effects, there is no *a priori* reason for believing that reducing inequality in the distribution of wealth, for example by an increase in the taxation of wealth, will decrease the amount of aggregate wealth available to be distributed. By contrast, in the case of an open economy there is such an *a priori* reason, as wealth may flow out to an economy with lower taxation of wealth. On the other hand, the closed economy conclusion may be the more relevant in the case of an otherwise open economy in which inter-country transfers of wealth are affected by restrictive legislation, or where there is a comprehensive and enforceable international agreement to prevent wealth-shifting to avoid taxation.

NOTES

1. Both federal and provincial gift and estate taxes in Canada have since been abolished, in the 1970s and 1980s (Duff, 2005).
2. Stiglitz (1994, p. 47) followed Marshall ([1890] 1961, p. 644) in overlooking the income effect. By contrast, Pigou (1920, p. 593) and Frank Knight (1921, pp. 117–18) overlooked the substitution effect. Robbins' article, while not actually using the terms 'income effect' and 'substitution effect', implied them.
3. Gross national product, not gross domestic product, is the appropriate concept here, as the latter measures the income generated within a country regardless of whether it accrues to residents or non-residents, whereas the former measures the income of residents, and therefore their capacity to save and accumulate wealth.
4. The 'Tobin tax' was named after its proponent, James Tobin (1978). For a recent appraisal see Arestis (2012).

9. Conclusion

[The piecemeal social engineer's] ends may be of diverse kinds, for example, . . . the distribution of wealth . . . . The piecemeal engineer knows, like Socrates, how little he knows. He knows that we can learn only from our mistakes. Accordingly, he will make his way step by step, carefully comparing the results expected with the results achieved, and always on the lookout for the unavoidable unwanted consequences of any reform. (Popper, [1944–45] 1957, pp. 66–7)

The title of this book, *The Distribution of Wealth – Growing Inequality?*, asks a question to which an answer is provided in Chapter 3. The extensive empirical material set out in that chapter led to the conclusion that 'there is substantial evidence that for most countries there was a tendency for inequality in the distribution of wealth to grow up until 1913, to fall fairly continuously thereafter until about the mid-1970s, and then to grow again, at least until the global financial crisis' (above, p. 86). And 'Piketty's thesis', which we discuss in Chapter 5, forecasts that there will be a further growth in this inequality during the twenty-first century. If, using one of the value systems outlined in Chapter 6, such growth in inequality in the distribution of wealth is judged to be undesirable, it can theoretically be stopped, or reversed, using means outlined in Chapter 7.

This theoretical possibility could become a feasible one under 'veil of ignorance' circumstances, as we now proceed to demonstrate. Suppose that a society's members, each veiled by ignorance in the sense that they do not know whether at the time of death they will be wealthy or destitute, gather in a convention organised for the purpose of deciding on a clause to be inserted in the constitution stating how much of the wealth of those who die in one year should be taxed and divided equally among those who are born in the next. It is highly improbable that the decision would result in a distribution of inherited wealth as unequal as that which currently prevails. No doubt some of those at the convention would favour a low or zero level of tax in the hope that they would turn out to be among the most wealthy, their descendants consequently starting life with more wealth than others. But casual observation suggests that such gamblers would be unlikely to be a majority in the convention. Others might be so risk-averse that they favoured a 100 per cent tax, knowing that regardless of whether they were wealthy or destitute at death, their immediate descendants and their descendants in turn would start life with the same wealth as everyone else. Those who are as risk-averse as this might even make up a majority. Even if they did not, the existence of various degrees of risk-aversion among its participants would make it highly probable that the convention would decide on a level of tax on inheritable wealth much higher than that actually prevailing in the country which at the present time has the highest level.

Why is it that lifting the veil of ignorance produces so different a distribution of inherited wealth? The answer, at least in part, is that those voting for a low or zero tax on inheritable wealth now include not only the gamblers, but also the wealthy, and if we include in the latter all those whose wealth is above the median level, taken together they make up a majority.

Of course, even if inherited wealth were equally divided, the outcome would not be equality in the distribution of wealth. There would still be heterogeneous choices between work and leisure, between saving and consumption, and between saving early in life and saving late in life, all contributing to unequal distribution of wealth among those who have begun their working life. However, such unequal distribution of wealth would be voluntary, merely reflecting the diversity of human behaviour. On the other hand, the unequal accumulation of wealth over a lifetime due to the unequal distribution of income resulting from unequal inherited ability would be involuntary. In a society in which there was equal distribution of inherited wealth, the road to reduction of involuntary unequal distribution of wealth would thus be a reduction in inequality in the distribution of income, brought about for example by the introduction of a more progressive income tax scale.

Both the veil-of-ignorance level of tax on inherited wealth and an acceptable degree of progression in the income tax scale might be revealed by piecemeal social engineering of the Popper type, that is to say step-by-step, as opposed to revolutionary, reforms.

Irving Fisher's statement that even if established, equality of wealth 'would not endure, because of unequal forces of thrift, ability, industry, luck and fraud . . . [and] inequality once established tends, by inheritance, to perpetuate itself in future generations' (Fisher, 1912, p. 482), would only partly apply to a society subject to such reforms. Inequality in the distribution of wealth due to unequal ability would be reduced; of the remaining 'unequal forces', thrift and industry generate what we have called voluntary unequal distribution, while not only luck but also at least a certain amount of fraud can be regarded as inescapable; and unequal inheritance would no longer apply.

Such piecemeal social engineering directed towards reducing inequality in the distribution of wealth is of course open to the objection that by sapping incentives it would necessarily reduce the amount of aggregate wealth available to be distributed. As demonstrated in Chapter 8, however, it is by no means certain that any such sacrifice would ensue, even if we assume that the goal of individuals is to maximise absolute wealth. Those who raise this objection either ignore the income effect on the wealthy of a tax on their income, or assume without proof that the income effect is always outweighed by the substitution effect, while at the same time they either ignore the substitution effect on the poor of a supplement to their income, or assume without proof that the substitution effect is always outweighed by the income effect. In the case of the wealthy, if the income effect is dominant, the response to a loss of after-tax income will be the sacrifice of some leisure, so that more time can be spent working in pursuit of income; in the case of the poor, if the substitution effect is dominant, the response to a gain in after-supplement income will likewise be more work at the expense of some leisure.

It may be more realistic, however, to assume that the goal of individuals is to maximise not absolute wealth but relative wealth. If this is so, the incentive to generate wealth will persist in the face of any redistribution of wealth which falls short of mandating complete equality.

There being no *a priori* reason for believing that a reduction in inequality in the distribution of wealth would reduce the amount of aggregate wealth available for distribution, there would be little risk in putting this proposition to the test by gradual implementation of an egalitarian distribution-of-wealth policy. According to most views of society, this would at the same time involve a movement towards distributive justice.

Finally, those who believe in democracy, including liberal democracy, are faced with the following dilemma. Beyond a certain point inequality in the distribution of wealth is incompatible with democracy, that is to say a society in which everyone has an equal say in political decision-making. While governments are elected by some form of majority vote, the decisions they make are influenced by pressure groups, and pressure groups tend to be more influential the greater their financial backing. The more concentrated the distribution of wealth, the smaller the number of people who provide funding for pressure groups, and the more government decision-making comes to resemble that at private company annual general meetings, where what rules is not 'one person, one vote' but 'one dollar, one vote'.

The serious adverse consequences of high and rising inequality have been emphasised by Steven Pressman (2016), who criticises Thomas Piketty for not discussing them in sufficient depth. Pressman distinguishes three dimensions: economic, political and social. The economic costs of inequality include lower rates of growth of both output and productivity, together with increased levels of household debt and therefore greater economic volatility. There are also undesirable, anti-Keynesian consequences for macroeconomic policy, since 'the monied interests' are able to exercise undue influence over university appointments in economics. As already noted, this shades into the political costs of inequality, with the rich enjoying disproportionate power over everything from electoral finance to party programmes and hence affecting the policy decisions of democratically elected governments. Finally there are social costs: greater inequality is associated with adverse health outcomes, higher levels of obesity and crime and reduced social mobility (Pressman, 2016, chapter 3). Some of these phenomena are more closely related to income inequality, but others – above all the political dimension – are clearly made substantially worse by high and increasing inequality in the distribution of wealth.

Bibliography

Alchian, Armen A. and Harold Demsetz (1972), 'Production, Information Costs, and Economic Organization', *American Economic Review*, **62**, pp. 777–95.

Alesina, Alberto and Dani Rodrik (1994), 'Distribution Politics and Economic Growth', *Quarterly Journal of Economics*, **109** (2), pp. 465–90.

Alvaredo, F. and E. Saez (2009), 'Income and Wealth Concentration from a Historical and Fiscal Perspective', *Journal of the European Economic Association*, **7** (5), pp. 1140–67.

Arestis, Philip (2012), 'Tobin Tax', in J.E. King (ed.), *The Elgar Companion to Post Keynesian Economics*, 2nd ed., Edward Elgar: Cheltenham, UK, and Northampton, MA, pp. 538–43.

Arrow, Kenneth (1951), *Social Choice and Individual Values*, New York: John Wiley.

Aspromourgos, T. (2015), 'Thomas Piketty, the Future of Capitalism and the Theory of Distribution: a Review Essay', *Metroeconomica*, **66** (2), pp. 284–305.

Atkinson, Anthony B. (1970), 'On the Measurement of Inequality', *Journal of Economic Theory*, **2** (3), pp. 244–63.

Atkinson, Anthony B. (1971), 'The Distribution of Wealth and the Individual Life-Cycle', *Oxford Economic Papers*, **23**, pp. 239–54.

Atkinson, Anthony B. (1973), 'On the Measurement of Inequality: Non-Mathematical Summary', in Anthony B. Atkinson (ed.), *Wealth, Income and Inequality*, Oxford: Oxford University Press, second edition, 1980, pp. 40–43.

Atkinson, Anthony B. (2015), *Inequality: What is to be Done?* Cambridge, MA: Harvard University Press.

Atkinson, Anthony B. and François Bourguignon (eds) (2000), *Handbook of Income Distribution*, volume 1, Amsterdam: Elsevier.

Atkinson, Anthony B. and François Bourguignon (eds) (2015), *Handbook of Income Distribution*, volume 2A, Amsterdam: Elsevier.

Atkinson, Anthony B. and Andrea Brandolini (2010), 'On Analyzing the World Distribution of Income', *World Bank Economic Review*, **24** (1), pp. 1–37.

Atkinson, Anthony B., James P.F. Gordon and Alan J. Harrison (1989), 'Trends in the Shares of Top Wealth-Holders in Britain, 1923–1981', *Oxford Bulletin of Economics and Statistics*, **51** (3), pp. 315–32.

Atkinson, Anthony B. and Alan J. Harrison (1974), 'Wealth Distribution and Investment Income in Britain', *Review of Income and Wealth*, **20** (2), pp. 125–42.

Atkinson, Anthony B. and Alan J. Harrison (1978), *Distribution of Personal Wealth in Britain*, Cambridge: Cambridge University Press.

Auerbach, A.J. and K. Hassett (2015), 'Capital Taxation in the Twenty-first Century', *American Economic Review*, **105** (5), pp. 38–42.

Australian Bureau of Statistics (2013), *6554.0 – Household Wealth and Wealth Distribution, Australia, 2011–12*, http://www.abs.gov.au/ausstats/abs@.nsf/mf/6554.0 (Accessed 17 December 2013).

Babeau, A. and D. Strauss-Kahn (1977), *La Richesse des Français*, Paris: Presses Universitaires de France.

Baekgaard, Hans (1997), 'The Changing Patterns of the Distribution of Household Wealth in Australia from 1986 to 1993', paper presented to the 1997 Conference of Economists, Hobart.

Bager-Sjögren, Lars and N. Anders Klevmarken (1998), 'Inequality and Mobility of Wealth in Sweden 1983/4–1992/3', *Review of Income and Wealth*, **44** (4), pp. 473–95.

Bardhan, Pranab, Samuel Bowles and Herbert Gintis (2000), 'Wealth Inequality, Wealth Constraints and Economic Performance', in Anthony B. Atkinson and François Bourguignon (eds) (2000), *Handbook of Income Distribution*, volume 1, Amsterdam: Elsevier, pp. 541–603.

Barro, Robert J. (2000), 'Inequality and Growth in a Panel of Countries', *Journal of Economic Growth*, **5** (1), pp. 5–32.

Barrow, Robin (1991), *Utilitarianism: A Contemporary Statement*, Aldershot, UK and Brookfield, VT: Edward Elgar.

Bauer, John and Andrew Mason (1992), 'The Distribution of Income and Wealth in Japan', *Review of Income and Wealth*, **38** (4), pp. 403–28.

Becker, Gary S. (1988), 'Family Economics and Macrobehavior', *American Economic Review*, **78** (1), pp. 1–13.

Becker, Gary S. and Nigel Tomes (1976), 'Child Endowments and the Quantity and Quality of Children', *Journal of Political Economy*, **84**, pp. S143–S162.

Becker, Lawrence C. and Charlotte B. Becker (eds) (1992), *Encyclopedia of Ethics*, New York: Routledge.

Beckerman, Wilfred (2011), *Economics as Applied Ethics*, New York: Palgrave Macmillan.

Bénabou, Roland (1996), 'Inequality and Growth', *NBER Macroeconomics Annual 1996, Volume 11*, pp. 11–92.

Bentham, Jeremy (1788), 'Essay on Representation', translated from the French in Mary P. Mack, *Jeremy Bentham: An Odyssey of Ideas, 1748–1792*, New York: Columbia University Press, 1962.

Bentham, Jeremy (1802), *Principles of the Civil Code*, in John Bowring (ed.), *The Works of Jeremy Bentham*, Volume I, New York: Russell and Russell, 1962, pp. 297–364.

Bentham, Jeremy (1825), *The Rationale of Reward*, in John Bowring (ed.), *The Works of Jeremy Bentham*, Volume II, New York: Russell and Russell, pp. 189–266.

Berlin, Isaiah (1956), 'Equality', *Proceedings of the Aristotelian Society*, **56**, pp. 301–26.

Bjerke, K (1956), 'Changes in Danish Income Distribution 1939–52', *Income and Wealth*, **IV**, pp. 98–154.

Blackorby, Charles and David Donaldson (1978), 'Measures of Relative Equality and Their Meaning in Terms of Social Welfare', *Journal of Economic Theory*, **18**, pp. 59–80.

Blinder, Alan S. (1973), 'A Model of Inherited Wealth', *Quarterly Journal of Economics*, **84** (4), pp. 608–26.

Blinder, Alan S. (1974), *Towards an Economic Theory of Income Distribution*, Cambridge, MA: MIT Press.

Blinder, Alan S. (1976), 'Inequality and Mobility in the Distribution of Wealth', *Kyklos*, **29** (4), pp. 607–38.

Blinder, Alan S. (1988), 'Comments on Chapter 1 and Chapter 2', in Denis Kessler and André Masson (eds), *Modelling the Accumulation and Distribution of Wealth*, Oxford: Oxford University Press, pp. 68–76.

Boadway, Robin and Michael Keen (2000), 'Redistribution', in Anthony B. Atkinson and François Bourguignon (eds), *Handbook of Income Distribution*, volume 1, Amsterdam: Elsevier, pp. 677–789.

Bonin, John P. and Louis Putterman (1987), *Economics of Cooperation and the Labor-Managed Economy*, Chur: Harwood Academic Publishers.

Bradford, Wylie Douglas (2000), 'Value and Justice: Property, Economic Theory and Rawls', unpublished Doctor of Philosophy thesis, University of Cambridge.

Brady, Rose (1999), *Kapitalizm*, New Haven, CT: Yale University Press.

Brandolini, Andrea, Luigi Cannari, Giovanni D'Alessio and Ivan Faiella (2002), 'Household Wealth Distribution in Italy', paper prepared for the 27th General Conference of the International Association for Research in Income and Wealth, Djurhhamn (Stockholm Archipelago), www.iariw.org.stockholm.htm (Accessed 30 June 2003).

Brickley, James A., Clifford W. Smith Jr. and Jerold L. Zimmerman (1996), *Organizational Architecture: A Managerial Economics Approach*, Chicago: Richard D. Irwin.

Burke, Edmund (1790), *Reflections on the Revolution in France 1790*, in L.G. Mitchell (ed.), *The Writings and Speeches of Edmund Burke*, Volume VIII, Oxford: Oxford University Press, 1989, pp. 53–293.

Cannan, Edwin (1893), *A History of the Theories of Production and Distribution*, London: P.S. King.

Cannan, Edwin (1897), 'What is Capital?', *Economic Journal*, 7, pp. 278–84.

Cannan, Edwin (1905), 'The Division of Income', *Quarterly Journal of Economics*, 19, pp. 341–69.

Cannan, Edwin (1914), *Wealth: A Brief Explanation of the Causes of Economic Welfare*, London: P.S. King.

Castello-Climent, Amparo (2010), 'Inequality and Growth in Advanced Economies: An Empirical Investigation', *Journal of Economic Inequality*, 8, pp. 293–321.

Chambers, S. (2012), 'Justice or Legitimacy, Barricades or Public Reason? The Politics of Property-owning Democracy', in M. O'Neill and T. Williamson (eds), *Property-Owning Democracy: Rawls and Beyond*, Chichester: Blackwell, pp. 17–32.

Chesher, Andrew D. and Patrick C. McMahon (1976), 'The Distribution of Personal Wealth in Ireland – the Evidence Re-examined', *Economic and Social Review*, 8, pp. 61–8.

Clay, Henry (1925), 'The Distribution of Capital in England and Wales', *Transactions of the Manchester Statistical Society*, pp. 53–80.

Cohen, G.A. (2009), *Why not Socialism?*, Princeton, NJ: Princeton University Press.

Collins, Chuck, Betsy Leondar-Wright and Holly Sklar (1999), *Shifting Fortunes: The Perils of the American Wealth Gap*, Boston, MA: United for a Fair Economy.

Cowell, Frank A. (1977), *Measuring Inequality*, Oxford: Philip Allan.

Cowell, Frank A. (2003), 'Theil, Inequality and the Structure of Income Distribution', Discussion Paper, http://eprints.lse.ac.uk/2288/1/Theil,_Inequality_and_the_Structure_of_Income_Distribution.pdf (Accessed 12 November 2014).

Crick, Bernard (1962), *In Defence of Politics*, Harmondsworth: Penguin, second edition, 1982.

Dagum, Camilo (1987), 'Gini Ratio', in John Eatwell, Murray Milgate and Peter Newman (eds), *The New Palgrave: A Dictionary of Economics*, Volume 2, Basingstoke: Macmillan, pp. 529–32.

Dalton, Hugh (1920), *Some Aspects of the Inequality of Income in Modern Communities*, London: G. Routledge.

Daniels, G.W. and H. Campion (1936), *The Distribution of National Capital*, Manchester: Manchester University Press.

Daumard, Adeline (1980), 'Wealth and Affluence in France since the

Beginning of the Nineteenth Century', in William D. Rubinstein (ed.), *Wealth and the Wealthy in the Modern World*, London: Croom Helm, pp. 90–121.

Davies, James B. (1979), 'On the Size Distribution of Wealth in Canada', *Review of Income and Wealth*, **25** (3), pp. 237–59.

Davies, James B. (1982), 'The Relative Impact of Inheritance and Other Factors on Economic Inequality', *Quarterly Journal of Economics*, **97** (3), pp. 471–98.

Davies, James B. (1988), 'Family Size, Household Production and Life Cycle Saving', *Annales d'Économie et de Statistique*, **9**, pp. 141–65.

Davies, James B. (1993), 'The Distribution of Wealth in Canada', in Edward N. Wolff (ed.), *Research in Economic Inequality, Volume 4, Studies in the Distribution of Household Wealth*, Greenwich, CT: JAI Press, pp. 159–80.

Davies, James B., Susannah Sandström, Anthony Shorrocks and Edward N. Wolff (2011), 'The Level and Distribution of Global Household Wealth', *Economic Journal*, **121**, March, pp. 223–54.

Davies, James B. and Anthony F. Shorrocks (2000), 'The Distribution of Wealth', in Anthony B. Atkinson and François Bourguignon (eds), *Handbook of Income Distribution*, Volume 1, Amsterdam: Elsevier, pp. 605–75.

Deininger, K, and L. Squire (1996), 'New Data Set Measuring Income Inequality', *World Bank Economic Review*, **10** (3), pp. 565–91.

Dell, Fabian, Thomas Piketty and Emmanuel Saez (2005), 'Income and Wealth Concentration in Switzerland over the 20th Century', London: Centre for Economic Policy Research, Discussion Paper No. 5090.

Demsetz, Harold (1965), 'Some Aspects of Property Rights', *Journal of Law and Economics*, **8**, pp. 61–70.

Demsetz, Harold (1967), 'Towards a Theory of Property Rights', *American Economic Review*, **57**, pp. 347–59.

Demsetz, Harold (1995), 'Enterprise Control, Wealth, and Economic Development', in *The Economics of the Business Firm: Seven Critical Commentaries*, Cambridge: Cambridge University Press, pp. 40–60.

De Soto, Hernando (2000), *The Mystery of Capital: Why Capitalism Triumphs in the West and Fails Everywhere Else*, New York: Basic Books.

Dilnot, A.W. (1990), 'The Distribution and Composition of Personal Wealth in Australia', *Australian Economic Review*, **89** (1), pp. 33–40.

Dolcerocca, Antoine and Gokhan Terzioglu (2015), *Interview: Thomas Piketty Responds to Criticisms from the Left*, http://www.potemkinreview. com/pikettyinterview.html (Accessed 2 February 2015).

Dorling, Danny (2014), *Inequality and the 1%*, London: Verso.

Duff, David (2005), 'Abolition of Wealth Transfer Taxes', *Pittsburgh Tax Review*, 3 (1), pp. 71–120.

Durán-Cabré, José and Alejandro Esteller-Moré (2007), 'The Recent Evolution of Wealth Concentration in Spain: An Analysis from Tax Data', University of Barcelona, mimeo.

Durán-Cabré, José and Alejandro Esteller-Moré (2010), 'Tax Data for Wealth Concentration Analysis: An Application to Spanish Wealth Tax', *Review of Income and Wealth*, 56 (3), pp. 620–31.

Dworkin, Ronald (1981a), 'What is Equality? Part 1: Equality of Welfare', *Philosophy and Public Affairs*, 10 (3), pp. 185–246.

Dworkin, Ronald (1981b), 'What is Equality? Part 2: Equality of Resources', *Philosophy and Public Affairs*, 10 (4), pp. 283–345.

Easton, Brian (1983), *Income Distribution in New Zealand*, New Zealand Institute of Economic Research, Research Papers 28, Wellington.

Ely, Richard T. (1903), *Studies in the Evolution of Industrial Society*, Reprint, London: Forgotten Books, 2013, pp. 256–7.

Esteban, Joan-Maria and Debraj Ray (1994), 'On the Measure of Polarization', *Econometrica*, 62 (4), pp. 819–51.

Fanning, Connell and David O'Mahony (1983), 'The Worker Co-operative', in Liam Kennedy (ed.), *Economic Theory of Co-operative Enterprises: Selected Readings*, Oxford: The Plunkett Foundation for Co-operative Studies, pp. 11–29.

Felipe, J. and J.S.L. McCombie (2013), *The Aggregate Production Function and the Measurement of Technical Change: 'Not Even Wrong'*. Cheltenham, UK, and Northampton, MA: Edward Elgar.

Fenna, Alan and Alan Tapper (2015), 'Economic Inequality in Australia: a Reassessment', *Australian Journal of Political Science*, 50 (3), pp. 393–411.

Finansdepartementet (1910), *Bouppteckningar efter aflidna, inregistrerade vid vederbörande domstolar åren 1906–1908*, Stockholm: Finansdepartementet.

Fisher, Irving (1896), 'What is Capital?', *Economic Journal*, 6, pp. 509–34.

Fisher, Irving (1912), *Elementary Principles of Economics*, New York: Macmillan.

Fleurbaey, M. (2008), *Fairness, Responsibility and Welfare*, Oxford: Oxford University Press.

Fleurbaey, M. and P.J. Hammond (2004), 'Interpersonally Comparable Utility', in S. Barberà et al. (eds), *Handbook of Utility Theory*, New York: Springer Science+Business Media, pp. 1179–1285.

Fleurbaey, M. and F. Maniquet (2009), 'Compensation and Responsibility', in K. Arrow, A. Sen and K. Suzumura (eds), *Handbook of Social Choice and Welfare*, Vol. 2, Amsterdam: Elsevier, pp. 507–604.

Fouquet, A. and D. Strauss-Kahn (1981), 'The Size Distribution of Personal Wealth in France (1977): A First Attempt at the Estate Duty Method', *Review of Income and Wealth*, **30** (4), pp. 403–18.

Frank, Robert (1985), *Choosing the Right Pond*, New York: Oxford University Press.

Frank, Robert (2011), *The Darwin Economy: Liberty, Competition, and the Common Good*, Princeton, NJ: Princeton University Press.

Frydman, Roman and Andrzej Rapaczynski (1994), *Privatization in Eastern Europe: Is the State Withering Away?*, Budapest: Central European University Press.

Frydman, Roman, Andrzej Rapacynski, John S. Earle et al. (1993), *The Privatization Process in Russia, Ukraine and the Baltic States*, Budapest: Central European University Press.

Fullbrook, Edward and Jamie Morgan (eds) (2014), *Piketty's Capital in the Twenty-First Century*, London: College Publications.

Galbraith, James K. (1998), *Created Unequal: The Crisis in American Pay*, New York: Free Press.

Galbraith, James K. (2014a), *'Kapital* for the Twenty-First Century', *Dissent*, **61** (2), pp. 77–82.

Galbraith, James K. (2014b), 'Unpacking the First Fundamental Law', *Real-World Economics Review*, **69**, 7 October, pp. 145–8.

Gallman, Robert E. (1969), 'Trends in the Size Distribution of Wealth in the Nineteenth Century', in Lee Soltow (ed.), *Six Papers on the Size Distribution of Wealth and Income*, New York: National Bureau of Economic Research, pp. 1–30.

Gini, C. (1914), 'Sulla misura della concentrazione e della variabilità dei caratteri', *Atti del R. Istituto Veneto di Scienze, Lettere ed Arti*, **LXXIII** (II), pp. 1203–48. Reprinted with additional footnotes in C. Gini, *Memorie di Metodologica Staistica, Vol. I, Variabilità e Concentrazione*, Milan: Dott. A Giuffrè Editore, 1939, pp. 359–408.

Giorgi, Giovanni M. (1999), 'Income Inequality Measurement: The Statistical Approach', in Jacques Silber (ed.), *Handbook on Income and Inequality Measurement*, Boston, MA: Kluwer Academic Publishers, pp. 245–67.

Good, F.J. (1990), 'Estimates of the Distribution of Wealth 1: Marketable Wealth of Individuals 1976 to 1988', *Economic Trends*, **444**, pp. 137–57.

Gottschalk, P. and Timothy M. Smeeding (2000), 'Empirical Evidence on Income Inequality in Industrial Countries', in Anthony B. Atkinson and François Bourguignon (eds), *Handbook of Income Distribution*, Volume 1, Amsterdam: Elsevier, pp. 261–307.

Graetz, Michael and Ian Shapiro (2005), *Death by a Thousand Cuts: The*

188   *The distribution of wealth – growing inequality?*

188   *The distribution of wealth – growing inequality?*

188   *The distribution of wealth – growing inequality?*

188   *The distribution of wealth – growing inequality?*

188 *The distribution of wealth – growing inequality?*

188   *The distribution of wealth – growing inequality?*

188   *The distribution of wealth – growing inequality?*

Fight Over Taxing Inherited Wealth, Princeton: Princeton University Press.

Groenewegen, Peter (1972), 'Consumer Capitalism', in J. Playford and D. Kirsner (eds), *Australian Capitalism: Towards a Socialist Critique*, Harmondsworth: Penguin, pp. 84–107.

Grubb, W. Norton and Robert H. Wilson (1992), 'Trends in Wage and Salary Inequality', *Monthly Labor Review*, **115** (6), pp. 23–39.

Gunton, Robert (1971), 'Distribution of Personal Wealth in Australia, 1967–68', unpublished manuscript cited in Alan Harrison, *The Distribution of Wealth in Ten Countries*, London: Her Majesty's Stationery Office, 1979.

Gunton, Robert (1975), 'Personal Wealth in Australia, 1953–69', unpublished Doctor of Philosophy thesis, University of Queensland.

Gustafsson, Björn, Li Shi and Wei Zhong (2006), 'The Distribution of Wealth in Urban China and in China as a Whole in 1995', *Review of Income and Wealth*, **52** (2), pp. 173–88.

Hammond, P.J. (1991), 'Interpersonal Comparisons of Utility: Why and How They Are and Should be Made', in J. Elster and J.E. Roemer (eds), *Interpersonal Comparisons of Well-Being*, Cambridge: Cambridge University Press, pp. 204–7.

Harcourt, Geoffrey C. (2015), 'Review Article' [on Piketty 2014a], *Economic and Labour Relations Review*, **26** (2), pp. 314–21.

Harrison, Alan (1979), *The Distribution of Wealth in Ten Countries*. Royal Commission on the Distribution of Income and Wealth: Background Paper to Report No. 7, Fourth Report on the Standing Reference. London: Her Majesty's Stationery Office.

Harsanyi, John C. (1955), 'Cardinal Welfare, Individualistic Ethics, and Interpersonal Comparisons of Utility', *Journal of Political Economy*, **63** (4), pp. 309–21.

Hausman, D.M. and M.S. McPherson (2006), 'How Could Ethics Matter to Economics?', *Applied Ethics: Critical Concepts in Philosophy*, **5**, pp. 354–65.

Hayek, Friedrich von (1960), *The Constitution of Liberty*, London: Routledge & Kegan Paul.

Henderson, Ronald F., Alison Harcourt and R.J.A. Harper (1975), *People in Poverty: A Melbourne Survey*, Melbourne: Cheshire for the Institute of Applied Economic and Social Research, University of Melbourne, revised edition with Supplement.

Her Majesty's Revenue and Customs (2012), *UK Personal Wealth Statistics 2008 to 2010*, https://www.gov.uk/government/statistics/uk-personal--wealth-statistics-2008-to-2010 (Accessed 5 February 2013).

Hicks, John R. (1939), 'The Foundations of Welfare Economics', *Economic Journal*, **49**, pp. 696–712.

Hillinger, C. (2014), 'Is *Capital in the Twenty-first Century Das Kapital* for the Twenty-first Century?, *Real-World Economics Review*, **69**, 7 October, pp. 131–7.

Hills, John, Francesca Bastagli, Frank Cowell, Howard Gelnnerster, Eleni Karagiannaki and Abigail McKnight (2013), *Wealth in the UK*, Oxford: Oxford University Press.

Hirsch, Fred (1976), *Social Limits to Growth*, London: Routledge & Kegan Paul.

Holmes, G.K. (1893), 'Measures of Distribution', *Journal of the American Statistical Association*, **III**, pp. 141–57.

Inland Revenue (1991), *Inland Revenue Statistics, 1991*, London: Her Majesty's Stationery Office.

Inland Revenue (2000), *Inland Revenue Statistics, 2000*, London: Her Majesty's Stationery Office.

Inland Revenue (2002), *Inland Revenue Statistics, 2002*, London: Her Majesty's Stationery Office.

Inland Revenue (2006), 'Distribution among the Adult Population of MarketableWealth', http://aka.hmrc.gov.uk/stats/personal_wealth/13-5-- table-2005.pdf (Accessed 12 December 2013).

Jäntti, Markus (2002), 'Trends in the Distribution of Income and Wealth – Finland 1987–1998', paper prepared for the 27th General Conference of the International Association for Research in Income and Wealth, Djurhhamn (Stockholm Archipelago), www.iariw.org.stockholm.htm (Accessed 30 June 2003).

Jevons, W. Stanley (1871), *The Theory of Political Economy*, 5th edition, New York: Augustus M. Kelley, 1957.

Johnson, Harry G. (1975), 'Equality and Economic Theory', *Nebraska Journal of Economics and Business*, **14**, pp. 3–17.

Jones, Alice Hanson (1977), *American Colonial Wealth: Documents and Methods*, 2nd edition, New York: Arno Press.

Jones, Derek C. (1980), 'Producer Co-operatives in Industrialised Western Economies', *British Journal of Industrial Relations*, **18** (2), pp. 141–68.

Kaldor, Nicholas (1939), 'Welfare Propositions in Economics and Interpersonal Comparisons of Utility', *Economic Journal*, **49**, pp. 549–52.

Kaldor, Nicholas (1955), *An Expenditure Tax*, London: Allen & Unwin.

Kaldor, Nicholas (1956), 'Alternative Theories of Distribution', *Review of Economic Studies*, **23** (2), pp. 83–100.

Katic, Pamela and Andrew Leigh (2013), 'Top Wealth Shares in Australia 1915–2012', mimeo.

Keister, Lisa A. (2000), *Wealth in America: Trends in Wealth Inequality*, Cambridge: Cambridge University Press.

Kelly, Simon (2001), 'Trends in Australian Wealth – New Estimates for the 1990s', http://www.natsem.canberra.edu.au/storage/cp2001_008.pdf (Accessed 2 November 2015).

Kelly, Simon (2002), 'Simulating Future Trends in Wealth Inequality', www.natsem.canberra.edu.au/storage/cp2002_010.pdf (Accessed 2 November 2015).

Kemp, Murray C. (2001), *International Trade and National Welfare*, London: Routledge.

Kennickell, Arthur B. (2000), 'An Examination of Changes in the Distribution of Wealth from 1989 to 1998: Evidence from the Survey of Consumer Finances', Jerome Levy Economics Institute, Working Paper No. 307, www.levy.org/docs/wrkpap/papers/307/html.

Kennickell, Arthur B. (2011), 'Tossed and Turned: Wealth Dynamics of U.S. Households 2007–09', Finance and Economics Discussion Series Working Paper 2011-51, Board of Governors of the Federal Reserve System, http://www.federalreserve.gov/pubs/feds/2011/201151/201151pap.pdf (Accessed 7 December 2014).

Kennickell, Arthur B. and R. Louise Woodburn (1999), 'Consistent Weight Design for the 1989, 1992 and 1995 SCFs, and the Distribution of Wealth', *Review of Income and Wealth*, **45** (2), pp. 193–215.

Kessler, Denis and André Masson (1987), 'Personal Wealth Distribution in France: Cross-Sectional Evidence and Extensions', in Edward N. Wolff (ed.), *International Comparisons of the Household Distribution of Wealth*: Oxford: Oxford University Press, pp. 141–76.

Kessler, Denis and André Masson (eds) (1988), *Modelling the Accumulation and Distribution of Wealth*, Oxford: Oxford University Press.

Kessler, Denis and Edward N. Wolff (1991), 'A Comparative Analysis of Household Wealth Patterns in France and the United States', *Review of Income and Wealth*, **37** (3), pp. 249–66.

Keynes, John Maynard (1936), *The General Theory of Employment, Interest and Money*, London: Macmillan.

King, John E. (2009), *Nicholas Kaldor*, Basingstoke: Palgrave Macmillan.

King, John E. (2016), 'The Literature on Piketty', *Review of Political Economy*, **28** (4), forthcoming.

Klevmarken, N. Anders (2004), 'On the Wealth Dynamics of Swedish Families. 1984–98', *Review of Income and Wealth*, **50** (4), pp. 469–91.

Knibbs, G.H. (1918), *The Private Wealth of Australia and its Growth as Ascertained by Various Methods, Together with a Report of the War Census of 1915*, Melbourne: Commonwealth Bureau of Census and Statistics.

Knight, Frank H. (1921), *Risk, Uncertainty and Profit*, New York: Augustus M. Kelley, 1964.

Kolm, S.C. (1976), 'Unequal Inequalities: I', *Journal of Economic Theory*, **12**, pp. 416–42.

Kolm, S.C. (2008), *Reciprocity*, Cambridge: Cambridge University Press.

Koo, Richard (2014), 'Piketty's Inequality and Local versus Global Lewis Turning Points', *Real-World Economics Review*, **69**, 7 October, pp. 89–99.

Kopczuk, Wojciech and Emmanuel Saez (2004), 'Top Wealth Shares in the United States 1916–2000: Evidence from Estate Tax Returns', *National Tax Journal*, **57** (2, part 2), pp. 445–88.

Kotlikoff, Laurence J. and Lawrence H. Summers (1981), 'The Role of Intergenerational Transfers in Aggregate Capital Accumulation', *Journal of Political Economy*, **89** (4), pp. 706–32.

Krugman, Paul (2014), 'Why We're in a New Gilded Age', *New York Review of Books*, 8, http://www.nybooks.com/articles/archives/2014/may/08/thomas-piketty-new-gilded-age/ (Accessed 15 November 2015).

Kuznets, Simon (1955), 'Economic Growth and Income Inequality', *American Economic Review*, **45** (1), pp. 1–28.

Lacey, Alan (2001), *Robert Nozick*, New York: Routledge.

Lafontaine, Francine (1992), 'Agency Theory and Franchising: Some Empirical Results', *Rand Journal of Economics*, **23** (2), pp. 263–83.

Lampman, Robert J. (1962), *The Share of the Top Wealth-Holders in National Wealth*, Princeton, NJ: Princeton University Press.

Langley, K.M. (1950–51), 'The Distribution of Capital in Private Hands in 1936–38 and 1946–47', *Bulletin of the Oxford University Institute of Economics and Statistics*, **12**, pp. 339–59, and **13**, pp. 33–54.

Lansing, John B. and John Sonquist (1969), 'A Cohort Analysis of Changes in the Distribution of Wealth', in Lee Soltow (ed.), *Six Papers on the Size Distribution of Wealth and Income*, New York: National Bureau of Economic Research.

Leigh, Andrew (2013), *Battlers and Billionaires: The Story of Inequality in Australia*, Melbourne: Redblack.

Leipziger, D.M., D. Dollar, A.F. Shorrocks and S.Y. Song (1992), *The Distribution of Income and Wealth in Korea*, Washington, DC: The World Bank.

Lerman, Donald L. and James J. Mickesell (1988), 'Rural and Urban Poverty: An Income/Net Worth Analysis', *Policy Studies Review*, **7**, pp. 765–81.

Letwin, William (1983), 'The Case against Equality', in William Letwin (ed.), *Against Equality: Readings on Economic and Social Policy*, London: Macmillan.

Li, Hongyi, Lyn Squire and Heng-fu Zou (1998), 'Explaining International and Intertemporal Variations in Income Inequality', *Economic Journal*, **108** (January), pp. 26–43.

Lindert, Peter H. (1986), 'Unequal English Wealth since 1670', *Journal of Political Economy*, **94**, pp. 1127–62.

Lindert, Peter H.(2000), 'Three Centuries of Inequality in Britain and America', in Anthony B. Atkinson and François Bourguignon (eds), *Handbook of Income Distribution*, Volume 1, Amsterdam: Elsevier, pp. 167–216.

Locke, John (1690), *Two Treatises of Government*, Peter Laslett (ed.), Cambridge: Cambridge University Press, 1960.

Lorenz, M.O. (1905), 'Methods of Measuring the Concentration of Wealth', *Journal of the American Statistical Association* (new series), **70**, pp. 209–17.

Lydall, Harold F. and D.G. Tipping (1961), 'The Distribution of Personal Wealth in Britain', *Bulletin of the Oxford University Institute of Economics and Statistics*, **23**, pp. 83–104.

Lyons, David (1977), 'The New Indian Land Claims and Original Rights to Land', *Social Theory and Practice*, **4** (3), pp. 249–72.

Lyons, Patrick M. (1975), 'Estate Duty Wealth Estimates and the Mortality Multiplier', *Economic and Social Review*, **6**, pp. 337–52.

MacIntyre, Alasdair C. (1964), 'Against Utilitarianism', in *Aims in Education: the Philosophic Approach*, Manchester: Manchester University Press, pp. 1–23.

Maddock, Rodney, Nils Olekalns, Janette Ryan and Margaret Vickers (1984), 'The Distribution of Income and Wealth in Australia 1914–1980: An Introduction and Bibliography', *Source Papers in Economic History*, No. 1, Canberra: Research School of Social Sciences, Australian National University.

Mankiw, N. Gregory (2015), 'Yes, $r > g$. So What?', *American Economic Review*, **105** (5), Papers and Proceedings, pp. 43–7.

Marshall, Alfred (1890–1920), *Principles of Economics*, London: Macmillan, ninth (variorum) edition, with annotations by C.W. Guillebaud.

Marx, Karl (1845), 'Theses on Feuerbach', in *Collected Works of Marx and Engels*, Volume 5, London: Lawrence & Wishart, 1976, pp. 197–228.

Marx, Karl (1849), *Wage Labour and Capital*, in *Collected Works of Marx and Engels*, Volume 9, London: Lawrence & Wishart, 1977, pp. 197–228.

Mazzaferro, Carlo and Stefano Toso (2006), 'The Effects of Social Security on the Distribution of Wealth in Italy', paper prepared for the 29th Conference of the International Association for Research in Income and Wealth, Joensuu, Finland, 20–26 August.

McCloskey, Deirdre (2014), 'Measured, Unmeasured, Mismeasured, and Unjustified Pessimism: A Review Essay on Thomas Piketty's *Capital in the Twenty-First Century'*, *Erasmus Journal for Philosophy and Economics*, 7 (2), pp. 73–115.

McCulloch, John R. (1825), *The Principles of Political Economy*, London: Routledge/Thoemmes Press, fourth edition with new introduction by Dennis P. O'Brien, 1995.

Meade, James E. (1964), *Efficiency, Equality and the Ownership of Property*, London: Allen & Unwin.

Meade, James E. (1976), *The Just Economy*, London: Allen & Unwin.

Mierheim, Horst and Lutz Wicke (1977), 'Die Veränderung der personellen Vermögensverteilung in der Bundesrepublik Deutschland zwischen 1969 und 1973' ['Changes in the Distribution of Personal Wealth in the Federal Republic of Germany between 1969 and 1973'], *Finanzarchiv*, 36 (1), pp. 59–92.

Milanovic, Branko (2005), *Worlds Apart: Measuring International and Global Inequality*, Princeton: Princeton University Press.

Milanovic, Branko (2014), 'The Return of "Patrimonial Capitalism": a Review of Thomas Piketty's *Capital in the Twenty-First Century'*, *Journal of Economic Literature*, 52 (2), pp. 519–34.

Milanovic, Branko and Shlomo Yitzhaki (2002), 'Decomposing World Income Distribution: Does the World Have a Middle Class?', *Review of Income and Wealth*, 48 (2), pp. 155–78.

Milgrom, Paul and John Roberts (1992), *Economics, Organization, and Management*, Englewood Cliffs, NJ: Prentice-Hall.

Mill, John Stuart (1838), 'Bentham', in *Essays on Ethics, Religion and Society*, in J.M. Robson (ed.), *Collected Works of John Stuart Mill*, Volume X, Toronto: University of Toronto Press, 1969, pp. 75–115.

Mill, John Stuart (1848), *Principles of Political Economy with Some of their Applications to Social Philosophy*, in J.M. Robson (ed.), *Collected Works of John Stuart Mill*, Volumes II and III, Toronto: University of Toronto Press, 1965.

Mill, John Stuart (1859), 'Liberty', in J.M. Robson (ed.), *Collected Works of John Stuart Mill*, Volume XVIII, Toronto: University of Toronto Press, 1977, pp. 213–310.

Mill, John Stuart (1861), 'Utilitarianism', in *Essays on Ethics, Religion and Society*, in J.M. Robson (ed.), *Collected Works of John Stuart Mill*, Volume X, Toronto: University of Toronto Press, 1969, pp. 203–59.

Modigliani, Franco and Richard Brumberg (1954), 'Utility Analysis and the Consumption Function: An Interpretation of Cross-Section Data', in Kenneth K. Kurihara (ed.), *Post-Keynesian Economics*, New Brunswick, NJ: Rutgers University Press, pp. 398–436.

Mohn, J.R. (1873), 'Statistiske bidrag til belysning af prviatformuens fordeling i Norge', *Norsk Retstitdende*, 1–2, pp. 1–32.

Mummery, A.F. and J.A. Hobson (1889), *The Physiology of Industry: Being an Exposure of Certain Fallacies in Existing Theories in Economics*, London: John Murray.

Natrella, Vico (1975), 'Wealth of Top Wealth-Holders', unpublished paper presented to the 135th Annual Meeting of the American Statistical Association, cited in Alan Harrison, *The Distribution of Wealth in Ten Countries*, London: Her Majesty's Stationery Office (1979).

Nevile, John W. and N.A. Warren (1984), 'How Much Do We Know About Wealth Distribution in Australia?', Sydney: Centre for Applied Economic Research, University of New South Wales, Working Paper No. 62.

Norton, Michael I. and Dan Ariely (2011), 'Building a Better America – One Wealth Quintile at a Time', *Perspectives in Psychological Science*, 6 (1), pp. 9–12.

Norton, Michael I., D.T. Neal, C.L. Govan, D. Ariely and E. Holland (2014), 'The Not-So-Common-Wealth of Australia: Evidence for a Cross-Cultural Desire for a More Equal Distribution of Wealth', *Analyses of Social Issues and Public Policy*, 14 (1), pp. 339–51.

Nove, Alec (1992), *An Economic History of the USSR: 1917–1991*, 3rd edition. Harmondsworth: Penguin.

Nozick, Robert (1974), *Anarchy, State, and Utopia*, Oxford: Blackwell.

Nozick, Robert (1989), *The Examined Life*, New York: Simon and Shuster.

Oakeshott, Michael (1951), 'Political Education', in Michael Oakeshott, *Rationalism in Politics and Other Essays*, London: Methuen, pp. 111–36.

Oakeshott, Michael (1956), 'On Being Conservative', in Michael Oakeshott, *Rationalism in Politics and Other Essays*, London: Methuen, pp. 168–96.

Office for National Statistics, *Statistical Bulletin: Wealth and Income, 2010–12*. http://www.ons.gov.uk/ons/rel/was/wealth-in-great-britain-wave-3/wealth-and-income--2010-12/stb--wealth-and-income--2010-12.html (Accessed 12 November 2014).

Ohlsson, Henry, Jesper Roine and Daniel Waldenström (2006), 'Long-run Changes in the Concentration of Wealth: An Overview of Recent Findings', Research Paper, UNU-WIDER, United Nations University (UNU), No. 2006/103, ISBN 9291908878.

Okun, Arthur M. (1975), *Equality and Efficiency: The Big Trade-Off*, Washington, DC: Brookings Institution.

Organisation for Economic Cooperation and Development (1988), *Taxation of Net Wealth, Capital Transfers and Capital Gains of Individuals*, Paris: OECD.

Organisation for Economic Cooperation and Development (2001), *Tax and the Economy: A Comparative Assessment of OECD Countries*, Paris: OECD.

Ostry, Jonathan D., Andrew Berg and Charlambos G. Tsangarides (2014), 'Redistribution, Inequality, and Growth', Washington, DC: International Monetary Fund, Staff Discussion Note, revised version, April.

Oxford English Dictionary (2015), http://www.oed.com/ (Accessed 14 June 2015).

Pareto, Vilfredo (1897), *Cours d'Économie Politique*, Volume II, Lausanne: F. Rouge.

Pasinetti, Luigi L. (1962), 'The Rate of Profit and Income Distribution in Relation to the Rate of Economic Growth', *Review of Economic Studies*, **29**, pp. 267–79.

Pasinetti, Luigi L. (1974), *Growth and Income Distribution*, Cambridge: Cambridge University Press.

Patton, Paul (2005), 'Historic Injustice and the Possibility of Supersession', *Journal of Intercultural Studies*, **26** (3), pp. 255–66.

Persson, T. and G. Tabellini (1994), 'Is Inequality Harmful for Growth?', *American Economic Review*, **84** (3), pp. 600–621.

Pigou, Arthur C. (1920), *The Economics of Welfare*, London: Macmillan.

Piketty, Thomas (1995), 'Social Mobility and Redistributive Politics', *Quarterly Journal of Economics*, **110** (3), pp. 551–84.

Piketty, Thomas (2014), *Capital in the Twenty-First Century*, Cambridge, MA: The Belknap Press of Harvard University Press.

Piketty, Thomas (2015a), 'About *Capital in the Twenty-First Century*', *American Economic Review*, **105** (5), pp. 48–53.

Piketty, Thomas (2015b), 'Putting Distribution Back at the Center of Economics: Reflections on *Capital in the Twenty-First Century*', *Journal of Economic Perspectives*, **29** (1), pp. 67–88.

Piketty, Thomas, G. Postel-Vinay and J.-L. Rosenthal (2004), 'Wealth Concentration in a Developing Economy: Paris and France, 1807–1994', *CEPR Working Paper* 4631, Centre for Economic Policy Research: London.

Piketty, Thomas and Emmanuel Saez (2003), 'Income Inequality in the United States, 1913–1998', *Quarterly Journal of Economics*, **118** (1), pp. 1–39.

Piketty, Thomas and Emmanuel Saez (2006), 'The Evolution of Top Incomes: A Historical and International Perspective', *American Economic Review*, **96** (2), pp. 200–205.

Piketty, Thomas and Gabriel Zucman (2015), 'Wealth and Inheritance in the Long Run', in Anthony B. Atkinson and François Bourguignon (eds), *Handbook of Income Distribution*, Volume 2B, Burlington, VT: Elsevier Science, pp. 1303–68.

Podder, N. and N.C. Kakwani (1976), 'Distribution of Wealth in Australia', *Review of Income and Wealth*, **22** (1), pp. 75–92.

Podoluk, J.R. (1974), 'Measurement of the Distribution of Wealth in Canada', *Review of Income and Wealth*, **22** (2), pp. 203–18.

Polanyi, George and John B. Wood (1974), *How Much Inequality? An Enquiry into the 'Evidence'*, London: Institute of Economic Affairs.

Popper, Karl R. (1944–45), *The Poverty of Historicism*, London: Routledge & Kegan Paul, 1957.

Pressman, S. (2016), *Understanding Piketty's Capital in the Twenty-First Century*, London and New York: Routledge.

Putterman, Louis (1996), 'Coupons, Agency and Social Betterment', in John E. Roemer (ed.), *Equal Shares*, London: Verso, pp. 139–58.

Putterman, Louis, John E. Roemer and Joaquim Silvestre (1998), 'Does Egalitarianism Have a Future?', *Journal of Economic Literature*, **36** (2), pp. 861–902.

Rae, John (1834), *Statement of Some New Principles on the Subject of Political Economy*, reprinted in Warren James (ed.), *John Rae: Political Economist. An Account of his Life and a Compilation of his Main Writings*, Volume II, Toronto: Toronto University Press, 1965.

Raskall, Phillip L. (1977), 'The Distribution of Wealth in Australia 1967–1972', Sydney: Planning Research Centre, University of Sydney.

Ravallion, Martin (2006), 'Should Poor People Care about Inequality?', *Equity and Development: Berlin Workshop Series 2006*, World Bank Publications.

Rawls, John (1971), *A Theory of Justice*, Cambridge, MA: Harvard University Press.

Rawls, John (1982), 'Social Utility and Primary Goods', in Amartya Sen and Bernard Williams (eds), *Utilitarianism and Beyond*, Cambridge: Cambridge University Press, pp. 159–85.

Rehm, Miriam and Matthias Schnetzer (2015), 'Property and Power: Lessons from Piketty and New Insights from the HFCS', *European Journal of Economics and Economic Policies: Intervention*, **12** (2), pp. 204–19.

Revell, Jack (1965), 'Changes in the Social Distribution of Property in Britain during the Twentieth Century', *Conference International d'Histoire Économique*, **3**, pp. 367–84.

Revell, Jack, assisted by Graham Hockley and John Moyle (1967), *The Wealth of the Nation: The National Balance Sheet of the United Kingdom, 1957–61*, Cambridge: Cambridge University Press.

Ricardo, David (1973), *The Works and Correspondence of David Ricardo, Volume 6*, edited by Piero Sraffa with the assistance of Maurice Dobb, Cambridge: Cambridge University Press.

Robbins, Lionel (1930), 'On the Elasticity of Demand for Income in Terms of Effort', *Economica*, **10** (29), pp. 123–9.

Robbins, Lionel (1932), *An Essay on the Nature and Significance of Economic Science*, London: Macmillan.

Robbins, Lionel (1963), 'An Essay on Art and the State', in Lionel Robbins, *Politics and Economics: Papers in Political Economy*, London: Macmillan, pp. 53–72.

Robbins, Lionel (1976), *Political Economy: Past and Present*, London: Macmillan.

Roemer, John E. (1994a), *A Future for Socialism*, Cambridge: Cambridge University Press.

Roemer, John E. (1994b), 'A Future for Socialism', *Politics and Society*, **22** (4), pp. 451–78.

Roemer, John E. (1996), *Theories of Distributive Justice*, Cambridge, MA: Harvard University Press.

Roemer, John E. (1998), 'Why the Poor do not Expropriate the Rich: An Old Argument in New Garb', *Journal of Public Economics*, **70**, pp. 399–424.

Roemer, John E. (2012), 'On Several Approaches to Equality of Opportunity', *Economics and Philosophy*, **28** (2), pp. 165–200.

Roine, Jesper and Daniel Waldenström (2015), 'Long-run Trends in the Distribution of Income and Wealth', IFN Working Paper 1021, http://papers.ssrn.com/sol3/papers.cfm?abstract_id=2505015 (Accessed 15 November 2015).

Rowthorn, Bob (2014), 'A Note on Piketty's *Capital in the Twenty-First Century*', *Cambridge Journal of Economics*, **38** (5), pp. 1275–84.

Royal Commission on the Distribution of Income and Wealth (1975), *Report No. 1: Initial Report on the Standing Reference*, London: Her Majesty's Stationery Office.

Ryan, Alan (2012), *On Politics: A History of Political Thought from Herodotus to the Present*, London: Penguin Books.

Saez, Emmanuel and Gabriel Zucman (2014), 'Wealth Inequality in the United States since 1913: Evidence from Capitalized Income Tax Data', Cambridge, MA: National Bureau of Economic Research, Working Paper 20625.

Sahlins, Marshall (1972), *Stone Age Economics*, Chicago: Aldine.

Salverda, Wiemer, Brian Nolan and Timothy M. Smeeding (eds) (2011), *The Oxford Handbook of Economic Inequality*, Oxford: Oxford University Press.

Scheve, Kenneth and David Stasavage (2012), 'Democracy, War and Wealth: Lessons from Two Centuries of Inheritance Tax', *American Political Science Review*, **106** (1), pp. 81–102.

Schneider, Michael P. (1987), 'Underconsumption', in John Eatwell, Murray Milgate and Peter Newman (eds), *The New Palgrave: A Dictionary of Economics*, Volume 4, Basingstoke: Macmillan, pp. 741–5.

Schneider, Michael (2004a), *The Distribution of Wealth*, Northampton, MA: Edward Elgar.

Schneider, Michael (2004b), 'Measuring Inequality: The Origins of the Lorenz Curve and the Gini Coefficient', Bundoora: La Trobe University School of Business, Discussion Papers 2004, A04.01.

Schneider, Michael (2007), 'The Nature, History and Significance of the Concept of Positional Goods', *History of Economics Review*, **45** (Winter), pp. 60–81.

Schneider, Michael and Mike Pottenger (2014), 'Do Personal Distribution of Wealth Facts Support Piketty's Thesis?', paper presented at the Society of Heterodox Economists Conference, University of New South Wales, December.

Schwartz, M. (1983), 'Trends in Personal Wealth, 1976–1981', *Statistics of Income Bulletin*, **3** (3), pp. 1–26.

Sen, Amartya (1970), *Collective Choice and Social Welfare*, San Francisco: Holden Day.

Sen, Amartya (1973), *On Economic Inequality*, expanded edition with James Foster, Oxford: Oxford University Press, 1997.

Sen, Amartya (1982), 'Equality of What?', in Amartya Sen, *Choice, Welfare and Measurement*, Oxford: Basil Blackwell, 1982, pp. 353–69.

Sen, Amartya (1984), 'Rights and Capabilities', in Amartya Sen, *Resources, Values and Development*, Oxford: Basil Blackwell, pp. 307–24.

Sen, Amartya (1987), 'The Standard of Living: Lecture I, Concepts and Critiques' and 'The Standard of Living: Lecture II, Lives and Capabilities', in Geoffrey Hawthorn (ed.), *The Standard of Living*, Cambridge: Cambridge University Press, pp. 1–19, 20–38.

Sen, Amartya (1992), *Inequality Reexamined*, Oxford: Oxford University Press.

Sen, Amartya (1993), 'Capability and Well-Being', in Martha Nussbaum and Amartya Sen (eds), *The Quality of Life*, Oxford: Oxford University Press.

Sen, Amartya (2001), *Development as Freedom*, Oxford: Oxford University Press.

Sen, Amartya (2009), *The Idea of Justice*, London: Allen Lane.

Shammas, C. (1993), 'A New Look at Long-Term Trends in Wealth Inequality in the United States', *American Historical Review*, **98** (4), pp. 412–32.

Shapiro, Carl and Joseph E. Stiglitz (1984), 'Equilibrium Unemployment as a Worker Discipline Device', *American Economic Review*, **74** (3), pp. 433–44.

Shorrocks, A.F. (1975), 'The Age-Wealth Relationship: A Cross-Section and Cohort Analysis', *Review of Economics and Statistics*, **57**, pp. 155–63.

Sierminska, Eva, Andrea Brandolini and Timothy M. Smeeding (2006a), 'The Luxembourg Wealth Study – A Cross-Country Comparable Database for Household Wealth Research', *Journal of Economic Inequality*, **6**, pp. 375–83.

Sierminska, Eva, Andrea Brandolini and Timothy M. Smeeding (2006b), 'Comparing Wealth Distribution Across Rich Countries: First Results from the Luxembourg Wealth Study', paper prepared for the 29th-Conference of the International Association for Research in Income and Wealth, Joensuu, Finland, 20–26 August.

Silber, Jacques (ed.) (1999), *Handbook on Income and Inequality Measurement*, Boston, MA: Kluwer Academic Publishers.

Sismondi, J.C.L. Simonde de (1824), 'On the Basis of Consumption and Production', translated by Elizabeth Henderson, *International Economic Papers*, **7**, 1957, pp. 20–39.

Smart, J.J.C. (1978), 'Distributive Justice and Utilitarianism', in John Arthur and William H. Shaw (eds), *Justice and Economic Distribution*, Englewood Cliffs, NJ: Prentice-Hall, pp. 103–15.

Smeeding, Timothy M. (2000), 'Changing Income Inequality in OECD Countries: Updated Results from the Luxembourg Income Study (LIS)', in Richard Hauser and Irene Becker (eds), *The Personal Distribution of Income in an International Perspective*, Berlin: Springer, pp. 205–24.

Smith, Adam (1776), *The Wealth of Nations*, edited W.B. Todd, Oxford: Oxford University Press, 1976.

Smith, James D. and S.D. Franklin (1974), 'The Concentration of Personal Wealth, 1922–1969', *American Economic Review*, **64**, pp. 162–7.

Smith, James D. (1984), 'Trends in the Concentration of Personal Wealth in the United States, 1958 to 1976', *Review of Income and Wealth*, **30** (4), pp. 419–28.

Smith, James D. (1987), 'Recent Trends in the Distribution of Wealth in the US: Data, Research Problems, and Prospects', in Edward N. Wolff (ed.), *International Comparisons of the Distribution of Household Wealth*, Oxford: Oxford University Press, pp. 72–89.

Smith, Louis P. (1983), 'Economists, Economic Theory, and Co-operatives', in Liam Kennedy (ed.), *Economic Theory of Co-operative Enterprises: Selected Readings*, Oxford: Plunkett Foundation for Co-operative Studies.

Solow, R.M. (2014), 'Thomas Piketty is right: everything you need to know about "Capital in the Twenty-First Century"', *New Republic*, 22 April.

Soltow, Lee (1972), 'The Censuses of Wealth of Men in Australia and in the United States in 1860 and 1870', *Australian Economic History Review*, **12** (2), pp. 125–41.

Soltow, Lee (1975), *Men and Wealth in the United States, 1850–1870*, New Haven, CT: Yale University Press.

Soltow, Lee (1980). 'Wealth Distribution in Norway and Denmark in 1789', *Historisk Tidsskrift (Oslo)*, **59**, pp. 221–35.

Soltow, Lee (1985). 'The Swedish Census of Wealth at the Beginning of the 19th Century', *Scandinavian Economic History Review*, **33** (1), pp. 1–24.

Spånt, Roland (1978), 'The Distribution of Wealth in Some Developed Countries: A Comparative Study of Sweden, Denmark, France, Germany and the UK and the USA', unpublished manuscript presented at the CREP-INSEE international meeting on Wealth Accumulation and Distribution, Paris, 1978, cited in Alan Harrison, *The Distribution of Wealth in Ten Countries*, London: Her Majesty's Stationery Office, 1979.

Spånt, Roland (1987), 'Wealth Distribution in Sweden: 1920–1983', in Edward N. Wolff (ed.), *International Comparisons of the Distribution of Household Wealth*, Oxford: Oxford University Press, pp. 51–71.

Statens Offentliga Utrednigar (1942), 'Förutsättningarna för och verkningarna av en engångsskatt å förmögenhet i Sverige', SOU 1942: 52, Stockholm: Finansdepartementet.

Statistics Canada (2013), *Assets and Debts held by Family Units*, http://www.statcan.gc.ca/tables-tableaux/sum-som/l01/cst01/famil115a-eng.htm (Accessed 13 November 2014).

Stewart, I. (1991), 'Estimates of the Distribution of Personal Wealth II: Marketable Wealth and Pension Rights of Individuals 1976 to 1989', *Economic Trends*, **457**, pp. 99–110.

Stiglitz, Joseph E. (1994), *Whither Socialism?*, Cambridge, MA: MIT Press.

Taussig, M.K. (1976), 'Wealth Inequality in the United States', unpublished manuscript cited in Alan Harrison, *The Distribution of Wealth in Ten Countries*, London: Her Majesty's Stationery Office, 1979.

Tawney, Richard H. (1931), *Equality*, London: Allen & Unwin, second edition, 1952.

Thirlwall, Anthony P. (1987), *Grand Masters in Economics: Nicholas Kaldor*, Brighton: Wheatsheaf.

Thompson, William (1824), *An Inquiry into the Principles of the Distribution of Wealth most Conducive to Human Happiness: Applied to the Newly Proposed System of Voluntary Equality of Wealth*, London: Longman, Hurst, Rees, Orme, Brown and Green, reprinted New York: Augustus M. Kelley, 1963.

Tobin, James (1978), 'A Proposal for International Monetary Reform', *Eastern Economic Journal*, **4**, pp. 153–9.

Tuomalo, Matti and Jouko Vilmunen (1988), 'On the Trends over Time in the Degree of Concentration of Wealth in Finland', *Finnish Economic Papers*, **1** (2), pp. 184–90.

Vanek, Jaroslav (1970), *The General Theory of Labor-Managed Economies*, Ithaca, NY: Cornell University Press.

Veblen, Thorstein (1899), *The Theory of the Leisure Class: An Economic Study of Institutions*, reprinted with a foreword by Stuart Chase, New York: Random House, 1934.

Vickrey, William (1945), 'Measuring Marginal Utility by Attitudes towards Risk', *Econometrica*, **13**, pp. 215–36.

Voitchovsky, Sarah (2009), 'Inequality and Economic Growth', in Wiemer Salverda, Brian Nolan and Timothy M. Smeeding (eds), *The Oxford Handbook of Economic Inequality*, Oxford: Oxford University Press, pp. 549–74.

Waldenström, Daniel (2009), *Lifting All Boats? The Evolution of Income and Wealth Inequality over the Path of Development*, Lund Studies in Economic History, https://lup.lub.lu.se/search/publication/1487895 (Accessed 13 November 2014).

Waldron, Jeremy (1992), 'Superseding Historical Injustice', *Ethics*, **103**, pp. 4–28.

Walras, Léon (1874), from *Eléments d'économie politique; ou théorie de la richesse sociale*, Paris: R. Pichon et R. Durand-Auzias, translated by W. Jaffé as *Elements of Pure Economics*, New York: Augustus M. Kelley, 1954, 1977.

Walravens, J. and P. Praet (1978), 'La distribution du patrimoine des particuliers en Belgique – 1969' ['The Distribution of Individual Wealth in Belgium – 1969'], unpublished manuscript presented at the CREP-INSEE international meeting on Wealth Accumulation and Distribution, Paris, 1978, cited in Alan Harrison, *The Distribution of Wealth in Ten Countries*, London: Her Majesty's Stationery Office, 1979.

Wedgwood, Josiah (1939), *The Economics of Inheritance*, London: Penguin.

Weil, David N. (2015), 'Capital and Wealth in the Twenty-First Century', *American Economic Review*, **105** (5), pp. 34–7.

White, Betsy Buttrill (1978), 'Empirical Tests of the Life Cycle Hypothesis', *American Economic Review*, **68**, pp. 547–60.

Whiteford, Peter (2014), 'Income and Wealth Inequality: How is Australia Faring?', *The Conversation*, http://theconversation.com/income-and-wealth-inequality-how-is-australia-faring-23483 (Accessed 13 June 2014).

Wilkins, Roger (ed.) (2013), *Families, Incomes and Jobs, Volume 8: A Statistical Report on Waves 1 to 10 of the Household, Income and Labour Dynamics in Australia Survey*, Melbourne: Melbourne Institute of Applied Economic and Social Research.

Williamson, Jeffrey G. and Peter H. Lindert (1981), 'Long-term Trends in American Wealth Inequality', in James D. Smith (ed.), *Modeling the Distribution and Intergenerational Transmission of Wealth*, Chicago: University of Chicago Press, pp. 9–94.

Wold, H.O.A. and P. Whittle (1957), 'A Model Explaining the Pareto Distribution of Wealth', *Econometrica*, **25**, pp. 591–5.

Wolff, Edward N. (1987), 'Estimates of Household Wealth Inequality in the US, 1962–1983', *Review of Income and Wealth*, **33** (3), pp. 231–56.

Wolff, Edward N. (1988), 'Life-Cycle Savings and the Individual Distribution of Wealth by Class', in Denis Kessler and André Masson (eds), *Modelling the Accumulation and Distribution of Wealth*, Oxford: Oxford University Press, pp. 261–85.

Wolff, Edward N. (1991), 'The Distribution of Household Wealth: Methodological Issues, Time Trends, and Cross-sectional Comparisons', in Lars Osberg (ed.), *Economic Inequality and Poverty: International Perspectives*, New York: M.E. Sharpe, pp. 92–133.

Wolff, Edward N. (1994), 'Trends in Household Wealth in the United States, 1962–83 and 1983–89', *Review of Income and Wealth*, **40** (2), pp. 143–74.

Wolff, Edward N. (1995), *Top Heavy: A Study of the Increasing Inequality of Wealth in America*, New York: Twentieth Century Fund.

Wolff, Edward N. (1996), 'International Comparisons of Wealth Inequality', *Review of Income and Wealth*, **42** (4), pp. 433–51.

Wolff, Edward N. (2000), 'Recent Trends in Wealth Ownership, 1983–1998', Jerome Levy Economics Institute, Working Paper No. 300.

Wolff, Edward N. (2006), *International Perspectives on Household Wealth*, Northampton, MA: Edward Elgar.

Wolff, Edward N. (2010), 'Recent Trends in Household Wealth, 1983–2009: The Irresistible Rise of Household Debt', *Review of Economics and Institutions*, **2** (1), pp. 1–31.

Wolff, Edward N. (2012), 'The Asset Price Meltdown and the Wealth of the Middle Class', Working Paper No. w18559, National Bureau of Economic Research.

Wolff, Edward N. and Marcia Marley (1989), 'Long-run Trends in U.S. Wealth Inequality: Methodological Issues and Results', in Robert E. Lipsey and Helen Stone Rice (eds), *The Measurement of Saving, Investment, and Wealth*, Chicago: University of Chicago Press.

Wolff, Jonathon (1991), *Robert Nozick: Property, Justice and the Minimal State*, Cambridge: Polity Press.

Wolfson, M.C. (1977), 'The Causes of Inequality in the Distribution of Wealth: A Simulation Analysis', unpublished Ph.D. dissertation, University of Cambridge.

Yntema, Dwight B. (1933), 'Measures of the Inequality in the Personal Distribution of Wealth or Income', *Journal of the American Statistical Association*, **28**, pp. 423–33.

Zamagni, Vera (1980), 'The Rich in a Late Industrialiser: The Case of Italy', in William D. Rubinstein (ed.), *Wealth and the Wealthy in the Modern World*, London: Croom Helm, pp. 122–66.

Zeuthen, Frederik (1928), *Den Økonomiske Fordeling*, Denmark: Nyt Nordisk Forlag.

Zucman, Gabriel (2014), 'Taxing across Borders: Tracking Personal Wealth and Corporate Profits', *Journal of Economic Perspectives*, **28** (4), pp. 121–48.

Zucman, Gabriel (2015), *The Hidden Wealth of Nations: The Scourge of Tax Havens*. Chicago: University of Chicago Press.

Name index

Alchian, Armen A. 165
Alesina, Alberto 156
Alvarado, Facundo 71, 88
Ariely, Dan 149–50
Arrow, Kenneth J. 117, 131–2, 136
Aspromourgos, Tony ix, 105, 115–16, 175
Atkinson, Anthony B. ix, 4, 7, 12, 15, 23–4, 27, 45–9, 54, 82, 87, 96–8, 108–9, 117, 131, 133–6, 143
Auerbach, Alan J. 109

Babeau, A. 79–80
Baekgaard, Hans 65
Bager-Sjögren, Lars 38, 40–41
Bardhan, Pranab 170–72
Barro, Robert J. 156–7
Barrow, Robin 126
Bauer, John 86
Becker, Gary S. 99–100
Bentham, Jeremy 124, 136, 155
Berlin, Isaiah 119, 128–9
Blackorby, Charles 136
Blinder, Alan 92, 99–100, 167
Bonin, John P. 165
Bourguignon, François ix, 4, 82
Bowles, Samuel 170–72
Bradford, Wylie x, 130
Brady, Rose 148
Brandolini, Andrea 12, 69–70
Brickley, James A. 161–2
Brumberg, Richard 5, 92
Burke, Edmund 119–20
Burley, Harry x

Campion, Henry 45, 69
Cannan, Edwin 2, 155
Cannari, Luigi 69–70
Cardak, Buly x
Castello-Climent, Amparo 157
Chesher, Andrew D. 77

Clay, Henry 45
Collins, Chuck 143
Cowell, Frank 11, 25–6
Crick, Bernard 121
Croft, Jane ix

Dagum, Camilo 24
D'Alessio, Giovanni 69–70
Dalton, Hugh 133
Daniels, George 45, 69
Daumard, Adeline 79
Davies, James B. ix, 9, 23–4, 73–5, 82–3, 85, 92, 95–6, 100, 167–8
Deiniger, K.156–7
Demsetz, Harold viii, x, 162–3, 165
De Soto, Hernando 7
Dilnot, A.W. 82
Donaldson, David 136
Dorling, Danny 52–3
Duràn-Cabré, José-M. 71–2, 88
Dworkin, Ronald 119, 126–9

Eaton, B.H. 77–8
Elgar, Edward ix
Ely, Richard T. 17
Esteban, Joan-Maria 164
Esteller-Moré, Alejandro 71–2, 88

Faiella, Ivan 69–70
Fanning, Connell 164–5
Fenna, Alan 67
Fisher, Irving 2, 89, 141, 178
Fouquet, A. 79
Frank, Robert 90–91, 123
Fraser, Malcolm 65
Frost, Lionel x
Frydman, Roman 147

Galbraith, James K. x, 24, 107–8, 115–16, 175
Gallman, Robert E. 55–7

Subject index

Printed and bound by CPI Group (UK) Ltd, Croydon, CR0 4YY

23/04/2025

14660980-0004